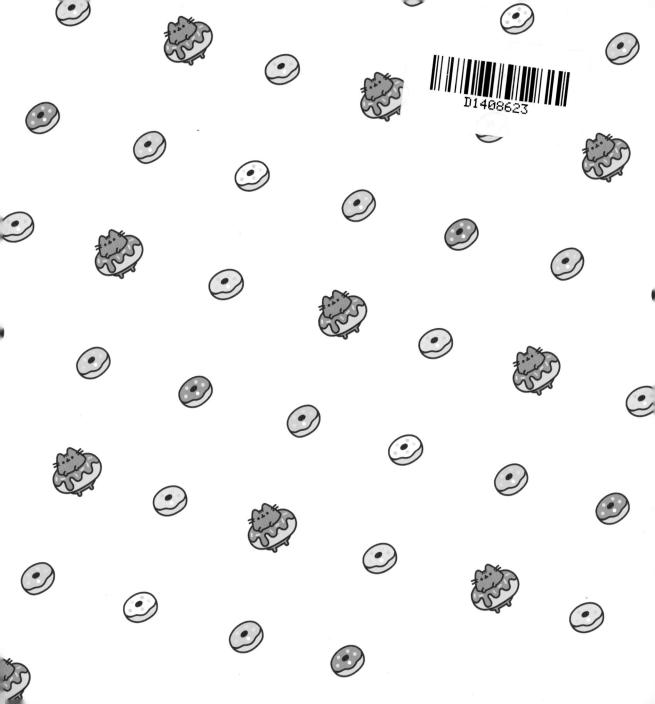

Let's Bake!

ALSO BY CLAIRE BELTON

I Am Pusheen the Cat

Pusheen Coloring Book

Mini Pusheen Coloring Book

ALSO BY SUSANNE NG

Creative Baking: Deco Chiffon Cake Basics

Creative Baking: Deco Chiffon Cakes

Creative Baking: Chiffon Cakes

Let's Bake!

A PUSHEEN COOKBOOK

Claire Belton
and Susanne Ng

GALLERY BOOKS

New York   London   Toronto   Sydney   New Delhi

Gallery Books
An Imprint of Simon & Schuster, Inc.
1230 Avenue of the Americas
New York, NY 10020

Copyright © 2020 by Pusheen Corp. and Susanne Ng

First Gallery Books hardcover edition June 2020

GALLERY BOOKS and colophon are registered trademarks of Simon & Schuster, Inc.

For information about special discounts for bulk purchases, please contact Simon & Schuster Special Sales at 1-866-506-1949 or business@simonandschuster.com.

The Simon & Schuster Speakers Bureau can bring authors to your live event. For more information or to book an event, contact the Simon & Schuster Speakers Bureau at 1-866-248-3049 or visit our website at www.simonspeakers.com.

Interior design by Jaime Putorti
Photographs by Liu Hongde and Claire Chin

Manufactured in the United States of America

3   5   7   9   10   8   6   4   2

Library of Congress Cataloging-in-Publication Data has been applied for.

ISBN 978-1-9821-3542-3
ISBN 978-1-9821-3543-0 (ebook)

To Pusheen:
Our constant muse, inspiration, delight, and companion
through many days of writing and baking.
You made it such a joy!

To the Pusheen fans:
Yes, this book is especially for you!

Contents

Pastries

Cakes

Breads & Breakfast

Introduction

Pusheen is a funny, mischievous, adorably plump tabby cat that brings smiles and laughter to people all around the world. She came to life through her animated comics and stickers on Pusheen.com, Facebook, Instagram, and other social media platforms! As you may have noticed, Pusheen is *really* into snacking! In this book, creator/artist Claire Belton and creative chef Susanne Ng have joined forces to create and share forty cute and delicious recipes, celebrating Pusheen's boundless love for treats!

In these super-fun recipes, you will find Pusheen everywhere, adorning sweet treats like cookies and marshmallows, yummy desserts like jelly, classical pastries such as tarts and éclairs, beautiful celebration cakes, and even Pusheen's favorite savory snack—pizza! There are basic recipes for beginners as well as more challenging projects for more advanced bakers.

Lots of love, laughter, and snacking "research and development" went into the creation of this cookbook. We hope that you will enjoy re-creating these recipes as much as Pusheen enjoys eating them!

All recipes have received the Pusheen Gold Beans of Approval.

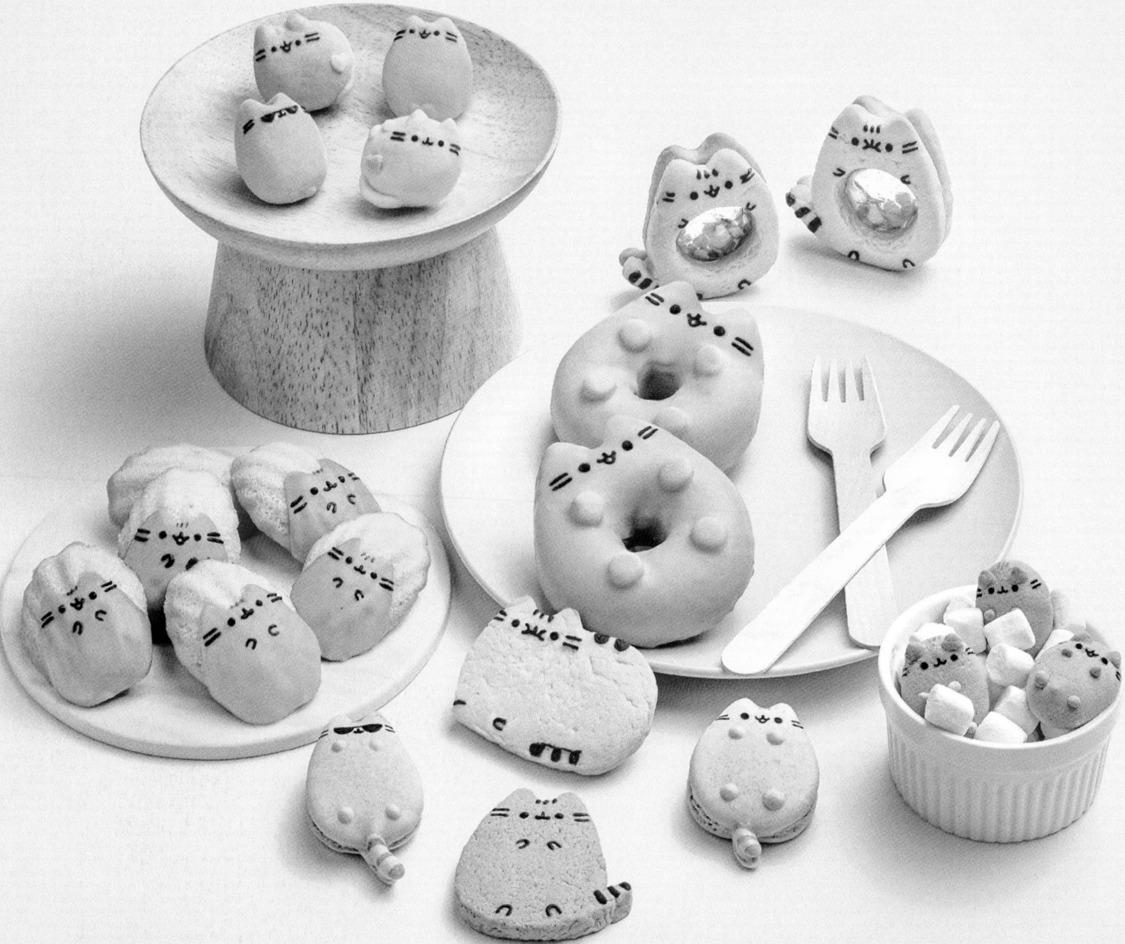

Cookies & Sweets

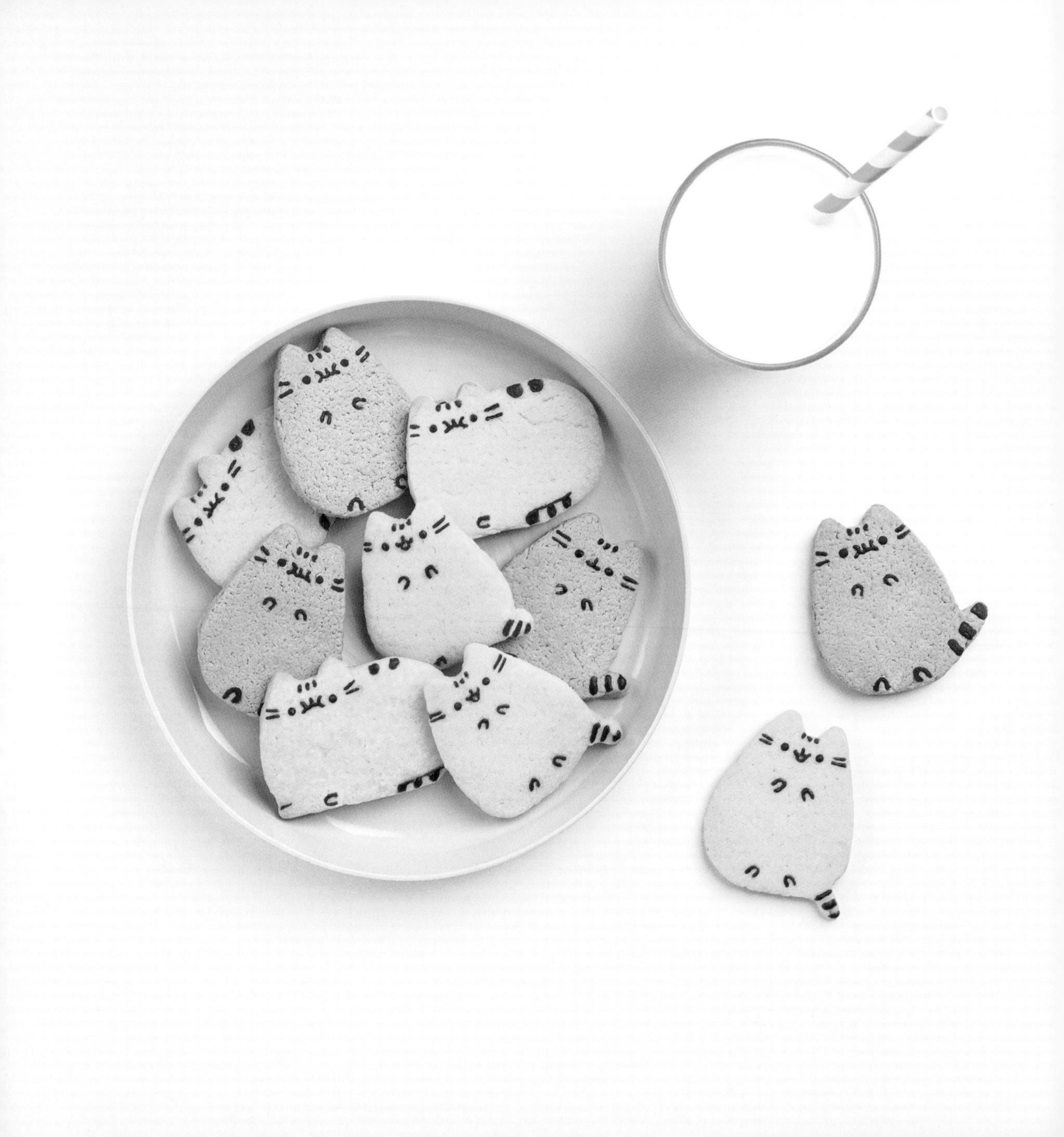

PUSHEEN BUTTER COOKIES

MAKES 18 TO 20 COOKIES • LEVEL OF DIFFICULTY: EASY

Tender and buttery, with a delightful infusion of vanilla and almond, these cookies are seriously addictive! They are extremely fuss-free to work with, too, retaining their shape well after baking. Use the templates at the back of the book to create your favorite Pusheen poses!

. . . .

INGREDIENTS

Butter Cookies

8 tablespoons (1 stick/115g) unsalted butter, cut into cubes and slightly softened but still cold

½ cup (100g) superfine sugar

1 large egg

2 cups (240g) all-purpose flour, sifted

¼ cup (30g) cornstarch

¼ teaspoon salt

¼ teaspoon pure vanilla extract

¼ teaspoon pure almond extract

Black food coloring or unsweetened black cocoa powder

Decorations

6 ounces (150g) dark coating/compound chocolate, chopped, or melting wafers

or

1 tablespoon meringue powder

1 ⅓ cups (165g) confectioners' sugar

2 tablespoons water

. . . .

1 MAKE THE COOKIES: In a large bowl, using an electric mixer, cream the butter and superfine sugar until pale and fluffy. Scrape down the bowl, add the egg, and beat until the egg is well incorporated and the mixture lightens in color.

2 With the mixer on low speed, beat in the flour, cornstarch, and salt. Add the vanilla and almond extract and mix well.

3 Divide the dough into two portions. To one portion, knead in a few drops of black food coloring or black cocoa powder pinch by pinch to tint the dough gray. Form the gray dough and plain dough into separate discs. Wrap in plastic wrap and chill for about 1 hour.

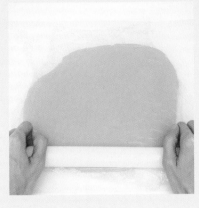

④ Preheat the oven to 340°F (170°C). Line 2 baking sheets with parchment paper or a silicone baking mat. Make a template by tracing Pusheen shapes from the Butter Cookies templates on page 197 (templates 1, 2, and 3) onto a piece of cake board or food-safe plastic and cutting them out.

⑤ Roll the dough out to ¼ inch (6mm) thick. Using a sharp knife, cut out your desired Pusheen shapes by placing your templates on top of the dough and using them as guides.

⑥ Place the cookies on the prepared baking sheets. Bake for 12 minutes. Remove from the oven and let the cookies cool completely on the pan.

⑦ DECORATE THE COOKIES: Paint or pipe on the Pusheen features using melted chocolate or royal icing. For melted chocolate, place the chocolate in a medium microwave-safe bowl and microwave in 30-second intervals, stirring after each to prevent burning, until melted and smooth. For royal icing, combine the meringue powder, confectioners' sugar, and water in a medium bowl and beat with an electric mixer on high speed until the icing forms peaks, about 10 minutes.

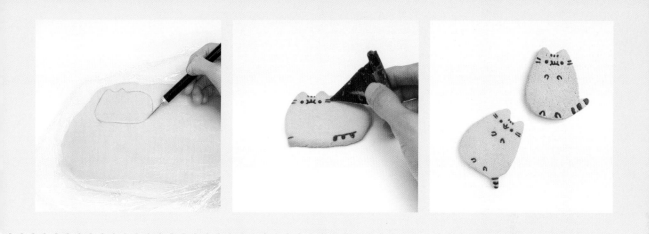

PUSHEEN 3D GERMAN COOKIES

MAKES 16 COOKIES · LEVEL OF DIFFICULTY: MEDIUM

Melt-in-your-mouth, crumbly, and pleasantly sweet, these 3D cookies will have you reaching for seconds. Using only five ingredients, the dough is extremely easy to shape into Pusheen.

1 Preheat the oven to 250°F (120°C). Line a baking sheet with parchment paper or a silicone baking mat.

2 In a large bowl, using an electric mixer, cream the butter and confectioners' sugar until pale and fluffy.

3 Sift the potato starch and cake flour together, add to the butter-sugar mixture, and mix with a spatula until the dough comes together.

4 Divide the dough into 4 equal portions. Tint each portion with a few drops of food coloring, using a different color (pink, green, purple, and black) for each,* and knead until the coloring is evenly incorporated. From each portion of dough, form 4 balls of ½ ounce (15g) each, for a total of 16 balls. You will have some dough scraps to use for the small parts like ears, hands, feet, and stripes.

*Optional: Instead of dividing the dough and coloring each portion separately, you can make just original gray Pusheens. Add

INGREDIENTS

- 5 tablespoons plus 1 teaspoon (75g) unsalted butter, cut into cubes and slightly softened but still cold
- 3 tablespoons confectioners' sugar
- ⅔ cup (100g) potato starch
- 6 tablespoons (50g) cake flour
- Food coloring: pink, green, purple, and black (or use natural food colorings: beet, matcha, purple sweet potato, and unsweetened black cocoa powders)

Decorations

- 3 ounces (80g) dark coating/compound chocolate, chopped, or melting wafers

or

- 1½ teaspoons meringue powder
- ⅔ cup (85g) confectioners' sugar
- 1 tablespoon water

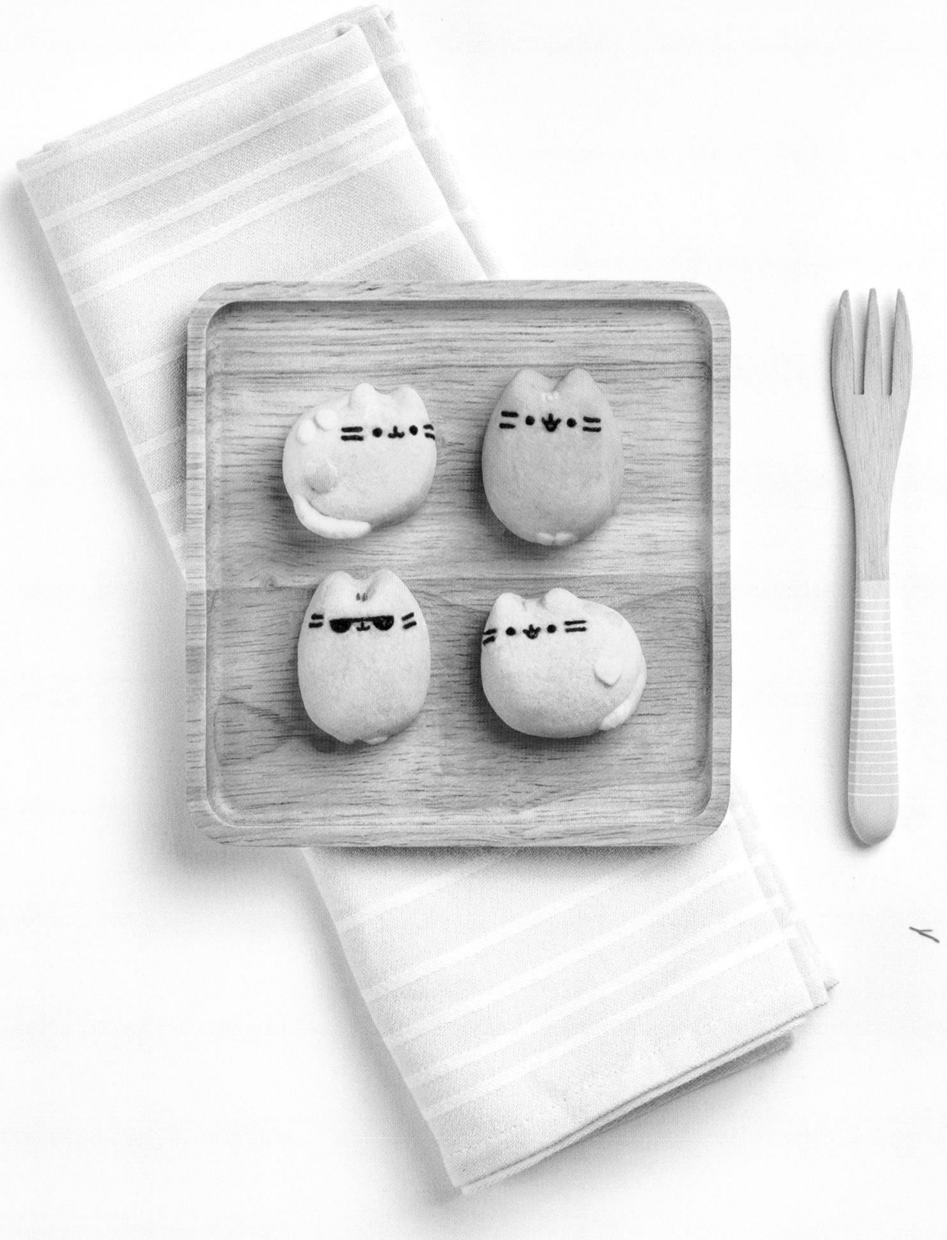

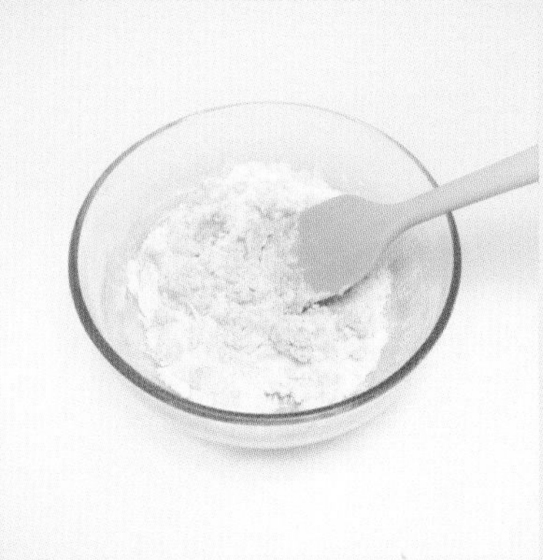
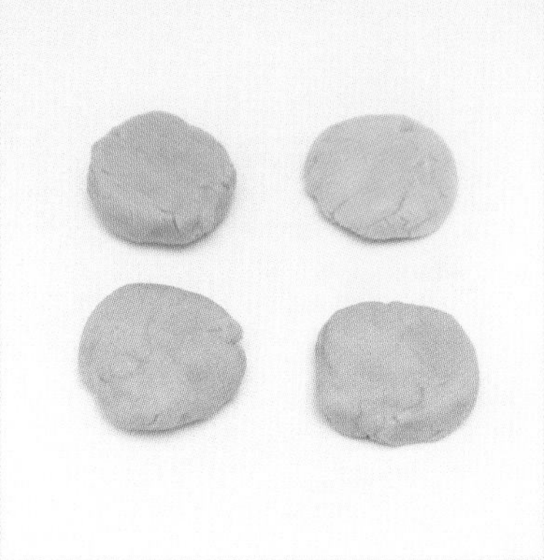
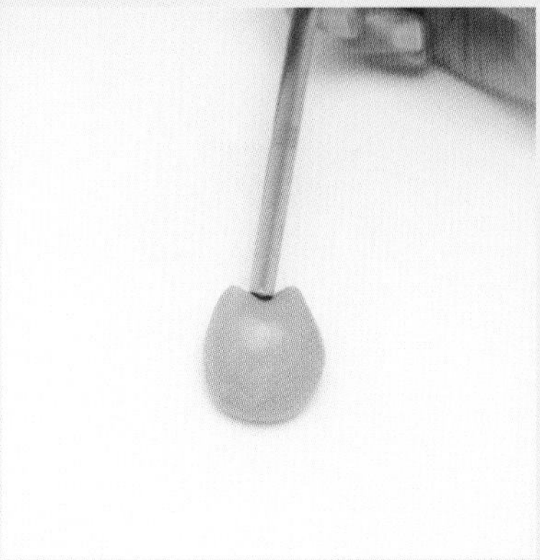

a few drops of black food coloring or a few pinches of black cocoa powder to the dough to color it gray, then shape Pusheens as directed.

5 MAKE THE PINK AND PURPLE PUSHEENS: Shape the balls of pink and purple dough into oval logs. Pinch two small pieces from the dough scraps* and shape them into small triangles for the ears. The bottoms of the ears should be wider than the tops. Attach the ears by pressing the wider portion to the top of the body. To create the tail, pinch tiny balls from two colors, press them together, roll them out into a tail shape, and attach it to the body. Finish by shaping dough into stripes and hearts and attaching them to Pusheen's body. Place the Pusheens on the prepared baking sheet.

*Tip: Lightly cover the dough scraps with plastic wrap to prevent the small parts from drying out. Usually the small parts stick to the body easily. If you have difficulty, just lightly brush them with some water.

6 MAKE THE GRAY AND GREEN PUSHEENS: Shape the balls of gray and green dough into egg shapes, with one end narrower than the other. Use the handle of a pastry brush or wooden spoon to push down the center of the narrower end to make the ears. Roll other colors of dough into thin strips for the head stripes. Pinch off tiny balls from the dough scraps for the feet and attach the feet to the body. Place the Pusheens on the prepared baking sheet.

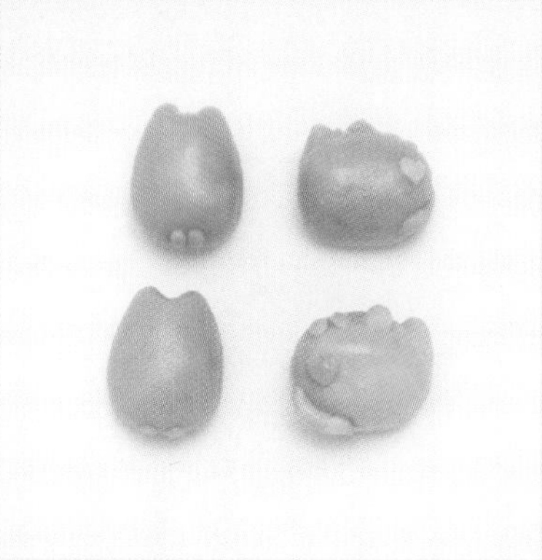

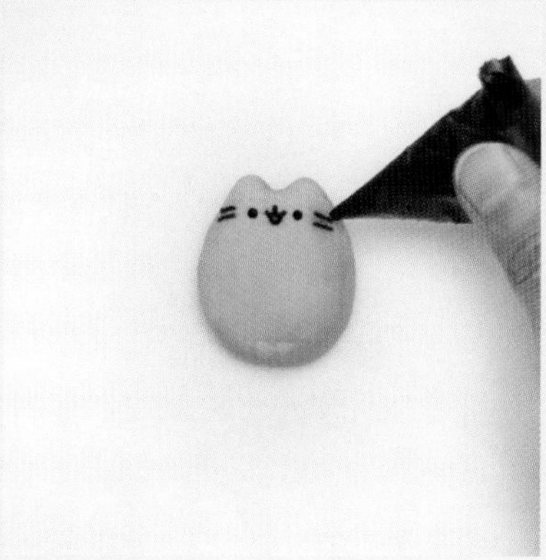

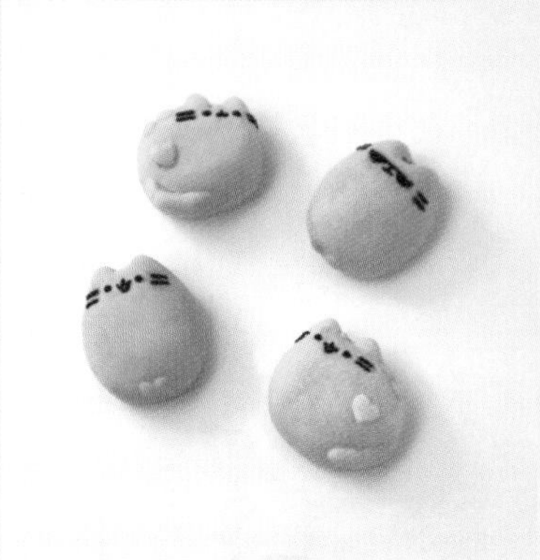

7 Bake for 25 minutes. Remove from the oven and let the cookies cool on the pan completely.

8 DECORATE THE COOKIES: Add the Pusheen features using melted chocolate or royal icing. For melted chocolate, place the chocolate in a small microwave-safe bowl and microwave in 30-second intervals, stirring after each to prevent burning, until melted and smooth. For royal icing, in a medium bowl, combine the meringue powder, confectioners' sugar, and water and beat with an electric mixer on high speed until the icing forms peaks, about 10 minutes. Place the chocolate or royal icing in a small piping bag. Snip a hole in the tip and pipe on Pusheen's features.

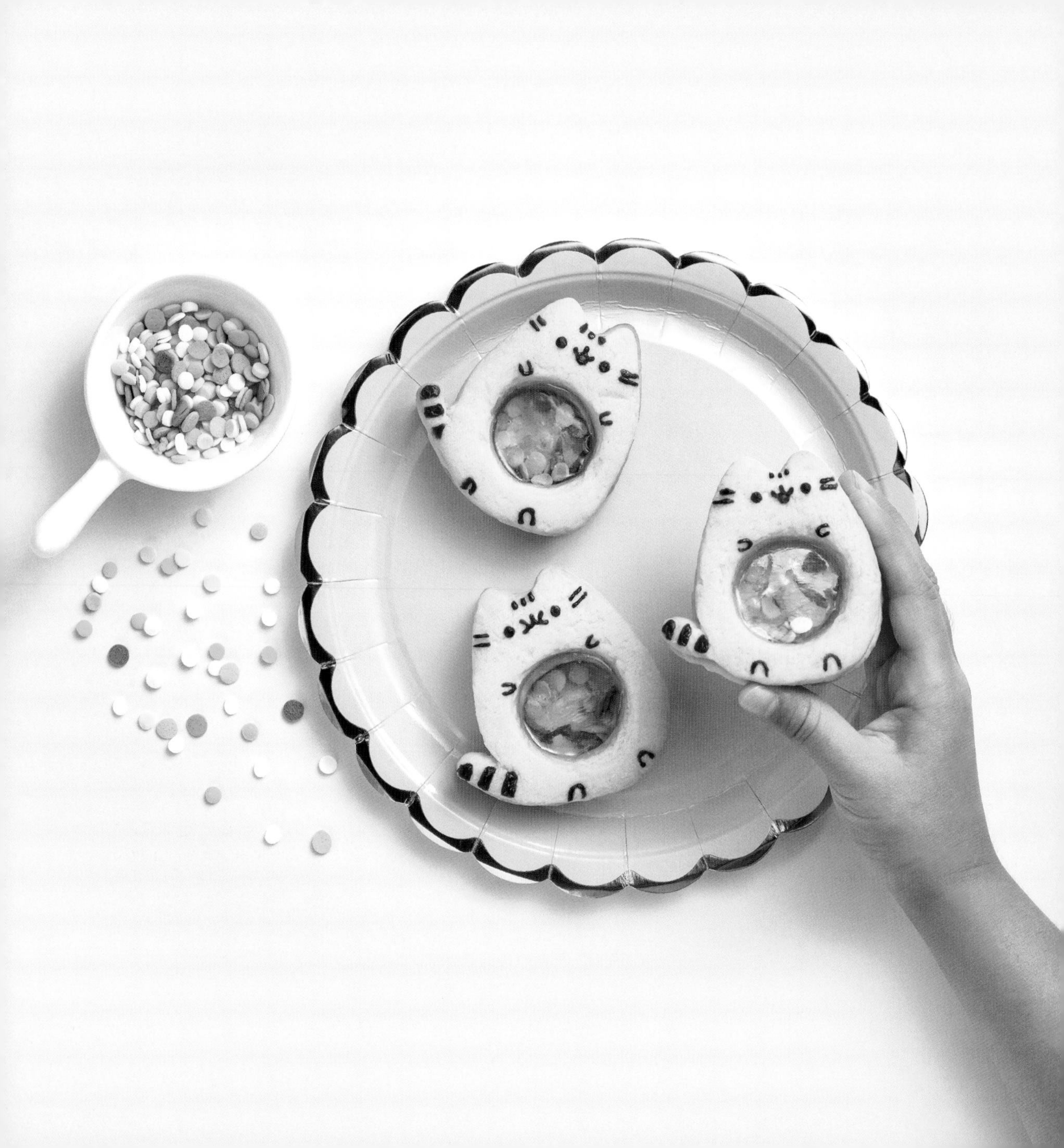

PUSHEEN SHAKER COOKIES

MAKES 9 COOKIES · LEVEL OF DIFFICULTY: EASY

The most adorable and tasty butter cookies transformed into Pusheen shaker toys, these are a great excuse to play with your food! Even better, you get to choose your favorite clear candies and sprinkles to complement and customize the cookies. This is truly as good as it gets!

. . . .

INGREDIENTS

Vanilla Butter Cookies

8 tablespoons (1 stick/115g) unsalted butter, cut into cubes and slightly softened but still cold

½ cup (100g) superfine sugar

1 large egg

2 cups (240g) all-purpose flour, sifted

¼ cup (30g) cornstarch

Generous ¼ teaspoon salt

½ teaspoon pure vanilla extract

3½ tablespoons crushed hard clear candies*

Assembly and Decorations

½ (3-ounce [85g]) bottle of rainbow-colored sprinkles

3 ounces (80g) dark coating/compound chocolate, chopped, or melting wafers

or

1½ teaspoons meringue powder

⅔ cup (85g) confectioners' sugar

1 tablespoon water

. . . .

*Tip: Choose any brand or flavor of hard clear candies that you enjoy. To crush the whole candies, place them in a zip-top bag and crush them into a fine powder using a mallet or rolling pin.

1 MAKE THE COOKIES: In a large bowl, using an electric mixer, cream the butter and superfine sugar until pale and fluffy. Scrape down the bowl and add the egg. Beat until the egg is well incorporated and the mixture lightens in color.

2 With the mixer on low speed, mix in the sifted flour, cornstarch, and salt. Add the vanilla and mix well.

3 Form the dough into a disc, wrap it in plastic wrap, and chill for about 1 hour.

④ Preheat the oven to 340°F (170°C). Line 2 baking sheets with parchment paper or a silicone baking mat. Make a template by tracing a Pusheen shape from the Shaker Cookies template on page 197 (template 1) onto a piece of cake board or food-safe plastic and cut it out.

⑤ Roll the dough out to ¼ inch (6mm) thick. Using a sharp knife, cut out the Pusheen shapes by placing your template on top of the dough and using it as a guide. You should have a total of 18 cookies. Place the cookies on the prepared baking sheets. Using a round cutter smaller than the Pusheen body (at least ¼ inch/6mm smaller on all sides), punch out a hole from the belly of each Pusheen cookie. Discard the dough rounds or bake them separately for a special treat.

⑥ Fill the center of each cookie with the crushed candies, distributing the candy evenly. The layer of crushed candies must be sufficiently thick, about ¼ inch (6mm).

⑦ Bake for 12 to 13 minutes, until lightly golden brown. When the cookies come out of the oven, immediately use a pin to pop any air bubbles in the candy center. Let the cookies cool completely on the pan to ensure that the candy has fully set before lifting them off.

8 ASSEMBLE AND DECORATE THE COOKIES: Use melted chocolate or royal icing. For melted chocolate, place the chocolate in a small microwave-safe bowl and microwave in 30-second intervals, stirring after each to prevent burning, until melted and smooth. For royal icing, in a medium bowl, combine the meringue powder, confectioners' sugar, and water and beat with an electric mixer on high speed until the icing forms peaks, about 10 minutes.

9 Place some of the sprinkles (about 24 to 28) inside the windowpane of one cookie. Transfer the melted chocolate or royal icing to a small piping bag and snip a small hole in the tip. Pipe a ring of melted chocolate or royal icing around the windowpane and sandwich it with another cookie. Repeat to assemble the remaining cookies.

10 Pipe on the Pusheen features with the remaining melted chocolate or royal icing.

PUSHEEN DIPPED SANDWICH COOKIES

MAKES 25 TO 30 COOKIES • LEVEL OF DIFFICULTY: MEDIUM

Dark chocolate cookies sandwiched with vanilla cream filling and then coated with more chocolate, these treats are satisfying and delicious! There's something so nostalgic about chocolate sandwich cookies with a glass of cold milk, whether you dunk them in the milk or eat them separately!

INGREDIENTS

Cookies

10 tablespoons (1¼ sticks/145g) unsalted butter, cut into cubes and slightly softened but still cold

½ cup (100g) superfine sugar

½ cup (100g) packed brown sugar

1 large egg

1 teaspoon pure vanilla extract

1¼ cups (150g) all-purpose flour

½ cup (50g) unsweetened dark cocoa powder

¼ teaspoon salt

Cream Filling

8 tablespoons (1 stick/115g) unsalted butter, cut into cubes and slightly softened but still cold

2 cups (250g) confectioners' sugar

1 tablespoon pure vanilla extract

White Chocolate Coating

10½ ounces (300g) white coating/compound chocolate, chopped, or Candy Melts

2 tablespoons coconut oil, plus more if needed

Black oil-based food coloring or unsweetened black cocoa powder

Decorations

3 ounces (80g) dark coating/compound chocolate, chopped, or melting wafers

1 **MAKE THE COOKIES:** In a large bowl, using an electric mixer, cream the butter, superfine sugar, and brown sugar until pale and fluffy. Add the egg and beat until the egg is incorporated and the mixture lightens in color. Add the vanilla and mix well.

2 Sift the flour, dark cocoa powder, and salt together into a separate large bowl. Fold the dry ingredients into the butter-sugar mixture with a spatula until they are well incorporated.

3 Scrape the soft dough out onto a piece of parchment paper. Cover with a second sheet of parchment paper and roll the dough into a sheet ¼ inch (6mm) thick. Freeze the dough for about 30 minutes.

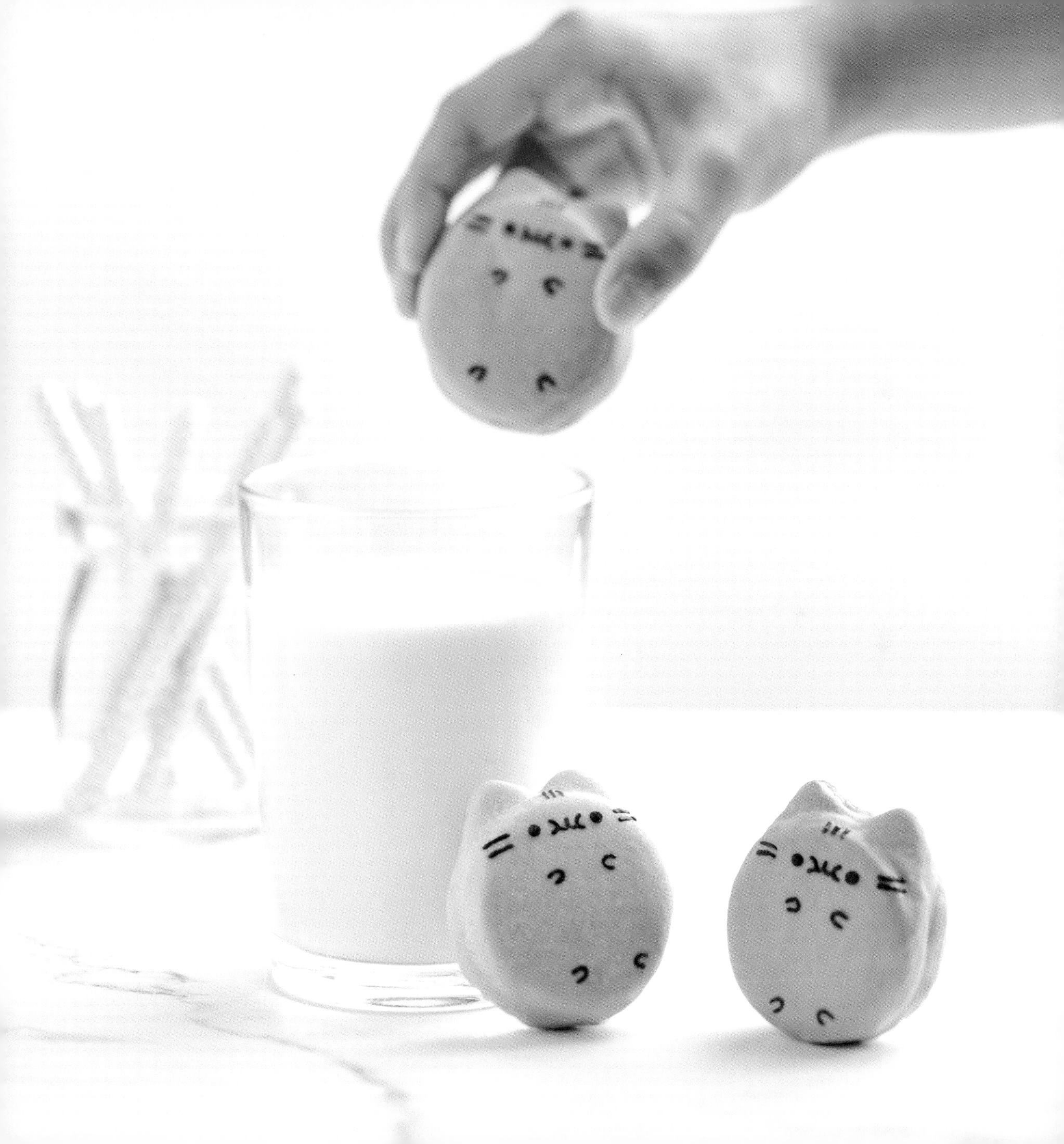

4 Preheat the oven to 325°F (160°C). Line 3 baking sheets with parchment paper.

5 Remove the top sheet of parchment paper from the chilled dough and cut the dough into 2-inch (5cm) rounds. Place them on 2 of the prepared baking sheets, leaving 1½ inches (4cm) between them. Gather up any scraps and form them into a disc; set aside.

6 Bake the cookies for 20 minutes. Remove from the oven and let the cookies cool completely on the pans. Keep the oven on.

7 Roll out the scraps to ⅛ inch (3mm) thick. Use a ½ x ⅓–inch (15 x 8mm) teardrop-shaped cutter to cut out shapes for the ears. If you do not have a teardrop-shaped cutter, pinch one side of a plastic straw and use that instead.

8 Place the teardrop shapes on the remaining lined baking sheet. Bake for 14 minutes. Remove from the oven and let the cookies cool completely on the pan.

9 MAKE THE CREAM FILLING: In a large bowl, using an electric mixer, cream the butter until soft, then sift in the confectioners' sugar and add the vanilla. Beat until the mixture is light and fluffy. Spread the filling over the bottom of one round cookie, then sandwich it with the bottom of another cookie. Press them together and clean off any excess filling with a knife. Insert 2 teardrop ears into the cream between

the round cookies, pointed ends facing out. Set the cookies on a baking sheet and refrigerate while you prepare the chocolate coating.

10 MAKE THE WHITE CHOCOLATE COATING: Place the white chocolate and 2 tablespoons coconut oil* in a medium microwave-safe bowl and microwave in 30-second intervals, stirring after each to prevent burning. If needed, add more coconut oil, 1 teaspoon at a time, until the chocolate is melted and has a dipping or pouring consistency. (Alternatively, use a double boiler to melt the chocolate and coconut oil.) Add drops of black food coloring or pinches of black cocoa powder and stir until smooth and evenly tinted the desired shade of gray.

*Tip: If you are using Candy Melts, you can use 1 tablespoon EZ Thin or shortening instead of the coconaut oil to thin the chocolate.

11 Line another baking sheet with parchment paper. Dip each chilled cookie in the white chocolate coating and place them on the prepared baking sheet, or place the cookies on the baking sheet and spoon over the coating. Let stand until the coating is set.

12 DECORATE THE COOKIES: When the chocolate coating has set, place the dark chocolate in a small microwave-safe bowl and microwave in 30-second intervals, stirring after each to prevent burning, until melted and smooth. Transfer the melted chocolate to a small piping bag, snip a small hole in the tip, and pipe Pusheen features onto the cookies.

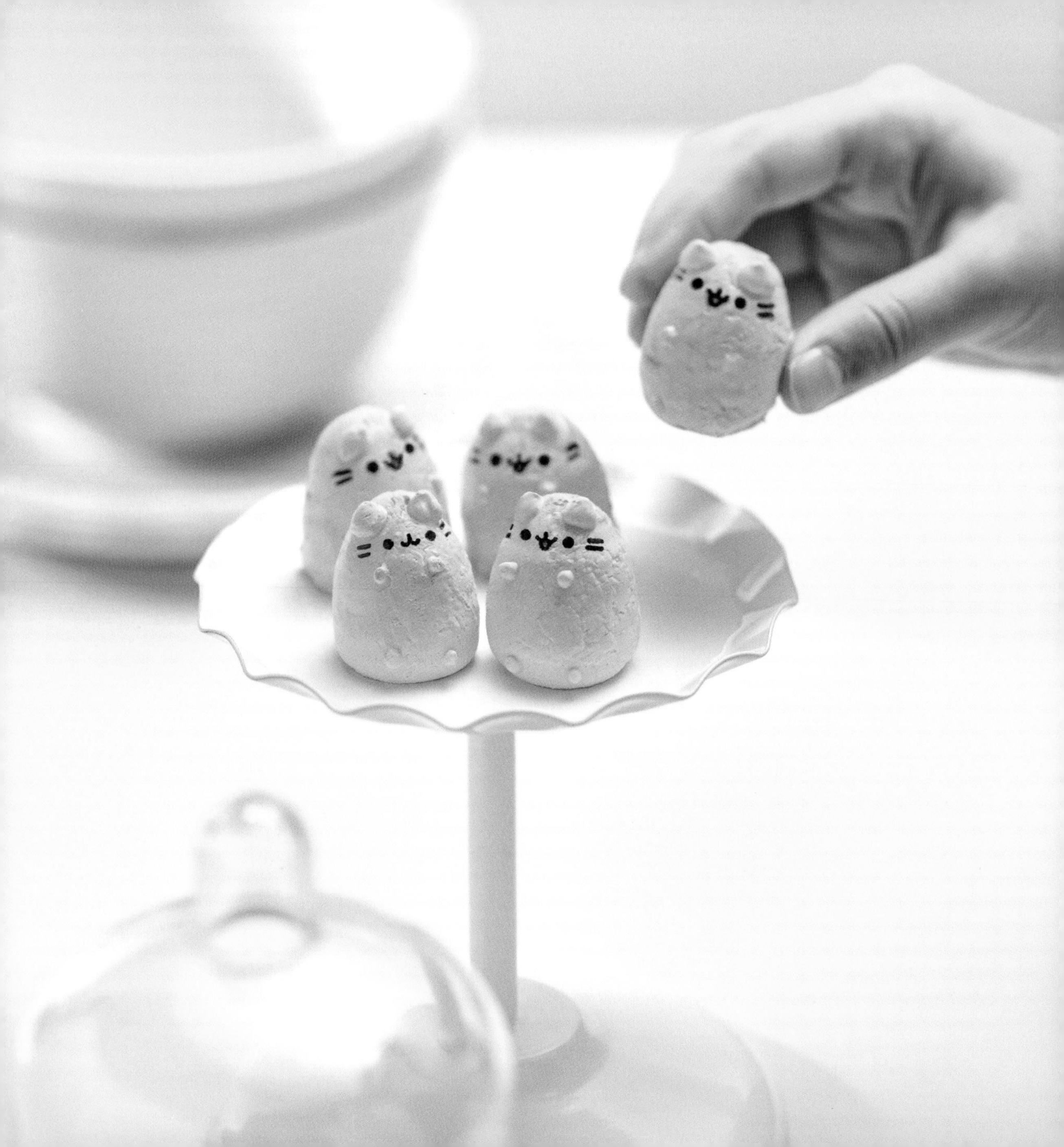

PUSHEEN MERINGUE COOKIES

MAKES 18 OR 19 COOKIES · LEVEL OF DIFFICULTY: DIFFICULT

Crispy on the outside but wonderfully soft on the inside, these sweet, airy, and cloudlike meringues are transformed into 3D Pusheens that are (almost) too cute to eat! Based on the recipe for Swiss meringue, these cookies are actually not difficult once you master the oven temperature control to prevent cracking.

1 Fill a medium saucepan with about 1 ½ inches (4cm) of water and bring it to a simmer over low heat. Place the egg white, sugar, and cream of tartar in a medium bowl. Place the bowl on top of the saucepan (make sure the water does not touch the bottom of the bowl). Cook the egg white mixture, whisking continuously, for 5 minutes, until the sugar has completely dissolved and the temperature of the mixture is 160°F (71°C). Do not allow the egg whites to scramble/coagulate. You can test if it is ready by rubbing a small amount of the mixture between your thumb and index finger. If it feels grainy, cook, whisking continuously, for 30 seconds to 1 minute more, then test again.

2 Immediately remove the bowl from the heat and beat the mixture with an electric mixer on medium speed until the meringue holds stiff peaks or the bowl is completely cool. Add a drop of black food coloring or a pinch of black cocoa powder and gently beat the color in until evenly incorporated.

3 Preheat the oven to 195°F (90°C). Line a baking sheet with parchment paper or a silicone baking mat.

INGREDIENTS

- 1 large egg white
- 5 tablespoons superfine sugar
- Pinch of cream of tartar
- Black food coloring or unsweetened black cocoa powder
- Edible ink markers (black and gray) or food coloring (dark brown and gray)

④ Transfer 1 tablespoon of the meringue into a small piping bag fitted with a 1mm round tip and set aside. Spoon the remaining meringue into a large piping bag fitted with a ¼-inch (6mm) round tip, or just snip a ¼-inch (6mm) hole. Pipe tall, round mounds of the meringue, about 1 inch (2.5cm) in diameter, onto the baking sheet at least 1 inch (2.5cm) apart, releasing the pressure on the bag before you lift it away. Use a toothpick to smooth the peak on each meringue. Using the meringue in the smaller piping bag, pipe tiny ears, hands, and feet onto the meringues. Bake for 1 hour, then turn off the oven and leave the meringues inside for 30 to 60 minutes to continue drying.

⑤ Remove the dried meringues from the oven. Using an edible ink marker or a toothpick dipped in dark brown food coloring,* draw on the Pusheen features. Dot on the head stripes with an edible ink marker or a toothpick dipped in gray food coloring.*

*Tip: You can make your own natural dark brown and gray food colorings using unsweetened dark or black cocoa powder dissolved in an equal quantity of hot water.

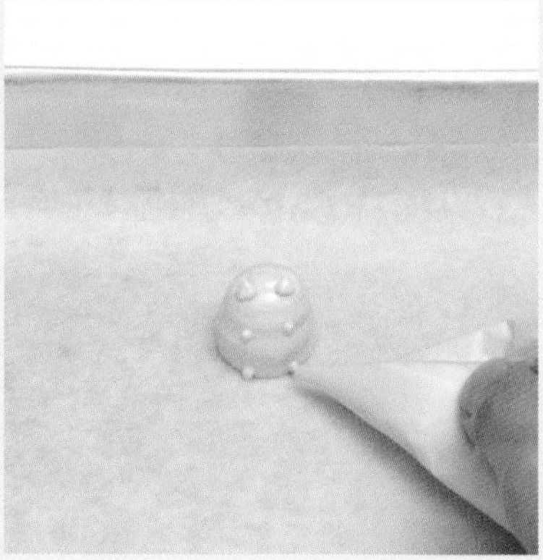

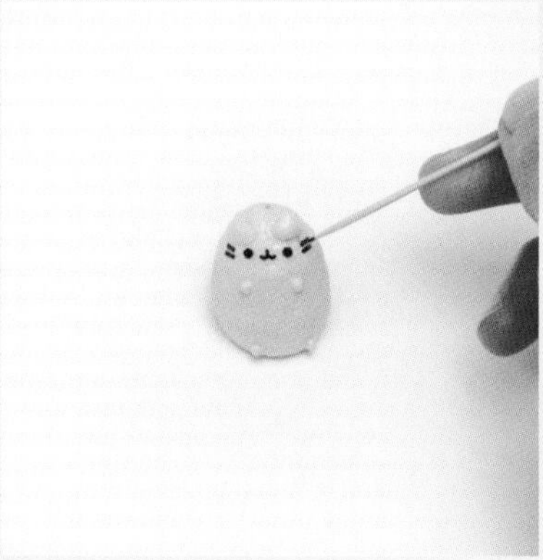

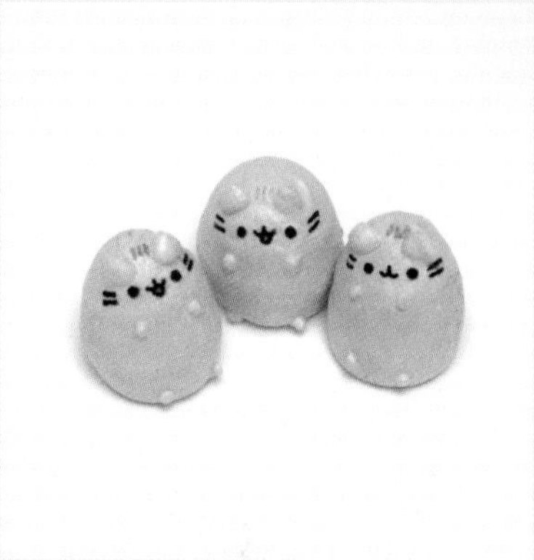

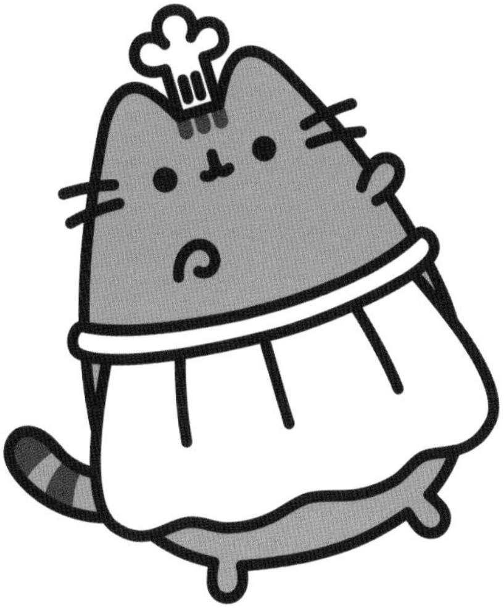

PUSHEEN MARSHMALLOWS

MAKES 25 TO 30 MARSHMALLOWS · LEVEL OF DIFFICULTY: MEDIUM

Nothing compares to the soft and pillowy fluffiness of homemade marshmallows! Scented with sweet vanilla, these marshmallow Pusheens are yummy and lovable, perfect on hot chocolate or just for popping into your mouth anytime!

· ·

1 Place the gelatin in the bottom of a medium heatproof bowl. Add 2 tablespoons of the cold water to the bowl. The amount should be sufficient to bloom the gelatin without needing to drain excess water. If it isn't, add more cold water, 1 teaspoon at a time. (See page 191.) Set aside to bloom for 5 to 10 minutes.

2 In a small saucepan, combine the remaining 2 tablespoons cold water, the honey, and the vanilla. If you have a candy thermometer, clip it to the side of the pan. Heat the mixture over medium heat until it reaches 239°F (115°C). Remove the saucepan from the heat.

3 Slowly pour the honey mixture into the bowl with the bloomed gelatin and whip the mixture using an electric mixer on high speed until slightly cooled, white, and foamy. With the mixer running, drizzle in the egg white and whip until the meringue is thick, white, and fluffy. Add a drop of black food coloring or a pinch of black cocoa powder and quickly beat in the color until the meringue is a uniform gray shade. Test the consistency of the meringue by lifting out the beaters: If it forms peaks or ribbons that

INGREDIENTS

- 3 gold gelatin sheets (2g each), cut into quarters
- 4 tablespoons cold water, plus more if needed to soak the gelatin
- 7 tablespoons (100g) light-colored honey
- 1 teaspoon pure vanilla extract
- ½ large egg white
- Black food coloring or unsweetened black cocoa powder
- Cornstarch, for dusting
- Black edible ink marker

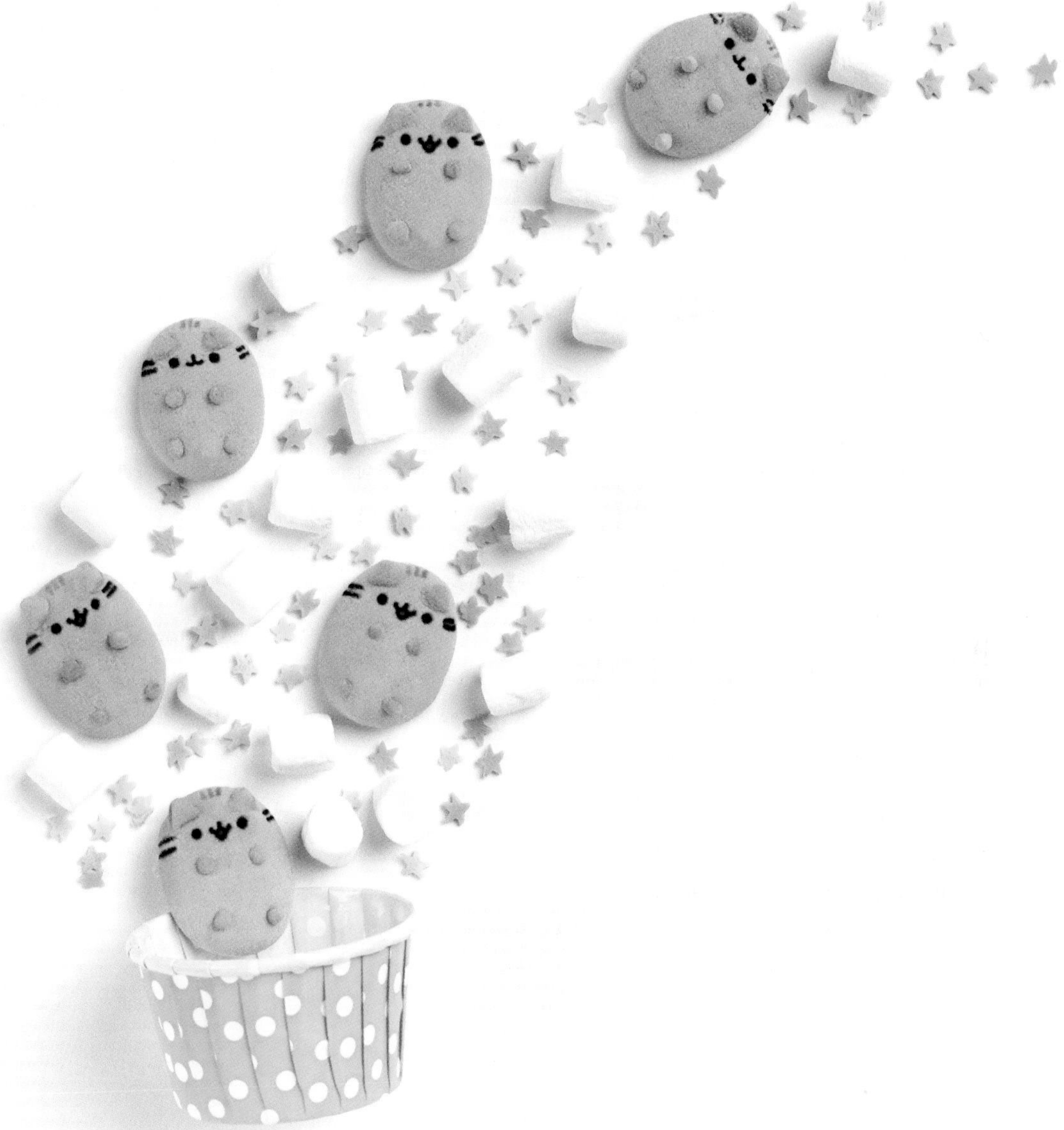

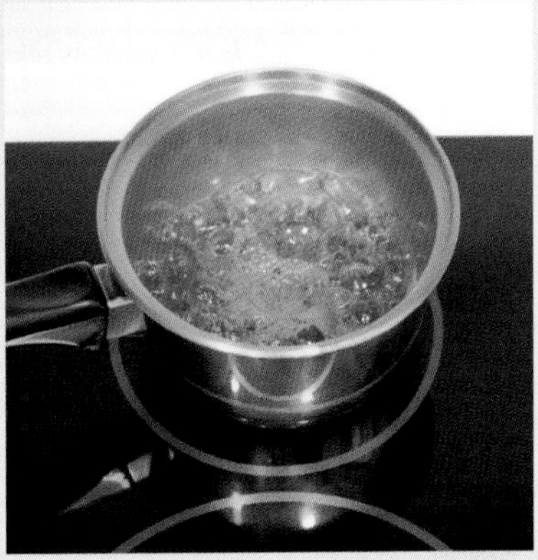
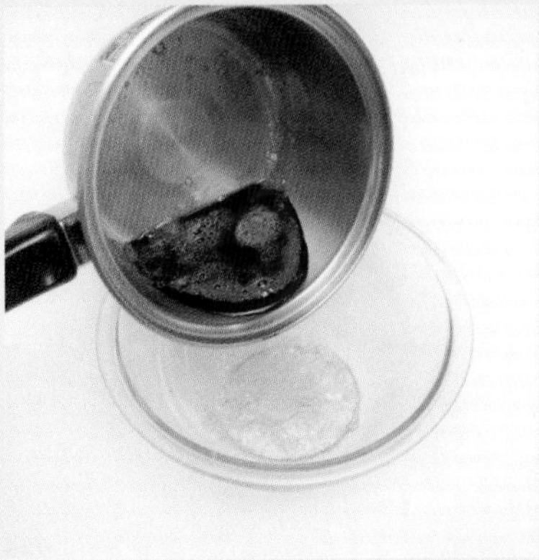
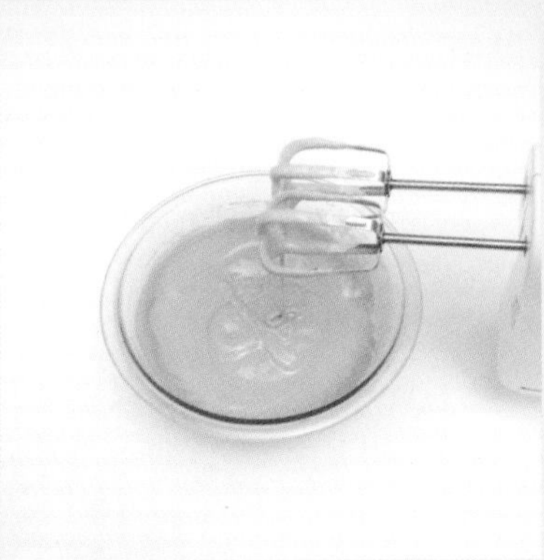
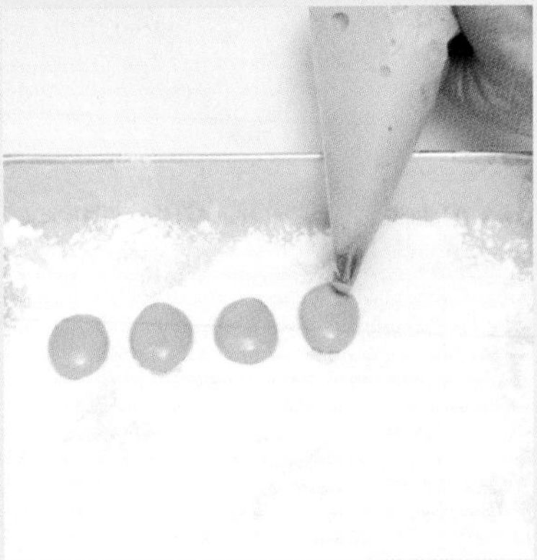
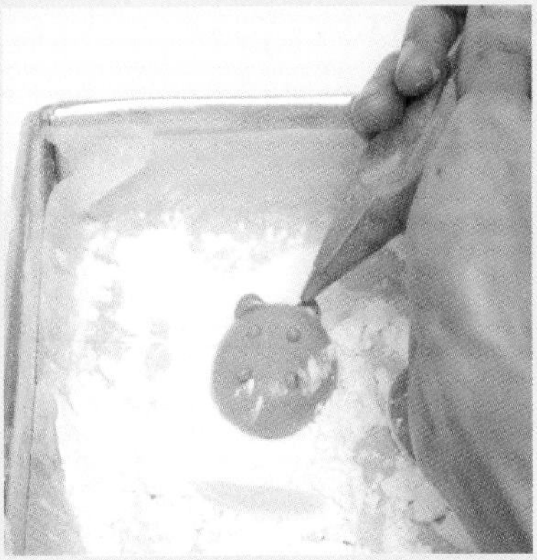
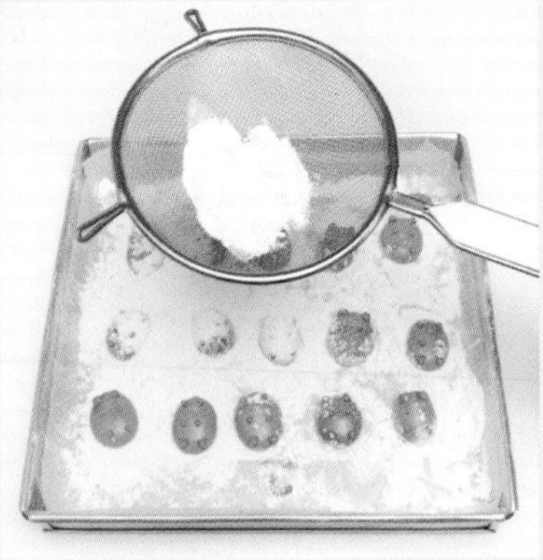
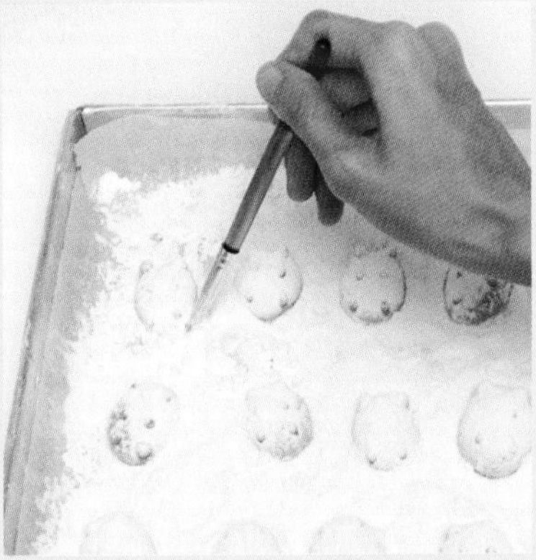
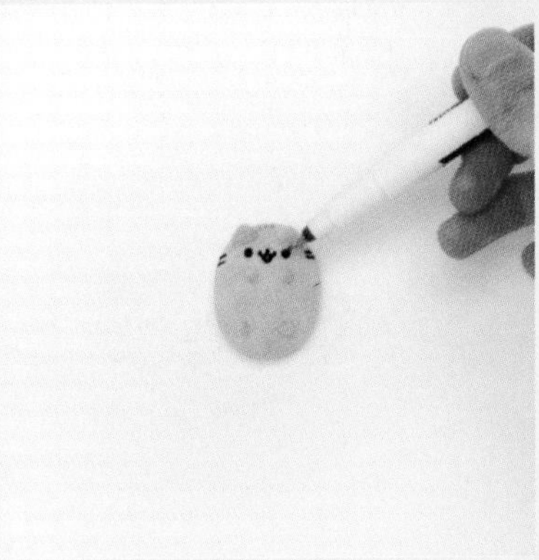
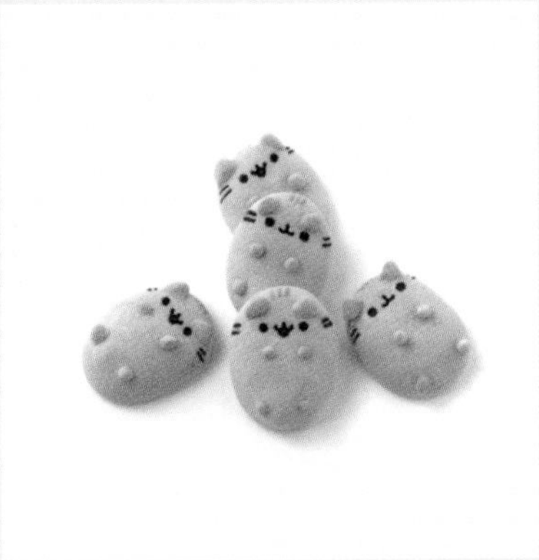

hold their shape as it falls from the beaters into the bowl, it is ready. If the meringue is not ready, beat in 10-second increments, testing again between each.

4 Spoon 1 tablespoon of the meringue into a small piping bag fitted with a 1mm round tip. Transfer the remaining meringue to a large piping bag fitted with a ¼-inch (6mm) round tip. Line a baking sheet with parchment paper and sift cornstarch over the parchment. Pipe ovals of the meringue about 1 inch (2.5cm) long onto the parchment, releasing the pressure on the bag before lifting it away. Using the meringue in the smaller piping bag, pipe tiny ears, hands, and feet onto each oval. Refrigerate for at least 6 hours to set.

5 Sift cornstarch over the marshmallows to remove stickiness and use a pastry brush to dust off any excess.

6 Draw Pusheen features on the marshmallows using the edible ink marker.

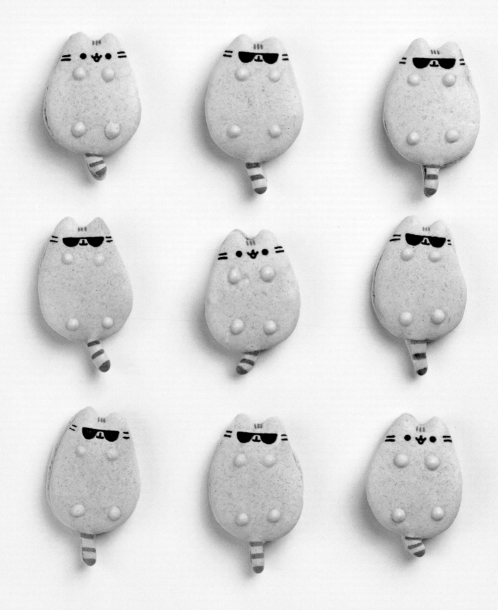

PUSHEEN MACARONS WITH WHITE CHOCOLATE GANACHE FILLING

MAKES 16 TO 20 MACARONS • LEVEL OF DIFFICULTY: MEDIUM

With a delicate almond-infused shell, a soft and chewy interior, and a burst of bold chocolate ganache flavor, these Pusheen macarons with pop-up hands and feet are guaranteed to both tickle your taste buds and please your other senses! Use the templates provided at the back of the book to make the top and bottom shells in cool Pusheen poses. Remember to pipe hands and feet only for the top shells!

*Tip: Aging egg whites dehydrates them slightly and makes them more stable when whipped. To age the egg whites, store them in a loosely covered container in the refrigerator for 24 hours.

1 Photocopy or scan and print the Macarons templates on pages 199 and 201 (templates 5 and 6). Ensure that there is an equal number of poses and their mirror images for making the top and bottom shells. Place the templates under the parchment paper or silicone baking mat on a baking sheet.

2 MAKE THE MACARON SHELLS: Sift the confectioners' sugar and almond flour into a medium bowl. Mix well with a spatula.

3 In a large bowl, using an electric mixer, whip the egg whites with the superfine sugar and cream of tartar until they hold stiff, dry peaks.

INGREDIENTS

Macaron Shells

1 cup (125g) confectioners' sugar

1 cup (85g) almond flour

2 large egg whites, aged for 24 hours (see tip*), at room temperature

3½ tablespoons superfine sugar

Pinch of cream of tartar

Black food coloring or unsweetened black cocoa powder

White Chocolate Ganache Filling

3 ounces (80g) white couverture chocolate, chopped

2 tablespoons heavy cream

Decorations

Black edible ink marker

4 Using a spatula, fold the dry mixture into the egg whites in a few additions. When all the dry mixture has been mostly incorporated (it's okay if some white streaks remain), tint the batter by adding drops of black food coloring or pinches of black cocoa powder to reach the desired gray shade, then continue folding until the batter falls from the spatula in ribbons or like molten lava.

5 Spoon 1 tablespoon of the batter into a small piping bag fitted with a 1mm round tip. Transfer the remaining batter into a large piping bag fitted with a ¼-inch (6mm) round tip. Pipe the batter perpendicularly onto the prepared baking sheet to fill the body. Using the smaller tip, pipe ears, joining them to the body. If necessary, use a toothpick to spread the batter evenly around the shape. Pipe on the tail.

6 Let the batter stand for 20 to 30 minutes, until it forms a thin skin, then, using the small piping tip, pipe dots for the hands and feet on half the bodies (these will be the macaron tops). Let stand for 30 minutes more, or until the batter forms a skin and is no longer sticky to the touch.

7 Preheat the oven to 285°F (140°C).

8 Bake for 13 to 14 minutes. Remove from the oven and let cool completely on the baking sheet, then gently remove the macaron shells from the pan with a small offset spatula.

9 MAKE THE GANACHE FILLING: Place the chocolate in a small microwave-safe bowl and microwave on medium power in 30-second intervals, stirring well after each, until melted and smooth.

10 Place the cream in another small microwave-safe bowl and microwave on medium power in 30-second intervals, until it starts to bubble. Pour the hot cream over the melted chocolate and stir with a spatula in one direction until smooth and well combined. Chill the ganache for at least 1 hour, until thickened, then transfer it to a large piping bag fitted with a ¼-inch (6mm) round tip, or just snip a ¼-inch (6mm) hole. Pipe some ganache on the flat side of each bottom macaron shell and sandwich with the flat side of the top shells (with hands and feet).

11 DECORATE THE MACARONS: Draw Pusheen features on the macarons using the edible ink marker.

PUSHEEN DONUTS

MAKES 5 DONUTS • LEVEL OF DIFFICULTY: EASY TO MEDIUM

Think soft, moist, vanilla cake donuts with a heavy coating of rich, smooth chocolate glaze! Inspired by Pusheen's adorable pool floats, these dreamy treats will have you drifting along. They are quick and simple to make, and baking them makes them a healthier alternative to fried yeast-batter donuts.

. . . .

INGREDIENTS

Donuts

2 tablespoons (¼ stick/30g) unsalted butter, cut into cubes and slightly softened but still cold

¼ cup (50g) superfine sugar

2½ tablespoons dark brown sugar

1 large egg

1 teaspoon baking powder

¼ teaspoon salt

1 teaspoon pure vanilla extract

1 cup (120g) all-purpose flour

6½ tablespoons whole milk

3 ounces (80g) dark coating/compound chocolate, chopped, or melting wafers

20 white chocolate chips

Chocolate Coating

8 ounces (225g) white coating/compound chocolate, chopped, or Candy Melts

1½ tablespoons coconut oil, plus more if needed

Black oil-based food coloring or unsweetened black cocoa powder

Decorations

3 ounces (80g) dark coating/compound chocolate, chopped, or melting wafers

. . . .

① MAKE THE DONUTS: Preheat the oven to 350°F (175°C). Lightly grease a standard 6-well donut pan to facilitate release of the donuts after baking.

② In a medium bowl, using an electric mixer, cream the butter, superfine sugar, and brown sugar until creamy. Add the egg and beat until fluffy and light, about 5 minutes.

③ Add the baking powder, salt, and vanilla and lightly stir them in by hand.

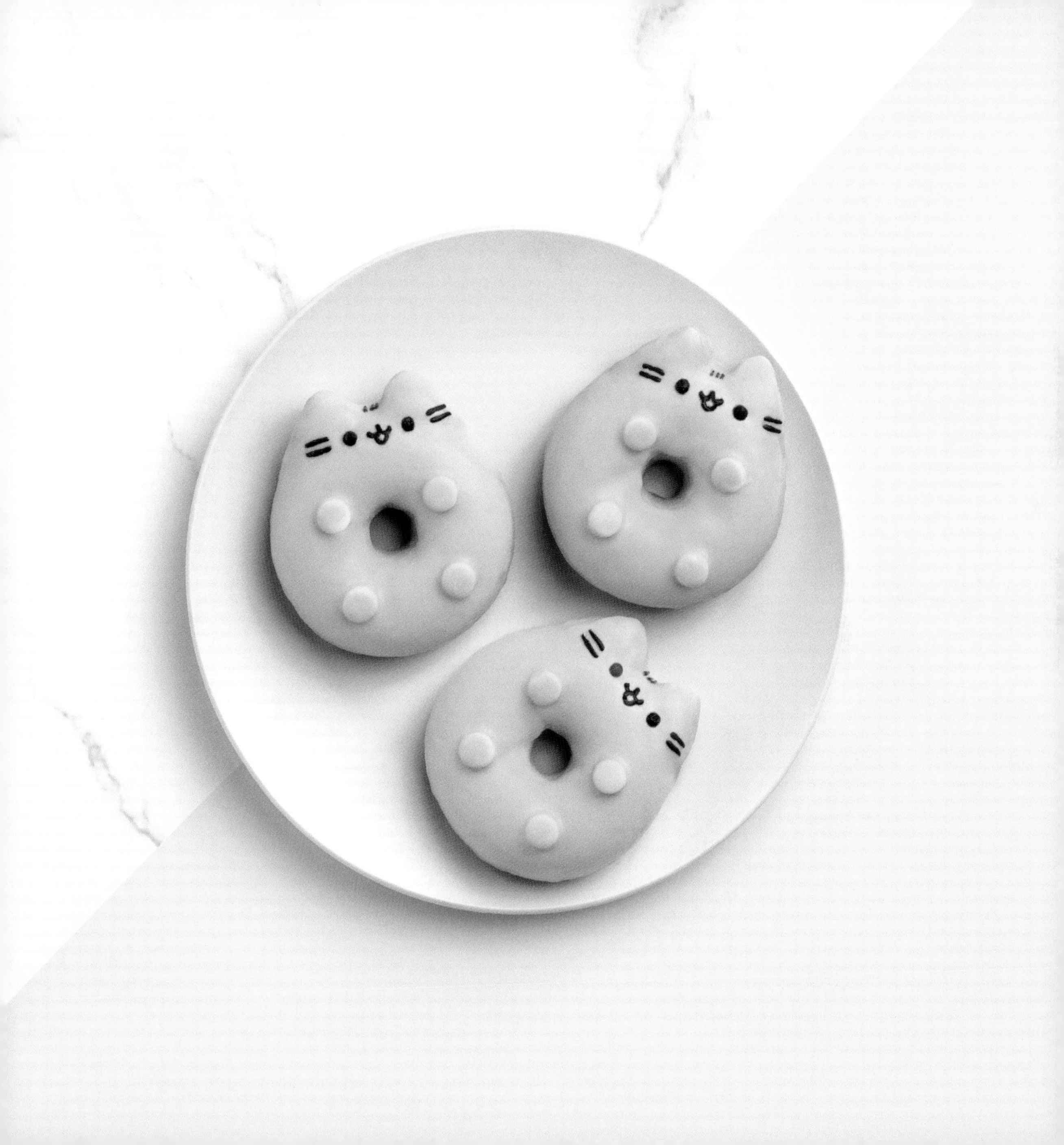

④ Fold in the flour, alternating with the milk, making sure everything is thoroughly combined. The batter will be fairly thick.

⑤ Pipe or spoon the batter into the prepared donut pan, filling the wells to about ¼ inch (6mm) from the rim. Bake the donuts for 12 to 13 minutes. Remove from the oven and let cool in the pan for 5 to 7 minutes, then turn them out of the pan onto a wire rack and let cool completely.

⑥ Place the dark chocolate in a small microwave-safe bowl and microwave in 30-second intervals, stirring after each to prevent burning, until melted and smooth. Slice small triangles out of one donut to make Pusheen's ears. Using the melted chocolate as glue, attach the ears to the remaining donuts, then attach 4 white chocolate chips to each donut for the hands and feet.

⑦ MAKE THE CHOCOLATE COATING: Place the white chocolate and coconut oil* in a medium microwave-safe bowl and microwave in 30-second intervals, stirring after each to prevent burning. If needed, add more coconut oil, 1 teaspoon at a time, until the chocolate is melted and has a dipping or pouring

consistency. Add drops of black food coloring or pinches of black cocoa powder and stir until smooth and evenly tinted the desired shade of gray.

*Tip: If you are using Candy Melts, you can use 1 tablespoon EZ Thin or shortening instead of the coconut oil to thin the chocolate.

8 Line a baking sheet with parchment paper. Working one at a time, hold a donut over the bowl of chocolate coating and spoon the coating over the top of the donut, letting the excess drip back into the bowl. Place the donuts onto the prepared baking sheet and let stand until the coating is set.

9 DECORATE THE DONUTS: Place the dark chocolate in a small microwave-safe bowl and microwave in 30-second intervals, stirring after each to prevent burning, until melted and smooth. Transfer the melted chocolate to a small piping bag, snip a small hole in the tip, and pipe Pusheen features onto the donuts.

PUSHEEN MADELEINES

MAKES 16 MADELEINES • LEVEL OF DIFFICULTY: EASY TO MEDIUM

Crunchy on the exterior, airy and soft inside, these iconic French butter cakes with their cute humps taste oh-so-good with coffee or tea! Decorated with adorable Pusheen faces, these are perfect accompaniments for any Pusheen tea party.

- -

INGREDIENTS

Madeleines

2 large eggs

⅓ cup (65g) superfine sugar

½ teaspoon pure vanilla extract

⅔ cup (80g) all-purpose flour

½ teaspoon baking powder

⅛ teaspoon salt

5 tablespoons plus 1 teaspoon (⅔ stick/75g) unsalted butter, melted and cooled, plus more for greasing

Chocolate Coating

5 ounces (150g) white coating/compound chocolate, chopped, or melting wafers

1 tablespoon coconut oil, plus more if needed

Black oil-based food coloring or unsweetened black cocoa powder

Decorations

3 ounces (80g) dark coating/compound chocolate, chopped, or melting wafers

1 tablespoon chopped white coating/compound chocolate

Black oil-based food coloring or unsweetened black cocoa powder

- -

1 MAKE THE MADELEINES: In a large bowl, using an electric mixer, beat the eggs and sugar until pale and fluffy. Beat in the vanilla.

2 Sift the flour, baking powder, and salt together into a medium bowl. Fold the flour mixture into the egg mixture with a spatula, then fold in the melted butter. Cover the bowl with plastic wrap and refrigerate the batter for 1 hour (this helps the madeleines bake up with the classic humps).

③ Preheat the oven to 350°F (175°C). Grease a madeleine pan with melted butter. (A 16-well madeleine pan would be ideal; however, you can also use a smaller pan with fewer wells and bake in batches until all the batter has been used up.)

④ Transfer the batter to a large piping bag, cut a ¼-inch (6mm) hole in the tip, and fill each well of the prepared pan 90 percent of the way. (Alternatively, you can spoon the batter into the pan with a 1-tablespoon measure.)

⑤ Bake for 9 to 10 minutes. Remove from the oven and turn the madeleines out onto a wire rack. Let the cakes cool completely.

⑥ MAKE THE CHOCOLATE COATING: Place the white chocolate and coconut oil in a medium microwave-safe bowl and microwave in 30-second intervals, stirring after each to prevent burning. If needed, add more coconut oil, 1 teaspoon at a time, until the chocolate is melted and has a dipping or pouring consistency. (Alternatively, use a double boiler to melt the chocolate and coconut oil.) Add a drop of black food coloring or a pinch of black cocoa powder and stir until smooth and evenly tinted gray.

⑦ Spoon the chocolate coating over the bottom third of each madeleine in an oval shape. Dip a toothpick in the chocolate coating and draw ears on each madeleine. Allow to set on a parchment-lined baking sheet or wire rack.

⑧ DECORATE THE MADELEINES: Place the dark chocolate in a medium microwave-safe bowl and microwave in 30-second intervals, stirring after each to prevent burning, until melted and smooth. Transfer the melted dark chocolate to a small piping bag, snip a small hole in the tip, and pipe eyes, mouth, whiskers, and hands onto the madeleines. Melt the white chocolate as you did the dark chocolate, add a drop of black food coloring or a pinch of black cocoa powder, and stir until evenly tinted dark gray. Transfer the dark gray chocolate to another small piping bag, snip a small hole in the tip, and pipe the head stripes between Pusheen's ears.

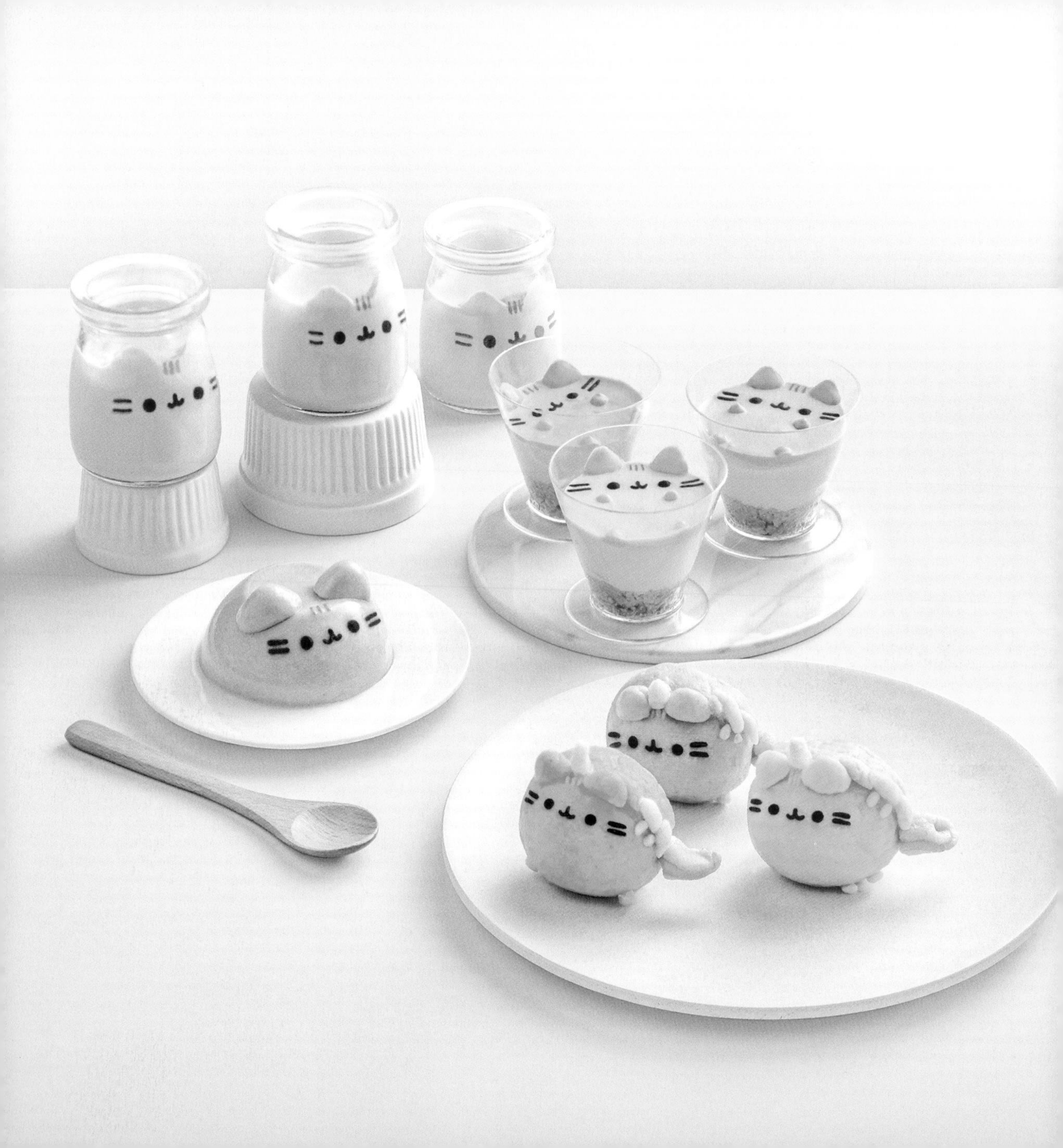

Desserts

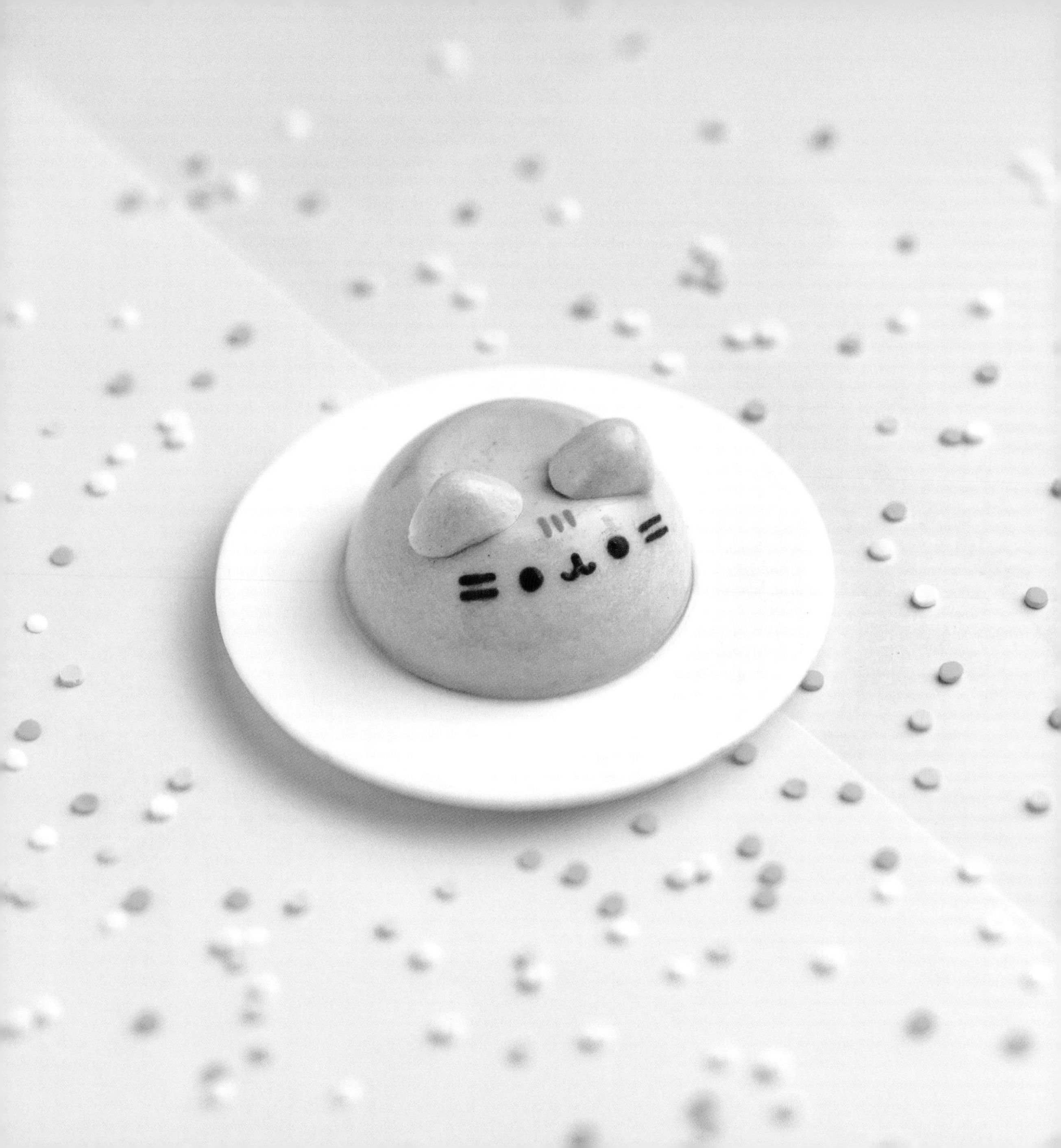

PUSHEEN MILK JELLIES

SERVES 4 · LEVEL OF DIFFICULTY: EASY TO MEDIUM

Sweet and refreshing, these milk jellies, made into 3D Pusheen faces, make attractive, gratifying desserts, especially in summer. Coconut milk adds extra creaminess and fragrance, as well as giving the jellies a milky effect, perfect for Pusheen.

. . . .

1 MAKE EAR MOLDS USING ALUMINUM FOIL: Fold a 2½-inch square piece of foil in half to make a rectangle (this reinforces the mold). Roll the rectangle into a cone and fold the ends into the cone to secure its shape (as pictured on page 42). Repeat to make a total of 8 ear molds.

2 MAKE THE MILK JELLIES: In a small saucepan, combine the water and milk and heat over medium heat. Gradually stir in the agar-agar powder, sugar, and a drop of black food coloring or a pinch of black cocoa powder and bring to a boil. Quickly turn off the heat and stir continuously until the agar-agar powder and sugar have fully dissolved.

3 Pour the mixture into 4 round-bottomed cups or silicone molds that are 3 inches (7.5cm) in diameter, filling them to the brim, and fill the 8 ear molds to ½ inch (1.25cm) deep. Let cool, then refrigerate until fully set, 2 to 4 hours.

4 Slightly warm the round molds using your hands and pop the jellies out. Place them on individual plates flat side down. Peel off the aluminum foil to unmold the ears. Dry the tops of

INGREDIENTS

Milk Jellies

1 cup (240g) water

1 cup (240g) whole milk or full-fat coconut milk

1½ teaspoons agar-agar powder

½ cup (100g) superfine sugar

Black food coloring or unsweetened black cocoa powder

Decorations

1 tablespoon chopped dark coating/compound chocolate

1½ teaspoons chopped white coating/compound chocolate

Black oil-based food coloring or unsweetened black cocoa powder

the round jellies and the bottoms of the ears by patting with a paper towel and place 2 ears on top of each jelly.

⑤ DECORATE THE JELLIES: Place the dark chocolate in a small microwave-safe bowl and microwave in 30-second intervals, stirring after each to prevent burning, until melted and smooth. Melt the white chocolate as you did the dark chocolate, add a drop of black food coloring or a pinch of black cocoa powder, and stir until evenly tinted gray. Transfer the melted dark chocolate and gray chocolate to separate small piping bags, snip a small hole in the tips, and pipe facial features onto the jellies, or use a toothpick to draw them on. Return to the refrigerator to chill for at least 1 hour before serving.

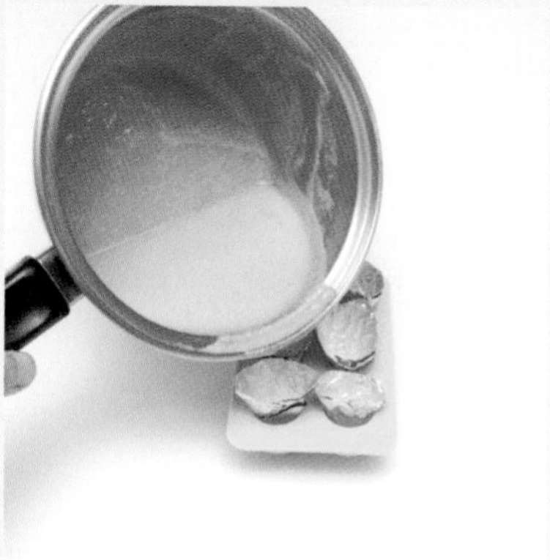
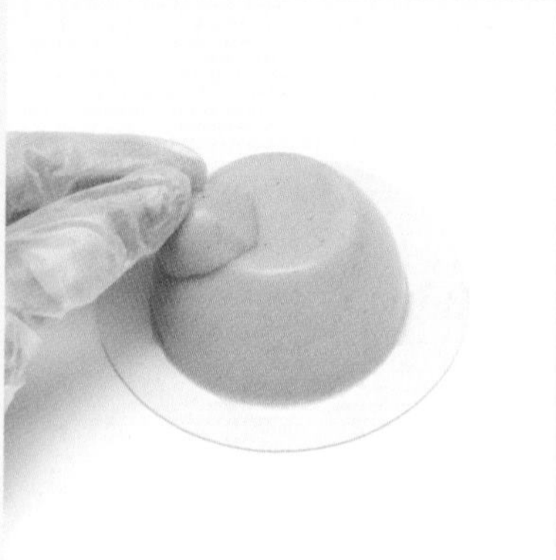
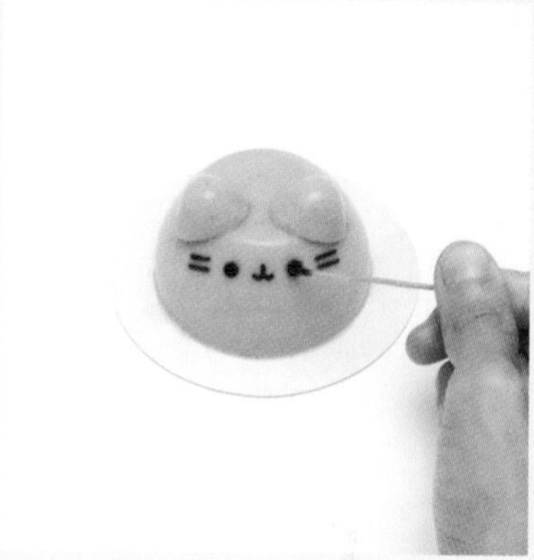
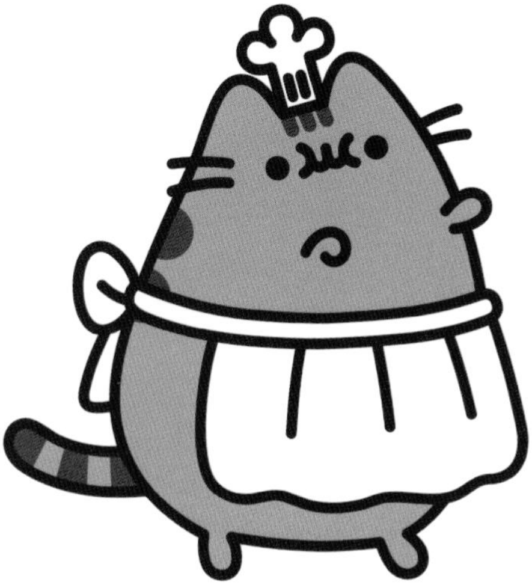

PASTEL PUSHEEN PANNA COTTA

SERVES 6 · LEVEL OF DIFFICULTY: MEDIUM

Smooth, silky, and melt-in-your-mouth, these classic Italian milk puddings are easy to make and can be prepared in advance. Transformed into pastel Pusheens, they make very yummy and pretty desserts!

. . . .

1 Using an erasable marker, draw a Pusheen face on the outside of six 3½-ounce (100ml) jars or cups. Place the dark chocolate in a small microwave-safe bowl and microwave in 30-second intervals, stirring after each to prevent burning, until melted and smooth. Using a toothpick, draw a Pusheen face on the inside of each jar or cup, using the marker-drawn face as a guide. Erase the marker drawings on the jars or cups and chill to set the chocolate.

2 MAKE THE PANNA COTTA: Place the gelatin in the bottom of a small bowl and add the cold water. The amount should be sufficient to bloom the gelatin without needing to drain excess water. If it isn't, add more cold water, 1 teaspoon at a time. (See page 191.) Set aside to bloom for 5 to 10 minutes.

3 In a small saucepan, combine the milk, cream, vanilla, and sugar over medium-low heat and bring just to a boil, stirring until the sugar dissolves. Remove from the heat.

4 Gently remove the bloomed gelatin sheets from the bowl and add them to the cream mixture, stirring well to make sure the gelatin dissolves. Let cool to room temperature.

INGREDIENTS

1 tablespoon chopped dark coating/ compound chocolate

Panna Cotta

3 gold gelatin sheets (2g each), cut into quarters

2½ tablespoons cold water, or more if needed, to soak the gelatin

1 cup (240g) whole milk

1 cup (240g) heavy cream

1 teaspoon pure vanilla extract

3 tablespoons superfine sugar

Food coloring: pink, purple, and green (or use natural food colorings: beet, purple sweet potato, and matcha powders)

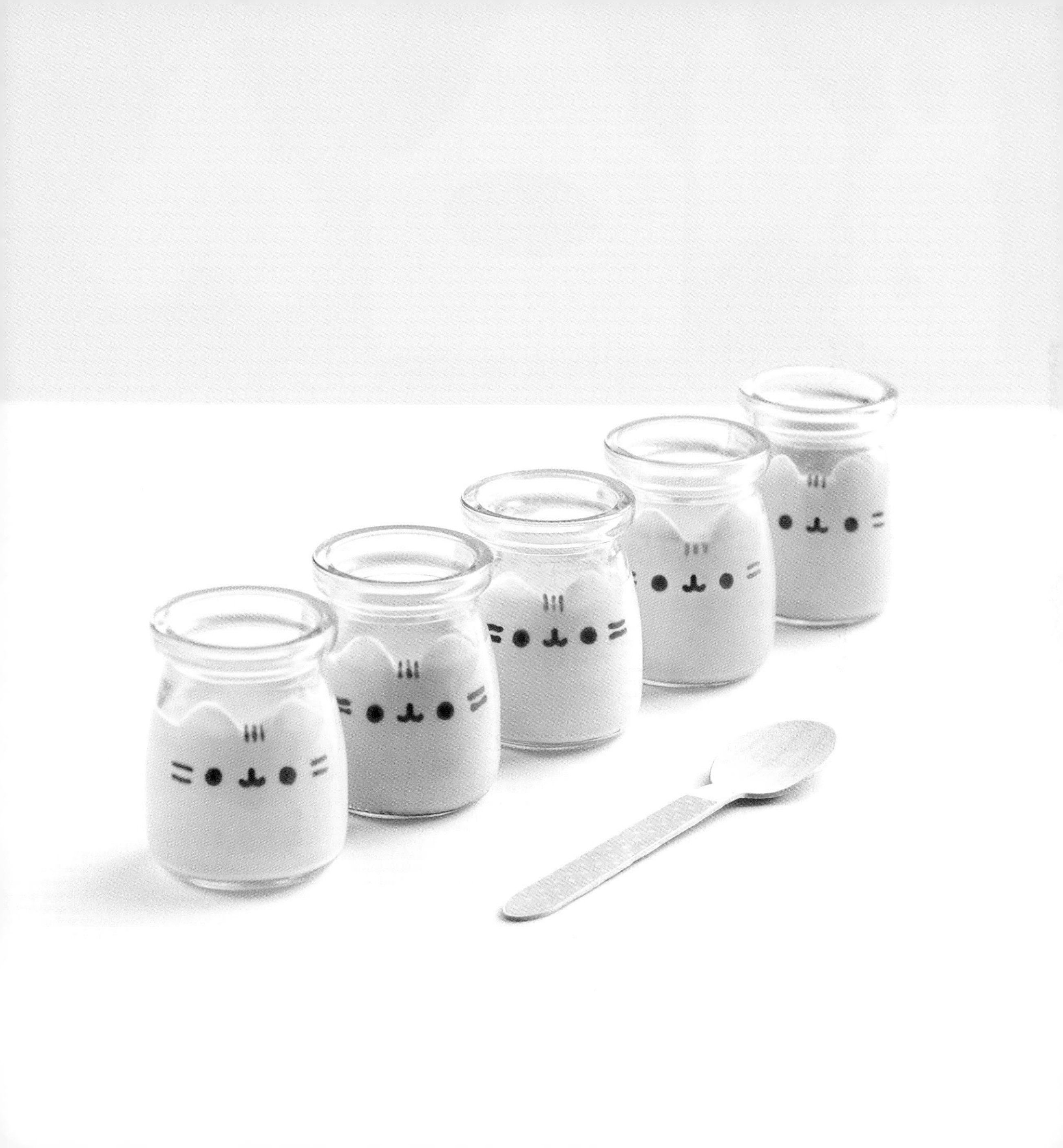

5 Divide the mixture among three medium bowls. Add a drop of food coloring* to each bowl, using a different color for each and adding just enough to tint the mixture pastel colors. Mix well.

*Tip: If you are using natural food coloring powder, dissolve each in an equal quantity of hot water before adding it to the panna cotta mixture to prevent uneven spots.

6 Remove the jars or cups from the refrigerator. Pour 5½ tablespoons (80g) of one of the colors of panna cotta mixture into each of two prepared jars (you will have some left over; see next step). Repeat for each color, pouring 5½ tablespoons (80g) into each jar, two jars per color. Refrigerate until set, about 4 hours.

7 Transfer the different colors of leftover panna cotta mixture to separate small piping bags and refrigerate them as well.

8 After the panna cotta has set, remove the piping bags from the fridge and let the panna cotta mixture in the piping bags soften slightly, about 5 minutes, before snipping a small hole from the tips. To form the ears, pipe the panna cotta mixture* from the piping bags into the jars as pictured above, then return the jars to the refrigerator to set for another 4 hours or more before serving.

*Tip: If the panna cotta mixture becomes too runny as you work, chill it again to thicken it.

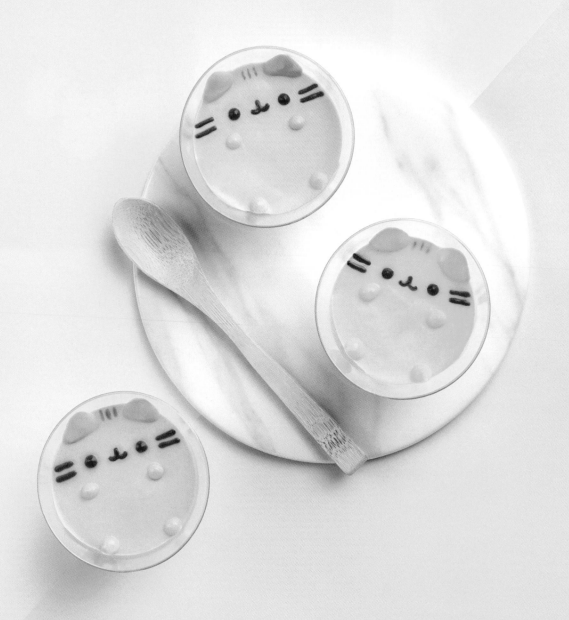

PASTEL PUSHEEN CHEESECAKE CUPS

SERVES 6 • LEVEL OF DIFFICULTY: EASY

The delicious combination of the creamy, tangy cheesecake and the buttery, crumbly graham cracker crust is a winner! This simple no-bake recipe makes for an easy yet super-impressive dessert for any Pusheen party!

1 In a medium bowl, combine the graham cracker crumbs and melted butter and mix well. Dividing evenly, spoon the crumb mixture (1 to 2 tablespoons) into the bottom of each of six 3½-ounce (100ml) custard cups and use the spoon to pack the crumbs into an even layer. Cover and refrigerate for at least 30 minutes to set the crust.

2 Meanwhile, place the gelatin in a small saucepan and pour over the milk. Soak for 5 to 10 minutes to soften. Heat the milk over low heat, stirring to dissolve the gelatin. Remove from the heat and let cool.

3 In a large bowl, using an electric mixer, beat the cream cheese and sugar until smooth. Add the lemon juice and vanilla and mix well. Add the heavy cream and mix well. Add the gelatin-milk mixture and mix until smooth and uniform.

INGREDIENTS

- ½ cup (45g) graham cracker crumbs or crushed cookies of your choice
- 2½ tablespoons (35g) unsalted butter, melted
- 3 gold gelatin sheets (2g each), cut into quarters
- 6½ tablespoons whole milk
- 7 ounces (200g) cream cheese
- ¼ cup (50g) superfine sugar
- 1 tablespoon fresh lemon juice
- 1 teaspoon pure vanilla extract
- ⅓ cup (80g) heavy cream
- Food coloring: pink, purple, and green (or use natural food colorings: beet, purple sweet potato, and matcha powders)
- Black food coloring or unsweetened black cocoa powder

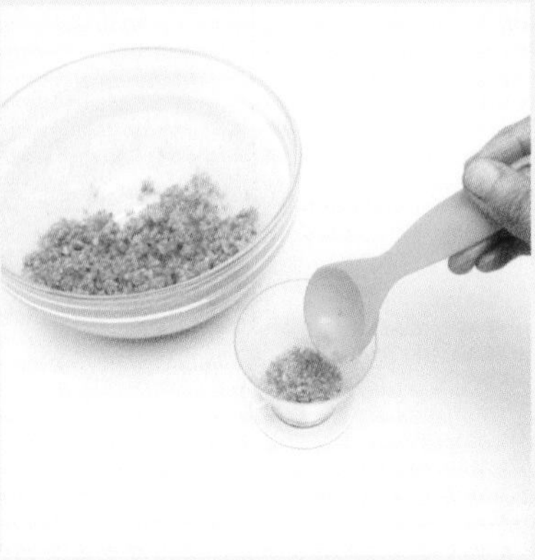
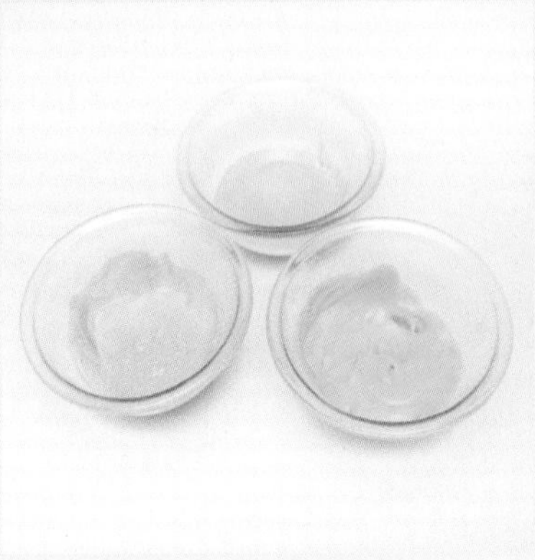
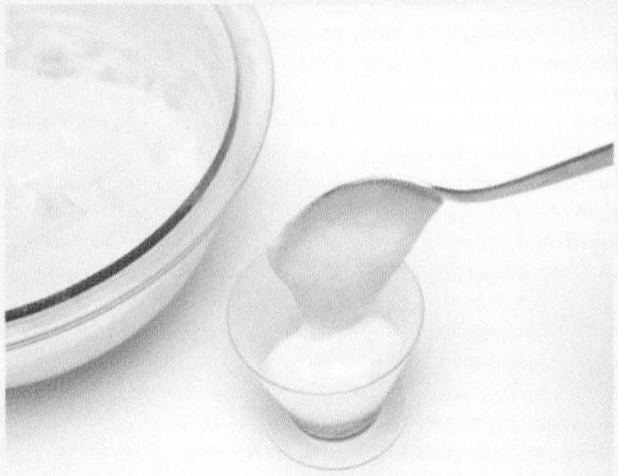

4 Spoon 2½ tablespoons of the batter into each of three small bowls. Add a drop of pink, purple, and green food coloring* to each bowl, using a different color for each, and mix well. (This will be the top layer of the cheesecakes.) Spoon 1 teaspoon of the batter into two separate small bowls. Add a drop of black food coloring or a pinch of black cocoa powder and a drop of purple food coloring to one bowl and stir until evenly tinted purple (this will be used for the facial features). Add a drop of black food coloring or a pinch of black cocoa powder to the second bowl and stir until evenly tinted gray (this will be used for the head stripes). You should still have some plain batter remaining.

*Tip: If you are using natural food coloring powders, dissolve each in an equal quantity of hot water before adding it to the batter to prevent uneven spots.

5 Spoon 2 tablespoons of the plain batter over the graham cracker crust in each cup. Top each with 1 tablespoon of pink, purple, or green batter; reserve the remaining pink, purple, and green batters. Gently level the batter by tapping the cups on the counter.

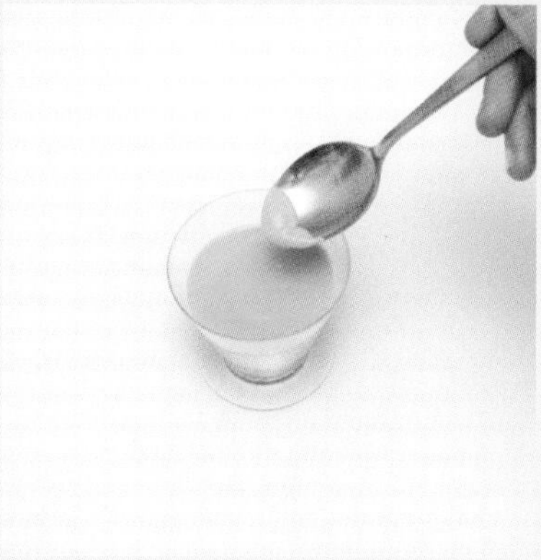
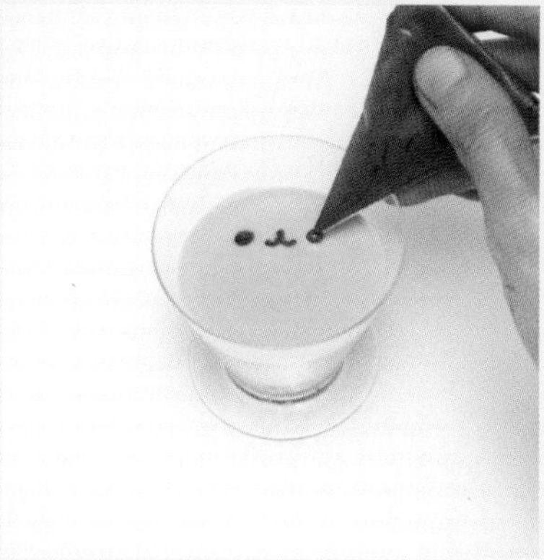
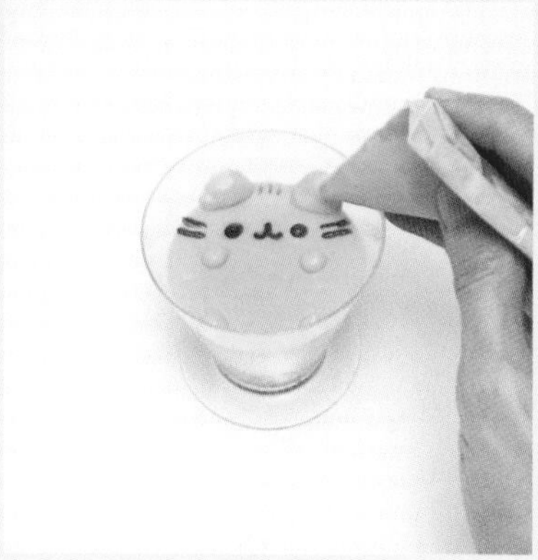

6 Transfer the dark purple and gray batters to separate small piping bags and snip a scant 1mm hole in the tips. Pipe dark purple facial features and gray head stripes onto the pastel Pusheen faces.

7 Transfer the remaining pink, purple, and green batter to separate small piping bags and snip a generous 2mm hole in the tips. Pipe ears, hands, and feet onto the top of the batter in the cups.

8 Cover and refrigerate for 1 to 2 hours until set before serving.

PASTEL PUSHEEN DANGO

MAKES 2 SERVINGS · LEVEL OF DIFFICULTY: EASY TO MEDIUM

These are inspired by *hanami dango*, a Japanese dessert in which three balls of sweet mochi are stacked on a skewer, and which is popular in springtime when the cherry blossoms are in bloom. These stacked pastel Pusheen *dango* are sweet, chewy, and oh-so-adorable! The rice flours can be ordered online or found in any Asian grocery store.

1. In a large bowl, mix together the rice flour, glutinous rice flour, and sugar.

2. Add the water little by little, mixing well after each addition, until the dough has the texture of an earlobe. (This is the traditional way to describe the perfect texture for your dango mixture.) If the dough is too wet and soft, add more rice flour (not glutinous) and knead again.

3. Divide the dough into three equal portions and tint each portion of dough* with a different color of food coloring. Knead each portion until the coloring is well combined and the dough is evenly tinted.

*Tip: The color will darken considerably after cooking, so make sure your colors are really light. Add the food coloring drop by drop or pinch by pinch until you get the desired shade.

INGREDIENTS

- ⅓ cup (40g) rice flour (not glutinous), plus more if needed
- ⅓ cup (40g) glutinous rice flour
- 3 tablespoons granulated or superfine sugar
- 3 to 4 tablespoons water, as needed
- Food coloring: pink, purple, and green (or use natural food colorings: beet, purple sweet potato, and matcha powders)
- Cornstarch, for dusting
- Black edible ink marker

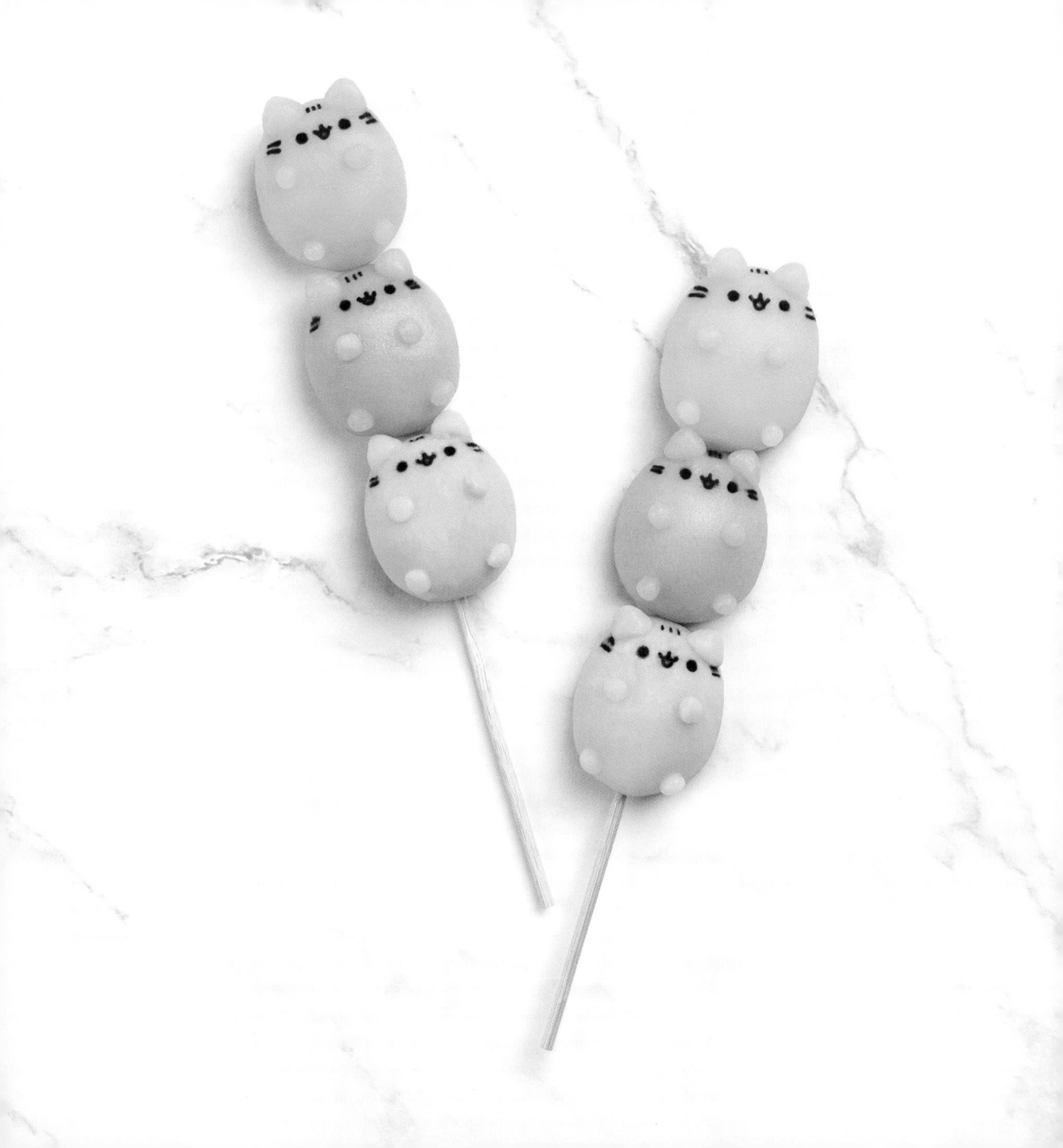

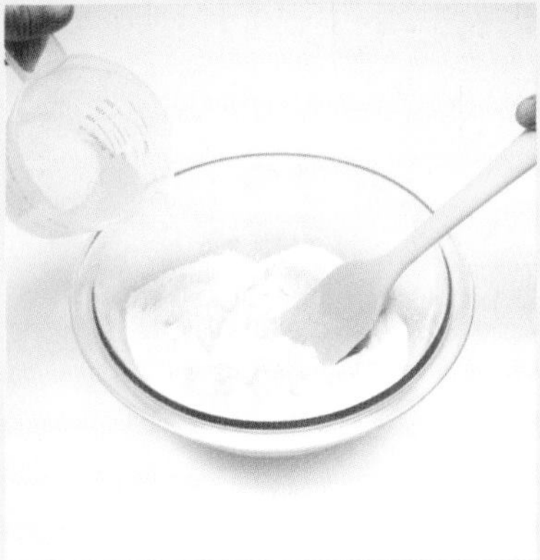
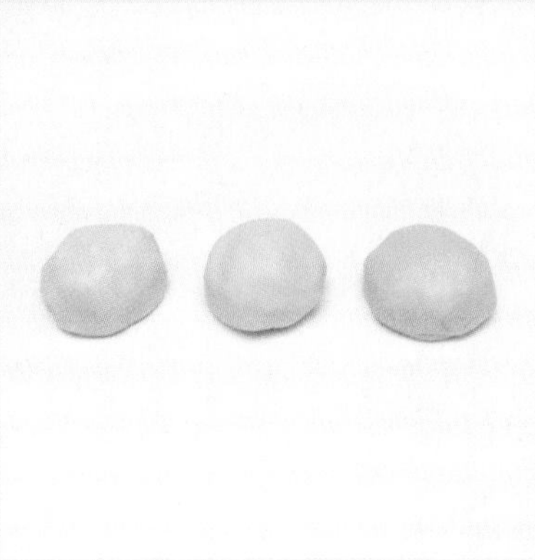
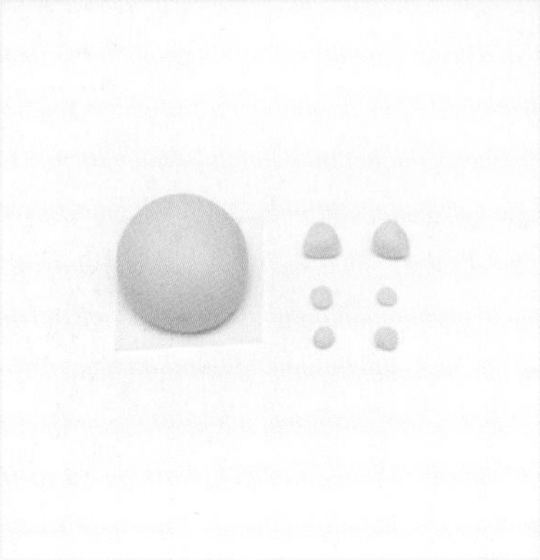

4 Dust the work surface and your hands with some cornstarch to prevent sticking. Pull off ¾-ounce (20g) pieces of dough and roll into oval balls, placing them on small pieces of parchment paper as you go and lightly covering them with plastic wrap to prevent them from drying out while you work. For each ball, pinch off 2 tiny bits of dough for the ears and 4 bits of dough for the hands and feet and attach them to the oval balls.

5 Using the edible ink marker, draw facial features onto the balls of dough.

6 To cook the dango, you can:

- BOIL THEM (THIS IS THE TRADITIONAL METHOD): Bring a large pot of water to a boil. Fill a large bowl with ice and water and set it nearby. Add the dango to the boiling water and cook, stirring so they don't stick to the bottom, until they start to float, 3 to 4 minutes, then cook for 1 minute more. Using a slotted spoon or skimmer, transfer the dango to the ice water to cool for 1 minute, then transfer to a plate.

- MICROWAVE THEM: Place the dango in a medium microwave-safe bowl, brush generously with water, and cover with plastic wrap. Microwave for 30 to 60 seconds, depending on your

microwave wattage. After 30 seconds, check if the dango are cooked (the skin should be dark and soft). Remove the dango from the microwave, brush with ice water, and let cool.

· STEAM THEM: Fill a saucepan with 1 to 2 inches (2.5 to 5cm) of water and bring it to a simmer. Place a steamer basket in the pan, add the dango, cover, and steam for 15 to 20 minutes, until the dango skin darkens and softens. Remove from the steamer and let cool.

7 Thread 3 dango onto each of two skewers, using one dango of each color on each skewer. Serve at room temperature. Leftover dango can be stored in an airtight container at room temperature for up to 2 days. If you live in a warm climate, store them in a cool place, but not in the refrigerator; refrigerating the dango will make them too tough. If desired, soften and reheat the dango by boiling, steaming, or microwaving them just before serving.

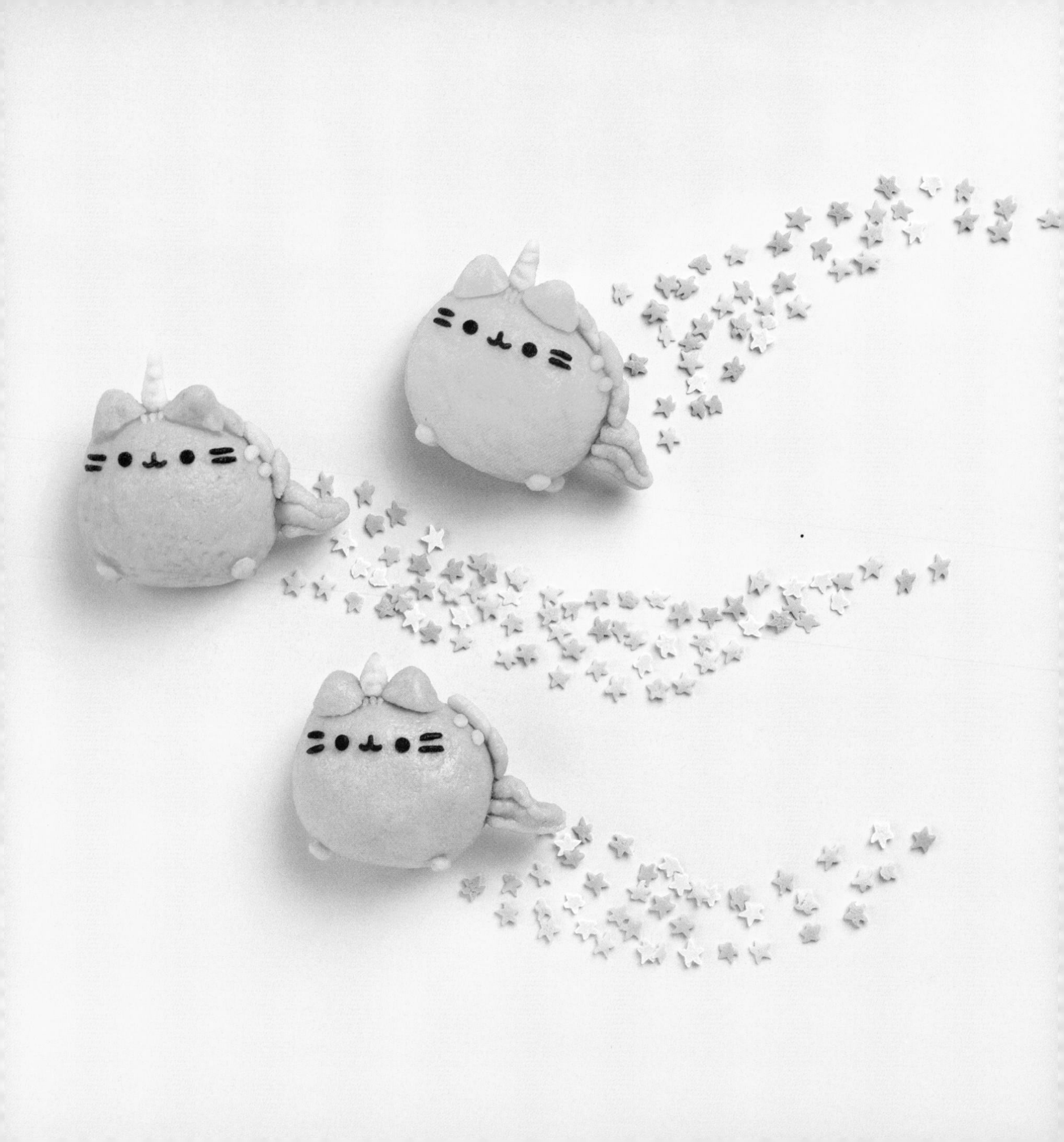

PUSHEENICORN SNOWSKIN MOONCAKES

MAKES 9 MOONCAKES · LEVEL OF DIFFICULTY: MEDIUM TO DIFFICULT

These magical Pusheenicorn mooncakes hide a lovely lotus paste filling beneath a soft, fragrant glutinous rice skin. Best served chilled, mooncakes are delectable and enchanting. You can use the same recipe for any Pusheen design.

. . . .

1 Divide the lotus paste into nine equal portions and roll them into oval balls. Cover with plastic wrap and set aside.

2 Toast the glutinous rice flour in a dry skillet over low heat until the flour turns light yellow. (You can also use store-bought cooked glutinous rice flour.) Sift the toasted glutinous rice flour and confectioners' sugar together into a large bowl. Mix well.

3 Add the shortening and, wearing gloves, quickly mix by hand until the mixture is uniform and resembles bread crumbs. Pour in the cold water. Using your gloved hands, knead the dough until it becomes soft and smooth; do not overknead the dough.

4 Divide the dough into 3 big portions, each weighing 4½ ounces (130g), and 2 much smaller portions, each weighing a scant ¼ ounce (5g). Using a different color for each larger portion, knead pink, green, and purple food coloring drop by drop or pinch by pinch into the dough until you reach the desired shade. Then knead a drop or pinch of black food coloring and

INGREDIENTS

- 1 cup (270g) white lotus paste, available online or from Asian grocery stores
- 1 cup (120g) glutinous rice flour, plus more for dusting
- 1 cup (125g) confectioners' sugar
- 3 tablespoons (40g) vegetable shortening
- ½ cup (120g) cold water
- Food coloring: pink, green, purple, and black (or use natural food colorings: beet, matcha, purple sweet potato, and black cocoa powders)

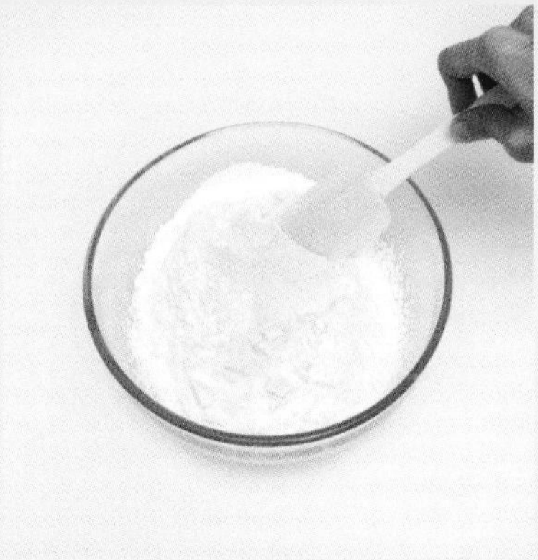
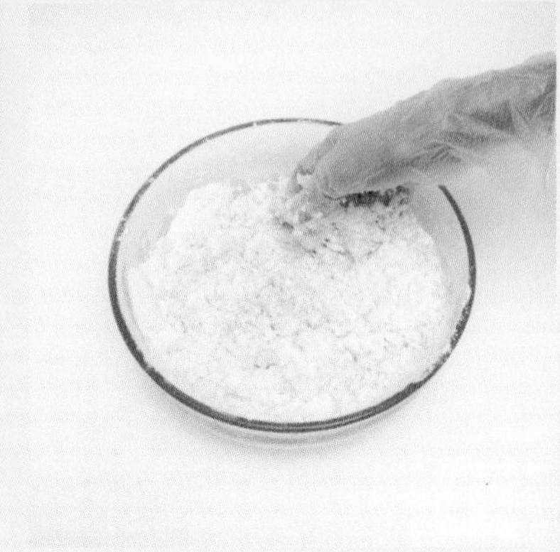
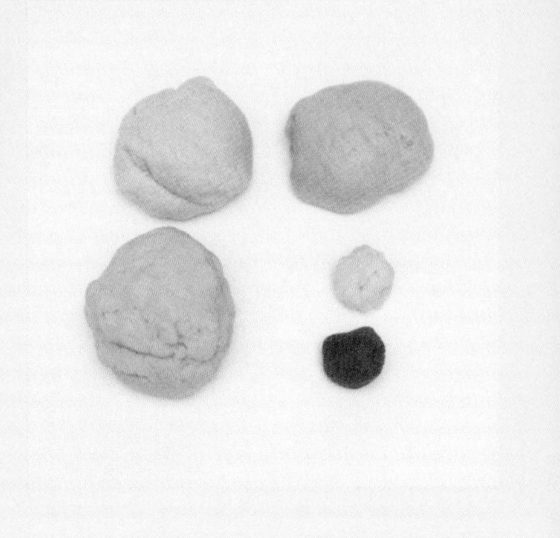

a drop or pinch of purple food coloring into one of the smaller portions until it is evenly tinted dark purple (leave the other smaller portion plain). Cover the dough with plastic wrap and let rest for 10 to 15 minutes.

5 From each larger portion of dough, pull off 3 small pieces, each weighing about 1¼ ounces (36g), and roll into balls (for a total of 9). Reserve the leftover dough for shaping the ears, hands, and feet later. Dust your hands and work surface with some glutinous rice flour.

6 For each mooncake, flatten one dough ball into an oval with the edges slightly thinner than the center (you can use plastic wrap around the ball to prevent sticking). Put a ball of lotus paste in the center of the dough and form the dough around the lotus paste to enclose it, pinching the edges tightly to seal. Roll the ball smooth. Pinch 2 triangles and 4 small balls from the reserved colored dough for the ears and feet and attach them to the body. Repeat with the remaining balls of dough and lotus paste.

7 Roll out the dark purple dough and cut into thin strips to form the facial features. For the eyes, form 2 generous 2mm balls of dark purple dough.

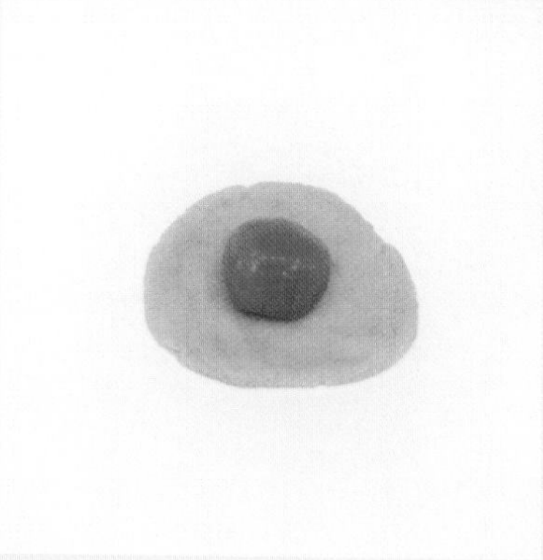
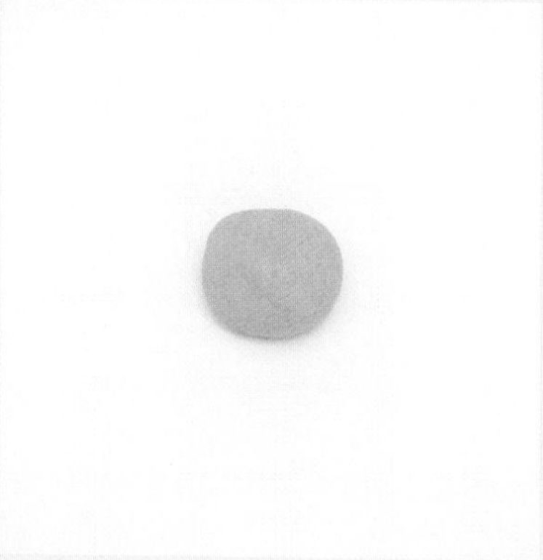
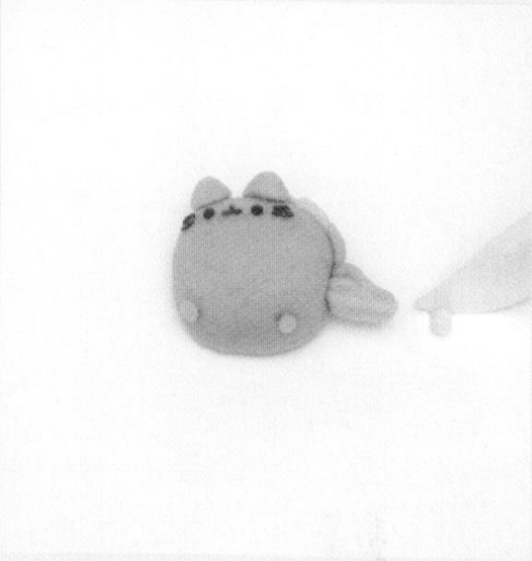

8 Pinch off small strips of pink, green, and purple dough to form the tricolored tail, the head stripes, and the back stripes.*

*Tip: Use a toothpick to cut out small features like stripes and attach them. The pieces should stick easily without needing any additional "glue." If you need to transport or move the mooncakes a lot, toast pieces of uncooked spaghetti in a 350°F (175°C) oven for a few minutes, then break them into smaller pieces and prop them under the tails to keep the tails supported.

9 Roll the plain dough into nine cones to make unicorn horns and make indents along the cones to complete the horn. Stick the horns on between the ears.

10 Place the mooncakes in an airtight container and refrigerate for about 2 hours to firm up before serving. The mooncakes will remain soft for about a week stored in the refrigerator.

PEPPERMINT PUSHEEN ICE CREAM

MAKES 8 TO 10 CONES • LEVEL OF DIFFICULTY: EASY TO MEDIUM

An easy, creamy, and delicious no-churn peppermint ice cream modeled into a Pusheen surprise popping out of a cone! Here, a round ice cube mold is used to obtain perfect spheres every time, but feel free to use an ice cream scoop.

. . . .

1 In a medium bowl, stir together the condensed milk, peppermint extract, vanilla, and a few drops of green food coloring. Set aside.

2 In a large bowl, using an electric mixer, beat the cream on high speed until it holds stiff peaks. With a spatula, gently fold the condensed milk mixture into the whipped cream.

3 Pour the ice cream mixture into eight 2-inch (5cm) spherical ice cube molds. (Alternatively, you can pour the mixture into any loaf pan or ice cream container and use an ice cream scoop to form it into balls later.) Cover with plastic wrap and freeze the ice cream until firm, about 6 hours.

4 MAKE THE DECORATIONS AND ASSEMBLE THE CONES: Place the dark chocolate in a small microwave-safe bowl and microwave in 30-second intervals, stirring after each to prevent burning, until melted and smooth. (Alternatively, use a double boiler to melt the chocolate.) Melt the white chocolate as you did the dark chocolate, then transfer 1 tablespoon to another small bowl, add

INGREDIENTS

- ¾ cup plus 2 tablespoons (200g) sweetened condensed milk
- 1 teaspoon pure peppermint extract
- 1 teaspoon pure vanilla extract
- Green food coloring
- 1½ cups (360g) heavy cream

Decorations

- 3 ounces (80g) dark coating/ compound chocolate, chopped, or melting wafers
- 3 ounces (80g) chopped white coating/compound chocolate
- Black oil-based food coloring or unsweetened black cocoa powder
- Green food coloring
- 8 to 10 ice cream cones, for serving

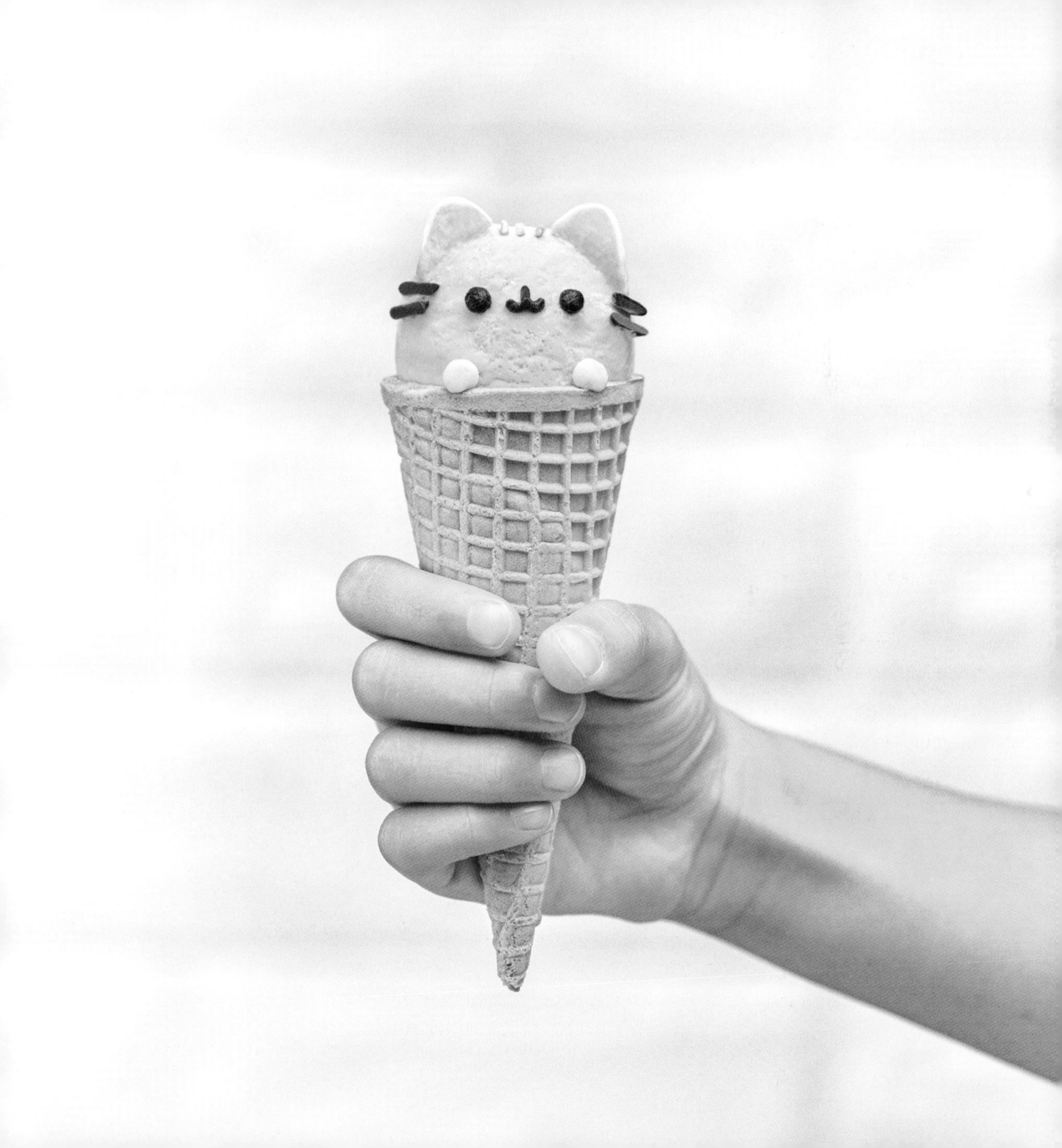

a drop of black food coloring or a pinch of black cocoa powder, and stir until smooth and evenly tinted gray. Add a drop of green food coloring to the remaining white chocolate and stir until evenly tinted to match the shade of the ice cream. Transfer the melted chocolates to separate small piping bags and snip small holes in the tips.

5 Photocopy or scan and print the Ice Cream template on page 203 (template 7) and place the template under a piece of parchment paper. Using the dark chocolate, pipe Pusheen facial features onto the parchment paper. Pipe ears and hands using the green chocolate, and head stripes using the gray chocolate. Set aside to harden.

6 Pop a round ball of ice cream from the mold or use a scoop to form a round ball of ice cream. Place the ball of ice cream in a cone and add the ears, hands, facial features, and head stripes. Serve immediately.

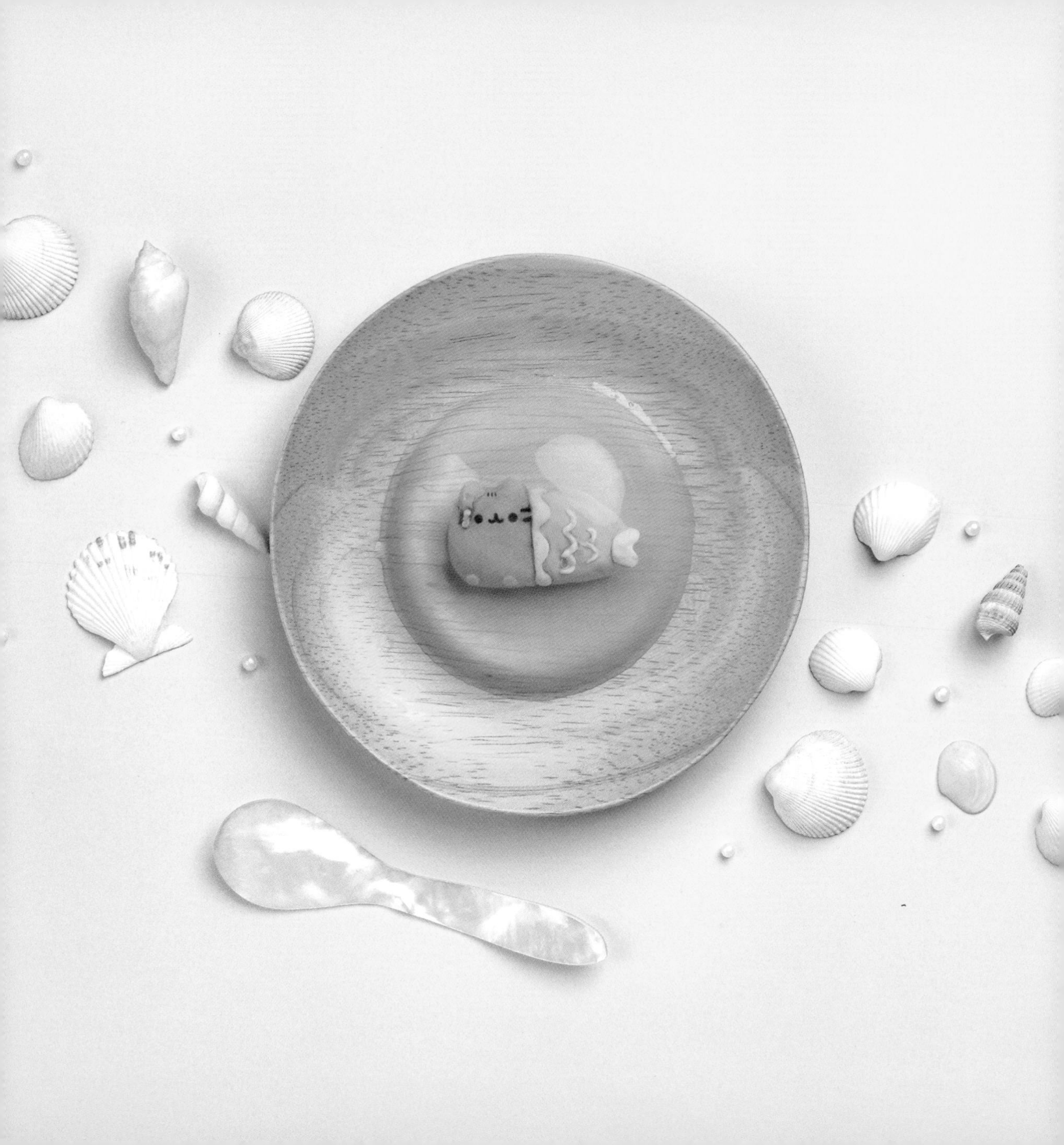

PUSHEEN MERMAID RAINDROP CAKES

MAKES TWO 3-INCH (7.5CM) CAKES · LEVEL OF DIFFICULTY: DIFFICULT

This creation is inspired by a Pusheen mermaid swimming literally in a drop of water. Watch the mermaid swim when you jiggle the raindrop cake! The clear and light-tasting raindrop cake is refreshing and complements the sweet mermaid rice cake.

. . . .

1 MAKE THE MERMAID FIGURES: In a medium bowl, mix together the glutinous rice flour and sugar. Add the water little by little and mix well until the dough takes on a moldable consistency. If the dough is too wet and soft, knead in more rice flour a little bit at a time.

2 Measure a 1-ounce (30g) portion of the dough and knead in black food coloring to tint it gray. Measure a ¾-ounce (20g) portion of the dough and knead in blue food coloring to tint it blue. Divide the remaining dough into 4 portions as shown in the first image on page 66. Set aside a plain portion weighing 2g and tint a 4g portion pink, a 2g portion yellow, and a 1g portion dark brown.*

*Tip: Since the dough volume is small, dip a toothpick into gel or liquid food coloring and use that to tint the dough, or use a small pinch of powdered natural food coloring. Be sure to knead in the colors until the dough is evenly tinted the desired shade.

INGREDIENTS

Mermaid Figures

¼ cup (30g) glutinous rice flour, plus more if needed

½ teaspoon superfine sugar

2 tablespoons water

Food coloring: black, blue, pink, dark brown, and yellow (or use natural food colorings: unsweetened black cocoa, butterfly blue pea flower, beet, unsweetened dark cocoa, and turmeric powders)

Raindrop Cakes

¼ teaspoon plus a pinch agar-agar powder

⅔ cup (160g) filtered or mineral water

Suggested Toppings (optional)

1 tablespoon simple syrup

1 tablespoon kinako (roasted soy flour)

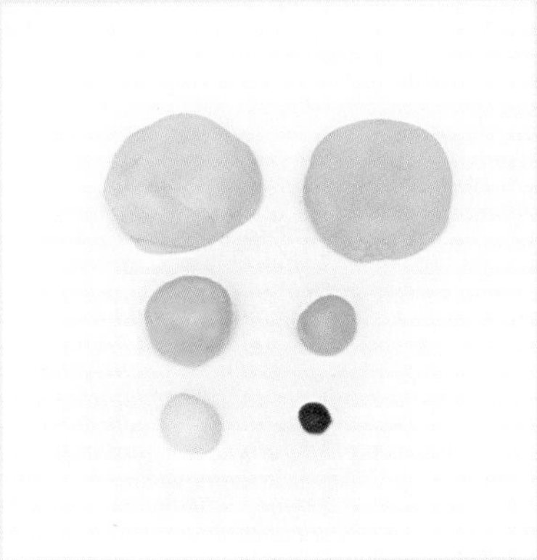

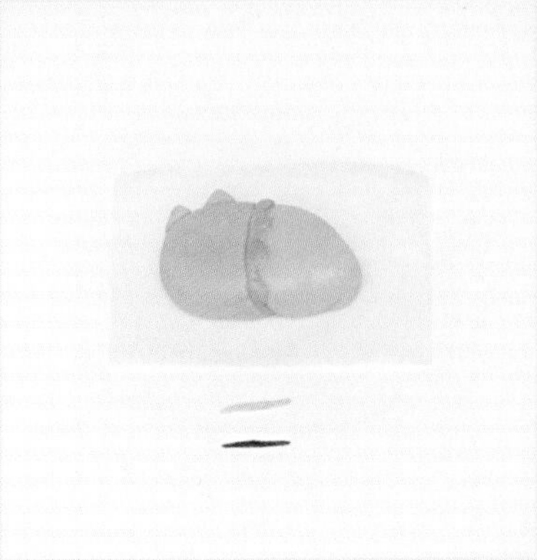

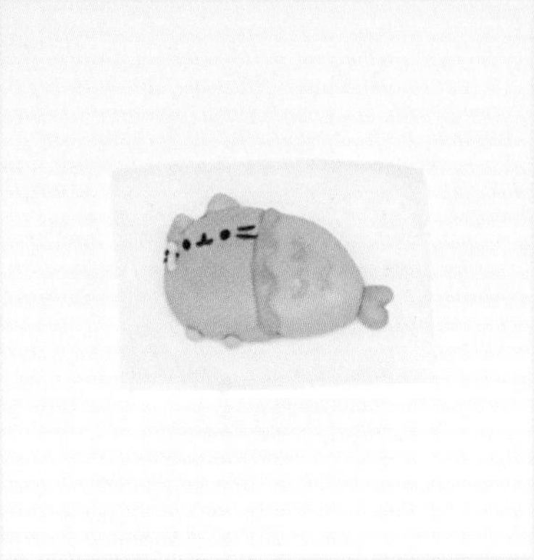

3 To assemble each mermaid figure, pull off a scant ½-ounce (12g) piece of the gray dough, roll it into a ball, join it to a ⅓-ounce (9g) ball of the blue dough, and place on a small piece of parchment paper. Roll 2 small balls of the gray dough into triangle shapes for the ears. Roll out a long strip of pink dough and use a wavy/fluted cutter to cut out waves. Stick this on the gray-blue boundary. Roll the dark brown and pink doughs into thin strips to make the facial details and scales. Pinch off a small portion of the yellow dough, press it flat, and use a star cutter to make star shapes. Roll tiny balls of the plain dough and stick them on for the pearls. Roll 2 more small balls of the gray dough for the hands.

4 Fill a large bowl with ice and water and set it nearby. Bring a large pot of water to a boil. Add the mermaid figures to the boiling water and cook until they start to float, 3 to 4 minutes, then cook for 1 minute more. Using a slotted spoon or skimmer, transfer the mermaids to the ice water to cool for 1 minute, then transfer to a plate.

⑤ MAKE THE RAINDROP CAKES: Place the agar-agar powder in a small saucepan. Add the filtered water bit by bit, stirring well so that no lumps form. Bring the mixture to a boil over medium heat. Boil for 2 minutes, then remove from the heat and stir to dissolve the agar-agar completely. Let the mixture cool until warm, about 20 minutes.

⑥ Prepare two 3-inch (7.5cm) round molds. Pour the agar-agar mixture into the molds to a depth of ½ inch (12mm), place a cooked mermaid figure facedown in each mold, then cover with more agar-agar mixture until the mermaid figure is fully submerged. Refrigerate for at least 1 hour to set.

⑦ After 1 to 3 hours, pop or turn the raindrop cakes out of the molds onto plates. Top each cake with some simple syrup or soy flour before serving, if desired.

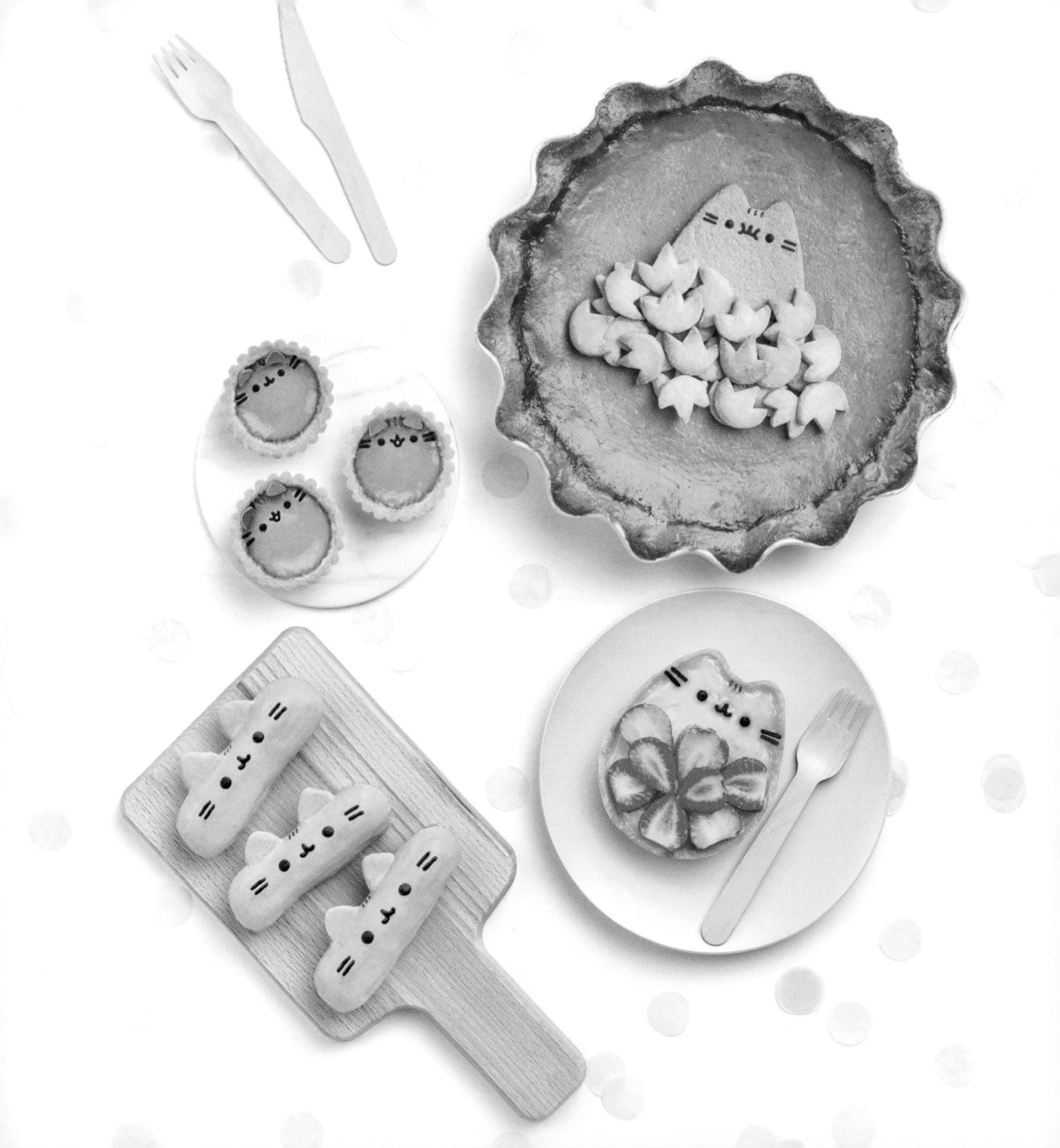

Pastries

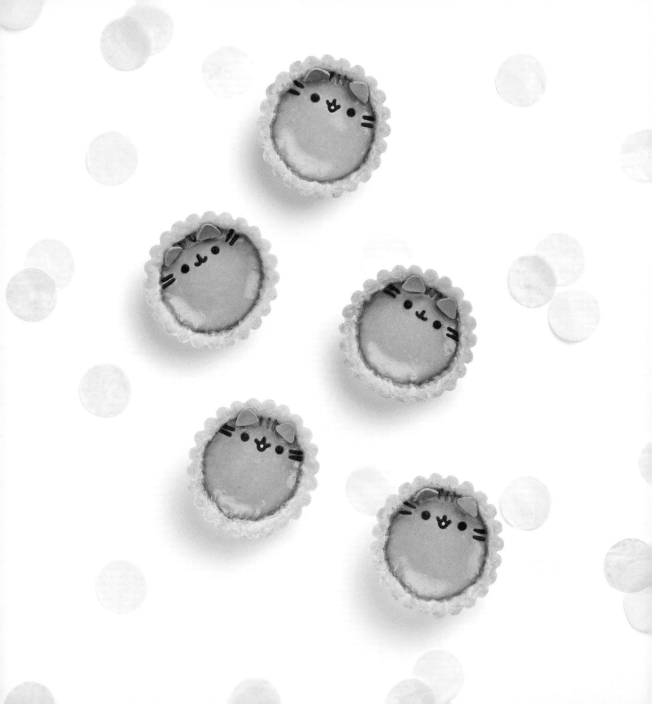

PUSHEEN BLACK SESAME TARTS

MAKES NINE 2-INCH (5CM) TARTS · LEVEL OF DIFFICULTY: MEDIUM

Rich and creamy black sesame pudding is balanced with a wonderful flaky, buttery tart crust. Combined with the cheerful Pusheen faces, these tarts are such a joy to eat and to look at!

. . . .

INGREDIENTS

Tart Crust

1½ cups (180g) all-purpose flour, plus more for dusting

⅔ cup (85g) confectioners' sugar

¼ teaspoon salt

8 tablespoons (1 stick/115g) unsalted butter, cut into small cubes and chilled

1 large egg

½ teaspoon pure vanilla extract

Black Sesame Tart Filling

1 gold gelatin sheet (2g), cut into quarters

1 tablespoon cold water, or more if needed, to soak the gelatin

½ cup (120g) whole milk

2¼ teaspoons sweetened black sesame paste

1½ teaspoons superfine sugar

Assembly and Decorations

3 ounces (80g) dark coating/ compound chocolate, chopped, or melting wafers

3 ounces (80g) white coating/ compound chocolate, chopped, or melting wafers

Black oil-based food coloring or unsweetened black cocoa powder

Pink oil-based food coloring

. . . .

1 MAKE THE TART CRUST: In a large bowl or in a food processor, combine the flour, confectioners' sugar, and salt. Add the cold butter and quickly cut it into the flour mixture using a pastry cutter or fork or by pulsing the food processor. Mix or pulse until the mixture becomes crumbly and resembles coarse meal. Add the egg and vanilla and mix or pulse until the dough is no longer dry and starts to clump together. Do not overmix the dough. The dough should be crumbly with large clumps.

2 Transfer the dough to a lightly floured surface and form it into a ball. Flatten the ball slightly to form a thick disc. Wrap the disc of dough in plastic wrap and refrigerate for 1 hour.

③ Take the dough out of the fridge and let it sit for a few minutes to soften slightly for easy rolling. Butter nine 2-inch (5cm) tart pans.

④ On a lightly floured surface, roll the dough out to ⅛ inch (3mm) thick. Use a round cutter that is 1 inch (2.5cm) wider than the bottom of your tart pans to cut out rounds of dough. Place a round of dough gently into each prepared tart pan, pressing gently to fit the dough into the pan.* With a sharp knife, trim the edges of the dough flush with the top of the pan. Prick the bottom of the shells with a fork to prevent them from puffing during baking. Cover the tart shells with plastic wrap, set them on a baking sheet, and freeze for 30 minutes. (Frozen dough is less prone to shrinking during baking.)

*Tip: If the dough becomes too soft to work with, chill it until firm again, then continue.

⑤ Preheat the oven to 355°F (180°C).

⑥ Remove the tart shells from the freezer, uncover them, and line each with a square of aluminum foil, pressing it tightly against the dough and covering the edges to prevent them from burning. Fill the foil

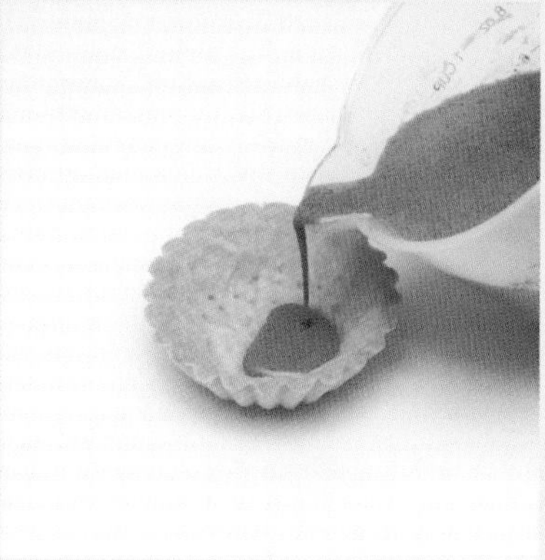
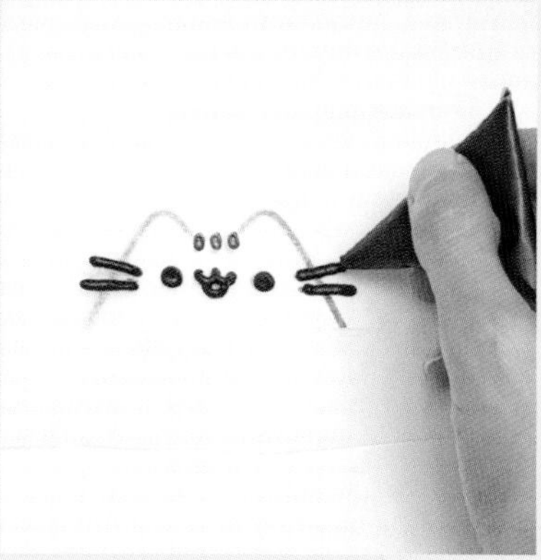
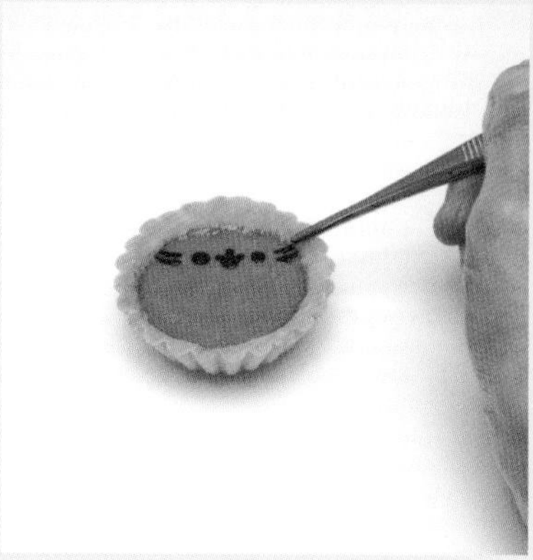

with pie weights, dried beans, or uncooked rice, making sure they're evenly distributed over the entire surface. Bake for 20 minutes, until the foil no longer sticks to the dough. Remove the tart shells from the oven, remove the weights and foil, and bake the shells for 10 minutes more until golden brown. Let the tart shells cool completely on the pan.

7 MAKE THE BLACK SESAME TART FILLING: Place the gelatin in the bottom of a small bowl and add the cold water. The amount should be sufficient to bloom the gelatin without needing to drain excess water. If it isn't, add more cold water, 1 teaspoon at a time. (See page 191.) Set aside to bloom for 5 to 10 minutes.

8 In another small bowl, combine 1½ teaspoons (8g) of the milk and the sesame paste and mix well. Combine the remaining milk, the softened sesame paste, and the superfine sugar in a small saucepan and bring to a gentle boil over medium-low heat.

9 Gently drain any excess water from the gelatin and add the gelatin to the milk mixture, stirring well to make sure it dissolves. Remove from the heat and let cool slightly.

10 Strain the black sesame filling through a fine-mesh sieve. Pour the filling into the cooled tart shells, filling them 90 percent of the way, and refrigerate until set, 3 to 4 hours.

11 MAKE THE DECORATIONS AND ASSEMBLE THE TARTS: Place the dark chocolate in a small microwave-safe bowl and microwave in 30-second intervals, stirring after each to prevent burning, until melted and smooth. (Alternatively, use a double boiler to melt the chocolate.) Melt the white chocolate as you did the dark chocolate and divide it between three small bowls. To one portion, add a drop of black food coloring or a pinch of black cocoa powder and stir until smooth and evenly tinted light gray. To the second portion, add 2 drops black food coloring or 2 pinches black cocoa powder and stir until smooth and evenly tinted dark gray. To the third portion, add a drop of pink food coloring and stir until smooth and evenly tinted pink to use for the mouth fill.

12 Transfer the melted dark chocolate and gray and pink chocolates to separate small piping bags and snip a scant ⅛-inch (2.5mm) hole in the tips. Photocopy or scan and print the Black Sesame Tarts templates on page 203 (templates 7 and 8) and place the templates under a piece of parchment paper. Using the dark chocolate, pipe Pusheen's eyes, nose, and whiskers onto the parchment paper, making one set for each tart. Using the light gray chocolate, pipe Pusheen's ears onto parchment paper. Using the dark gray chocolate, pipe on Pusheen's head stripes. Using the pink chocolate, pipe on the pink mouth fill. Set aside to harden.

13 Add the Pusheen features by gently peeling the chocolate off the parchment paper and transferring them to the tarts using a pair of forceps or tweezers.

PUSHEEN FRUIT TARTS

MAKES THREE 5–INCH (7.5CM) TARTS • LEVEL OF DIFFICULTY: MEDIUM

Fresh, bright, and bursting with juicy strawberries, with luscious pastry cream and a flaky, buttery crust, this Pusheen fruit tart is an all-time favorite! Use our template to create your own Pusheen-shaped pan.

INGREDIENTS

Pusheen-Shaped Tart Crust

1½ cups (180g) all-purpose flour

⅔ cup (85g) confectioners' sugar

¼ teaspoon salt

8 tablespoons (1 stick/115g) unsalted butter, cut into small cubes and chilled

1 large egg

½ teaspoon pure vanilla extract

Pastry Cream Filling

¾ cup plus 2 tablespoons (215g) whole milk

1½ teaspoons pure vanilla extract

¼ cup (50g) superfine sugar

2 tablespoons cornstarch or custard powder

3 large egg yolks

2 tablespoons (¼ stick/30g) unsalted butter, cut into small cubes and chilled

Assembly and Decorations

3 tablespoons chopped dark coating/compound chocolate

½ cup (160g) apricot jam

1 tablespoon water

1 cup (about 9) strawberries, sliced lengthwise into thirds

1 MAKE 4 PUSHEEN-SHAPED TART PANS FROM ALUMINUM FOIL: Fold a sheet of foil into a strip ½ inch (1.5cm) wide, then bend the strip into a Pusheen shape, following the Fruit Tarts template on page 205 (template 12) as a guide. Cut another piece of foil into an oval shape 2 inches (5cm) bigger than the Pusheen-shaped foil outline. Cut slits around the oval (to make it easier to fold in), then place it under the Pusheen-shaped foil. Wrap the oval foil over the Pusheen-shaped strip to reinforce the shape and make the bottom of the tart pan. Repeat this process to make another two pans.

2 MAKE THE TART CRUST: In a large bowl or in a food processor, combine the flour, confectioners' sugar, and salt. Add the cold butter and quickly cut it into the flour mixture using a pastry cutter or fork

or by pulsing the food processor. Mix or pulse until the mixture becomes crumbly and resembles coarse meal. Add the egg and vanilla and mix or pulse until the dough is no longer dry and starts to clump together. The dough should be crumbly with large clumps.

3. Transfer the dough to a lightly floured surface and form it into a ball. Flatten the ball slightly to form a thick disc. Wrap the disc of dough in plastic wrap and refrigerate for 1 hour.

4. Take the dough out of the fridge and let it sit for a few minutes to soften slightly for easy rolling. Butter your tart pans by brushing lightly with a silicone pastry brush greased with butter.

5. Divide the dough into three portions. On a lightly floured surface, roll out each portion of the dough into an oval shape that is 1 inch (2.5cm) wider than the tart pans on all sides and ⅛ inch (3mm) thick. Place a dough oval gently into each tart pan, pressing very gently to fit the dough into the pan.* With a sharp knife, trim the edges of the dough flush with the top of the pans. Prick the bottom of the shells with a fork to prevent them from puffing during baking. Cover the tart shells with plastic wrap, set them on a baking sheet, and freeze for 30 minutes. (Frozen dough is less prone to shrinking during baking.)

*Tip: If the dough becomes too soft to work with, chill it until firm again, then continue.

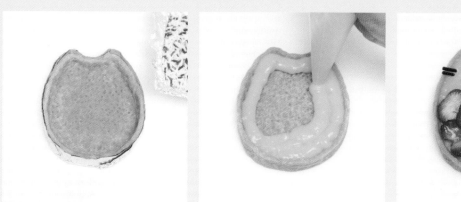

6 Preheat the oven to 355°F (180°C).

7 Remove the tart shells from the freezer, uncover them, and line each with a piece of aluminum foil, pressing it tightly against the dough and covering the edges to prevent them from burning. Fill the foil with pie weights, dried beans, or uncooked rice, making sure they're evenly distributed over the entire surface. Bake for 20 minutes, or until the foil no longer sticks to the dough. Remove the tart shells from the oven, remove the weights and foil, and bake for 10 minutes more, until golden brown. Let the tart shells cool completely on the pan.

8 MAKE THE PASTRY CREAM FILLING: In a small saucepan, combine the milk, vanilla, and half the superfine sugar and heat over medium heat until it comes to a boil.

9 In a medium bowl, whisk together the remaining superfine sugar, the cornstarch or custard powder, and the egg yolks until light and creamy. While whisking continuously, slowly drizzle half of the hot milk mixture into the egg yolk mixture to temper them, then pour the tempered egg yolk mixture back into the saucepan with the remaining milk mixture and whisk to combine. Reduce the heat to low and cook, whisking continuously, until the custard is thick, 20 to 25 minutes. Remove from the heat and stir in the butter until melted and well combined. Transfer to a clean medium bowl and cover with plastic wrap,

pressing it directly against the surface of the pastry cream to prevent skin from forming, and refrigerate for 3 hours.

10 MAKE THE DECORATIONS AND ASSEMBLE THE TARTS: Place the Fruit Tarts template (template 12) under a piece of parchment paper. Place the dark chocolate in a small microwave-safe bowl and microwave in 30-second intervals, stirring after each to prevent burning, until melted and smooth. Transfer the melted dark chocolate to a small piping bag, snip a small hole in the tip, and pipe Pusheen features onto the parchment paper. Set aside to harden.

11 In a small saucepan, stir together the apricot jam and water over medium-low heat for about 2 minutes, until mostly liquid. Strain the glaze through a fine-mesh sieve and let cool.

12 Transfer the chilled pastry cream to a large piping bag and snip a ½-inch (1.5cm) hole in the tip. Fill the tart shells evenly with the pastry cream. Decorate the tops of the tarts with the sliced strawberries. Add the chocolate Pusheen features by gently peeling the chocolate off the parchment paper and transferring them to the tarts using a pair of forceps or tweezers. Lightly brush the apricot glaze over the tarts.

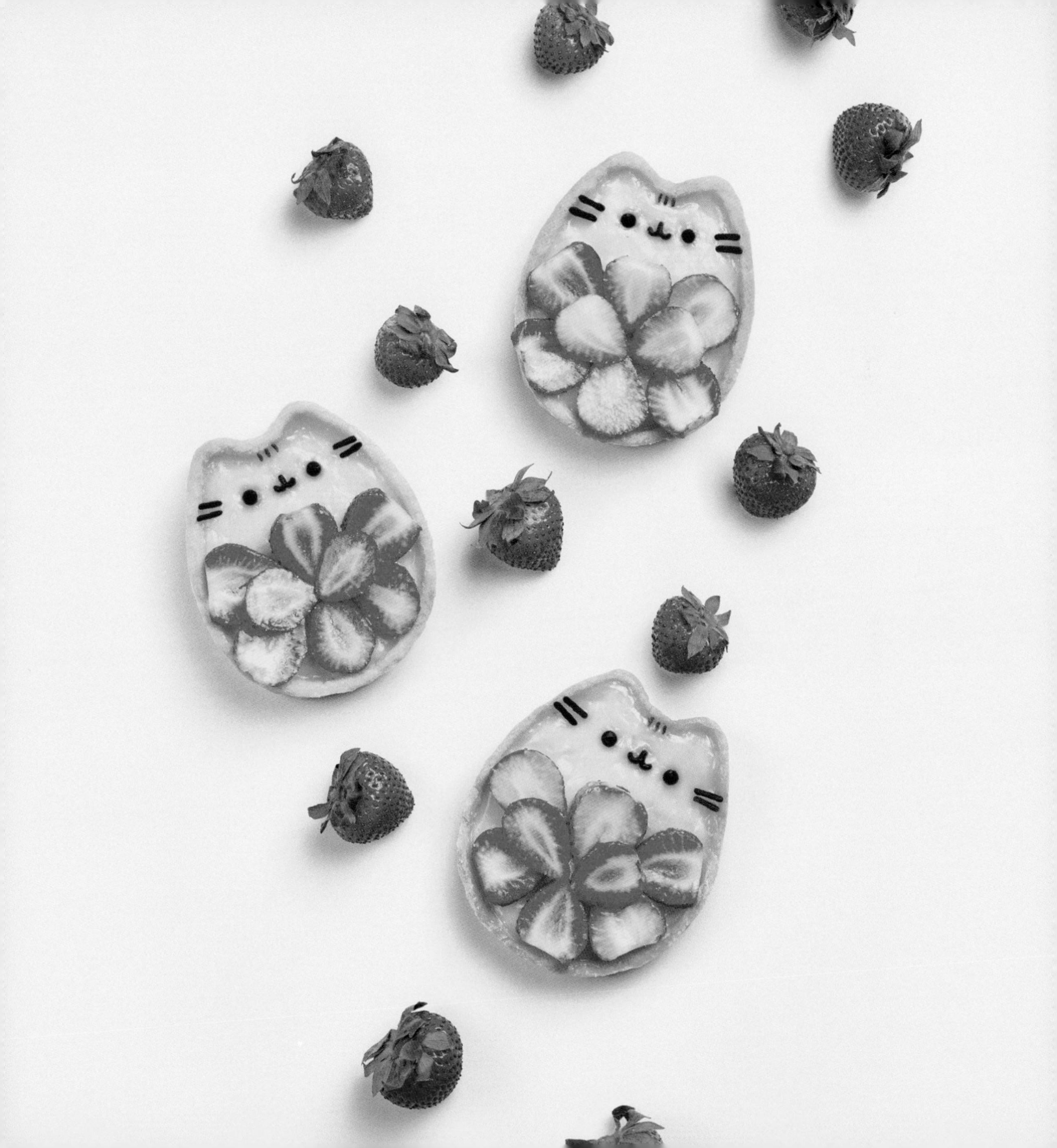

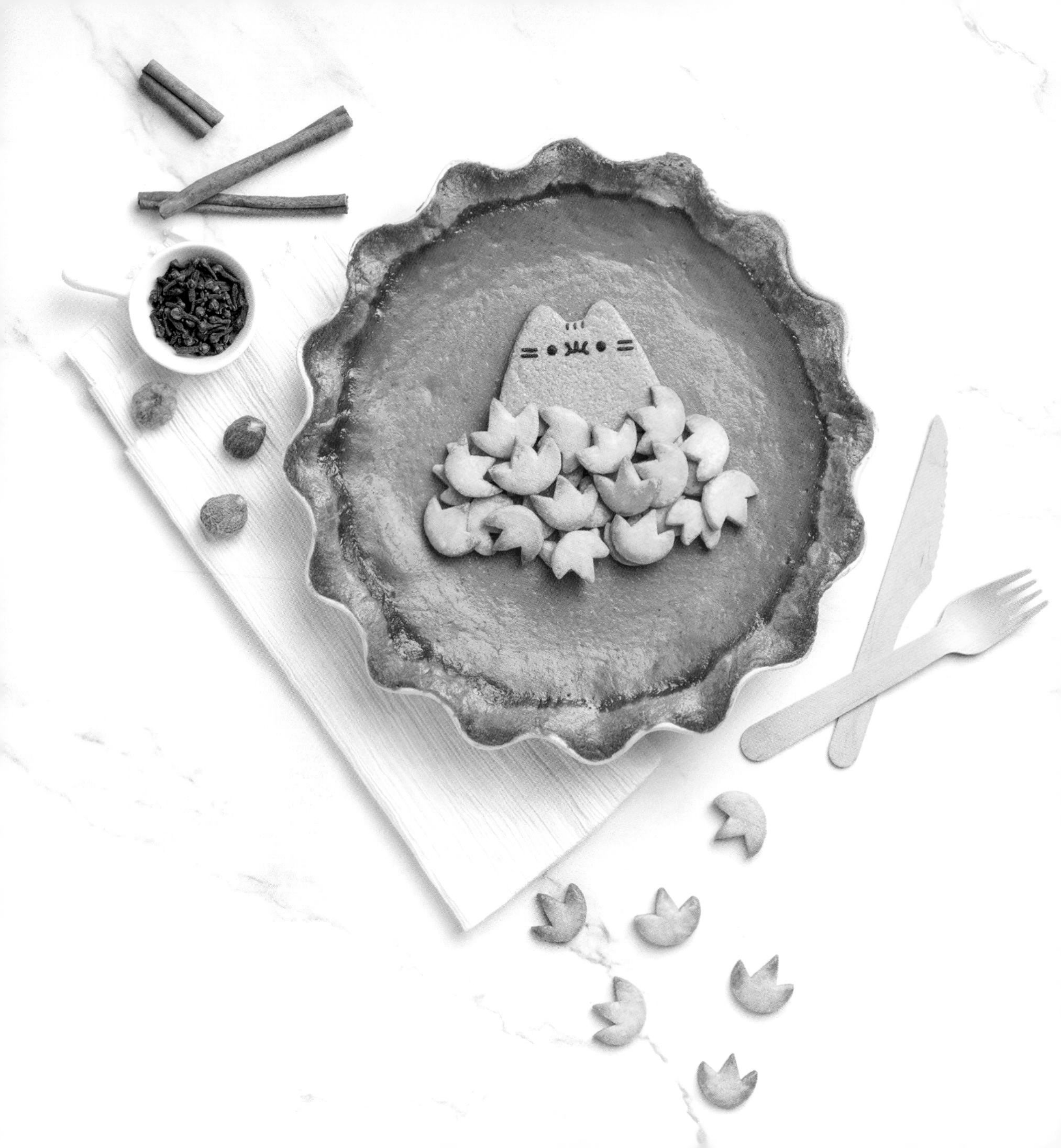

PUSHEEN PUMPKIN PIE

MAKES ONE 9-INCH (23CM) PIE • LEVEL OF DIFFICULTY: MEDIUM TO DIFFICULT

Bursting with flavor, this rich, velvety, sweet-and-spicy pumpkin filling coupled with a winning flaky piecrust is a hit during Thanksgiving. The double crust is woven into the adorable design of Pusheen peeking out from a huge pile of autumn leaves.

INGREDIENTS

Piecrust

2½ cups (300g) all-purpose flour, plus more for dusting

1 tablespoon superfine sugar

1 teaspoon salt

8 tablespoons (1 stick/115g) unsalted butter, cut into small cubes and chilled

8 tablespoons (115g) shortening, cut into small cubes and chilled

¼ cup (60g) cold water

Black food coloring or unsweetened black cocoa powder

Egg Wash

1 large egg

1 tablespoon water

Pumpkin Pie Filling

1 (15-ounce/454g) can unsweetened pumpkin puree

1 (12-ounce/340g) can evaporated milk

¾ cup (150g) superfine sugar

1 teaspoon ground cinnamon

½ teaspoon ground nutmeg

½ teaspoon ground ginger

½ teaspoon salt

¼ teaspoon ground cloves

2 large eggs

Decorations

1 tablespoon chopped dark coating/compound chocolate

① MAKE THE PIECRUST: In a large bowl or in a food processor, combine the flour, superfine sugar, and salt. Add the cold butter and shortening and quickly cut them into the flour mixture using a pastry cutter or fork or by pulsing the food processor. Mix or pulse until the mixture becomes crumbly and resembles coarse meal. Work in 1 tablespoon of cold water at a time until the dough isn't dry and starts to clump together, adding more water as needed.

② Turn the dough out onto a lightly floured surface and form it into a ball. It should come together easily without being sticky. Divide the ball in half, then divide one portion in half again so you have one

large portion and two smaller portions. Knead a drop of black food coloring or a pinch of black cocoa powder into one smaller portion until the dough is evenly tinted gray (leave the other portions plain).

3 Flatten each ball of dough slightly with your hands to form discs 1 inch (2.5cm) thick. Wrap each disc separately in plastic wrap and refrigerate for at least 1 hour.

4 Flour your work surface and rolling pin generously to prevent sticking (or roll out the dough between two pieces of plastic wrap or parchment paper). Remove the larger disc of chilled dough from the fridge and roll it out to about a ¼-inch (6mm) thickness or into a round at least 2 inches (5cm) wider than the bottom of your pie pan. Place the round of dough over the pie pan and press it gently into the pan to fit. Tuck under or cut away any overhanging dough and crimp the edge. Prick the bottom of the piecrust with a fork to prevent it from puffing during baking. Cover the piecrust with plastic wrap and freeze for 30 minutes. (Frozen dough is less prone to shrinking during baking.)

5 Preheat the oven to 375°F (190°C).

6 Remove the piecrust from the freezer, uncover it, and line it with aluminum foil, pressing the foil against the dough and covering the edges to prevent them from burning. Fill the foil with pie weights, dried beans, or uncooked rice, making sure they're evenly distributed over the entire surface. Bake for 20 minutes, or until the foil no longer sticks to the dough.

7 MEANWHILE, MAKE THE EGG WASH: In a small bowl, whisk together the egg and water.

8 Remove the piecrust from the oven, remove the foil and weights, lightly brush the crust with the egg wash, and bake for 10 minutes more, until golden brown. Reserve the remaining egg wash.

9 MAKE THE PUMPKIN PIE FILLING: In a medium saucepan, combine the pumpkin puree, evaporated milk, superfine sugar, cinnamon, nutmeg, ginger, salt, and cloves. Heat over very low heat, stirring until smooth. Remove from the heat and let cool slightly, then stir in the eggs. (This step helps to produce a very smooth filling.)

10 Fill the piecrust with the filling. Cover with a pie shield to prevent the crust from burning. Bake for 40 to 50 minutes, until the filling is set but still jiggles slightly in the center

11

MAKE THE DECORATIONS: Make templates by tracing a Pusheen shape from the Pumpkin Pie half Pusheen template on page 203 (template 10) onto food-safe plastic and cutting it out, and by tracing the Maple Leaf template on page 203 (template 11) onto food-safe plastic and cutting it out.

12 On a lightly floured surface, roll out the disc of gray dough to ¼ inch (6mm) thick. Place the Pusheen-shaped template on top of the dough and use it as a guide to cut out the shape with a sharp knife. Roll out the disc of plain dough to ¼ inch (6mm) thick. Place the maple leaf–shaped template on top of the dough and use it as a guide to cut out as many maple leaves as you can with a sharp knife. Place the cut-out decorations on a parchment-lined baking sheet, cover with plastic wrap, and chill for about 1 hour. Remove the decorations from the fridge, lightly brush them with the reserved egg wash, and bake for 14 minutes. Remove from the oven and let cool completely.

13 Place the dark chocolate in a small microwave-safe bowl and microwave in 30-second intervals, stirring after each to prevent burning, until melted and smooth. Transfer the melted dark chocolate to a small piping bag, snip a small hole in the tip, and pipe facial features onto the Pusheen shape.

14 Top the pumpkin pie with the Pusheen shape and leaves.

PUSHEEN CREAM PUFFS

MAKES 25 TO 30 CREAM PUFFS · LEVEL OF DIFFICULTY: MEDIUM

Crisp, airy, and hollow rounds of choux pastry, spilt in two and filled with sweetened whipped cream, are styled into Pusheens playing peekaboo. These heavenly bite-size French pastries are guaranteed to bring smiles to everyone!

INGREDIENTS

Choux Pastry

½ cup (60g) bread flour*

½ cup (60g) all-purpose flour*

1 cup (240g) water

8 tablespoons (1 stick/115g) unsalted butter, cut into cubes and slightly softened but still cold

1½ teaspoons superfine sugar

½ teaspoon salt

3 large eggs

Egg Wash (optional)

1 large egg

1½ tablespoons water

Chantilly Cream Filling

1 cup (240g) heavy cream

1 teaspoon pure vanilla extract or vanilla bean paste

3 tablespoons confectioners' sugar

Black food coloring or unsweetened black cocoa powder

Decorations

3 ounces (80g) white coating/ compound chocolate, chopped, or melting wafers

Black oil-based food coloring or unsweetened black cocoa powder

3 ounces (80g) dark coating/ compound chocolate, chopped, or melting wafers

*Tip: You can also use only bread flour, or only all-purpose flour, depending on the texture you like. Bread flour produces superior structure, while all-purpose flour gives a more melt-in-your-mouth quality.

1 MAKE THE CHOUX PASTRY: Preheat the oven to 355°F (180°C). Line a baking sheet with parchment paper or a silicone baking mat.

2 Sift the bread flour and all-purpose flour together into a small bowl.

3 In a medium saucepan, combine the water, butter, superfine sugar, and salt. Bring to a boil over medium heat, stirring continuously, then remove from the heat and pour the flours into the mixture. Using a wooden spatula, mix well until a ball of dough forms, about 2 minutes. Reduce the heat to low and cook the dough for 3 minutes more, stirring continuously. (This ensures that more moisture is removed from the dough.) Remove from the heat and transfer the dough to a medium bowl. Let the dough cool for about 10 minutes, pressing it against the side of the bowl to cool and remove bubbles.

4 Add 2 of the eggs, one at a time, mixing well after each addition. In a small bowl, lightly beat the last egg and add it little by little, testing the consistency as you add it (you may not need to add the entire egg); the dough should form a V at the tip of the spatula when you lift it. (Another sign is that when you pull the spatula through the dough, it leaves a streak in the dough that doesn't collapse on itself.)

5 Transfer the dough to a piping bag fitted with a ½-inch (1.5cm) round tip. Press the air out of the dough by flattening the dough in the piping bag. Gather the dough in the bag and pipe 1-inch (2.5cm) rounds at least 2 inches (5cm) apart onto the prepared pan. Hold the piping bag perpendicular to the pan, moving the bag up as you pipe so that the piping tip always touches the top of the dough.

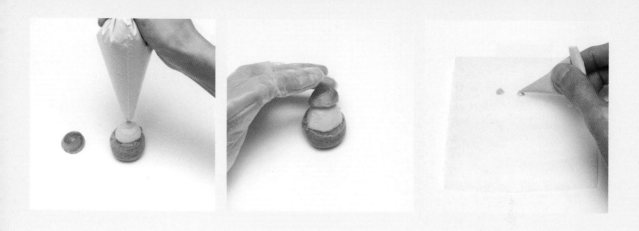

6 MAKE THE OPTIONAL EGG WASH: In a small bowl, whisk together the egg and water, if desired. Using a pastry brush, flatten the tips of the dough using the egg wash (or just water). Use a clean pastry brush to dot water onto the parchment paper or silicone baking mat around the dough (not touching the dough; this will create steam that will help cause expansion as the pastries bake).

7 Bake the choux pastries for 20 minutes, then reduce the oven temperature to 320°F (160°C) and bake for 20 minutes more, until the pastries are crisp and golden brown. While they are still hot, use a skewer or toothpick to pierce the side or bottom of the pastries to release any steam.

8 MAKE THE CHANTILLY CREAM FILLING: In a chilled large bowl, combine the cream, vanilla, and confectioners' sugar. Whisk until the cream holds stiff peaks. Add a drop of black food coloring or a pinch of black cocoa powder and whisk lightly until evenly tinted gray.

9 Transfer the Chantilly cream to a piping bag fitted with a ½-inch (1.5cm) round tip. Slice off the top third of each pastry and set aside. Pipe the Chantilly cream into the bottom of the pastries to form Pusheen's head. Top with the pastry tops. Place the filled cream puffs on a baking sheet and refrigerate while you prepare the chocolate decorations.

10 MAKE THE DECORATIONS AND ASSEMBLE THE CREAM PUFFS: Place the white chocolate in a small microwave-safe bowl and microwave in 30-second intervals, stirring after each to prevent burning, until melted and smooth. Tramsfer half of the melted white chocolate to another bowl. To one portion, add a small drop of black food coloring or a small pinch of black cocoa powder and stir until evenly tinted the same shade of light gray as the Chantilly cream. To the second portion, add a drop of black food coloring or a pinch of black cocoa powder and stir until evenly tinted dark gray. Pipe small triangles and small rounds of the light gray chocolate onto a piece of parchment paper for Pusheen's ears and hands, making one set for each cream puff, and set aside to harden. Melt the dark chocolate as you did the white chocolate.

11 Place the light gray ears onto the cream filling using a pair of forceps or tweezers. Use a toothpick to draw on the facial features and head stripes using the dark chocolate and the dark gray chocolate.

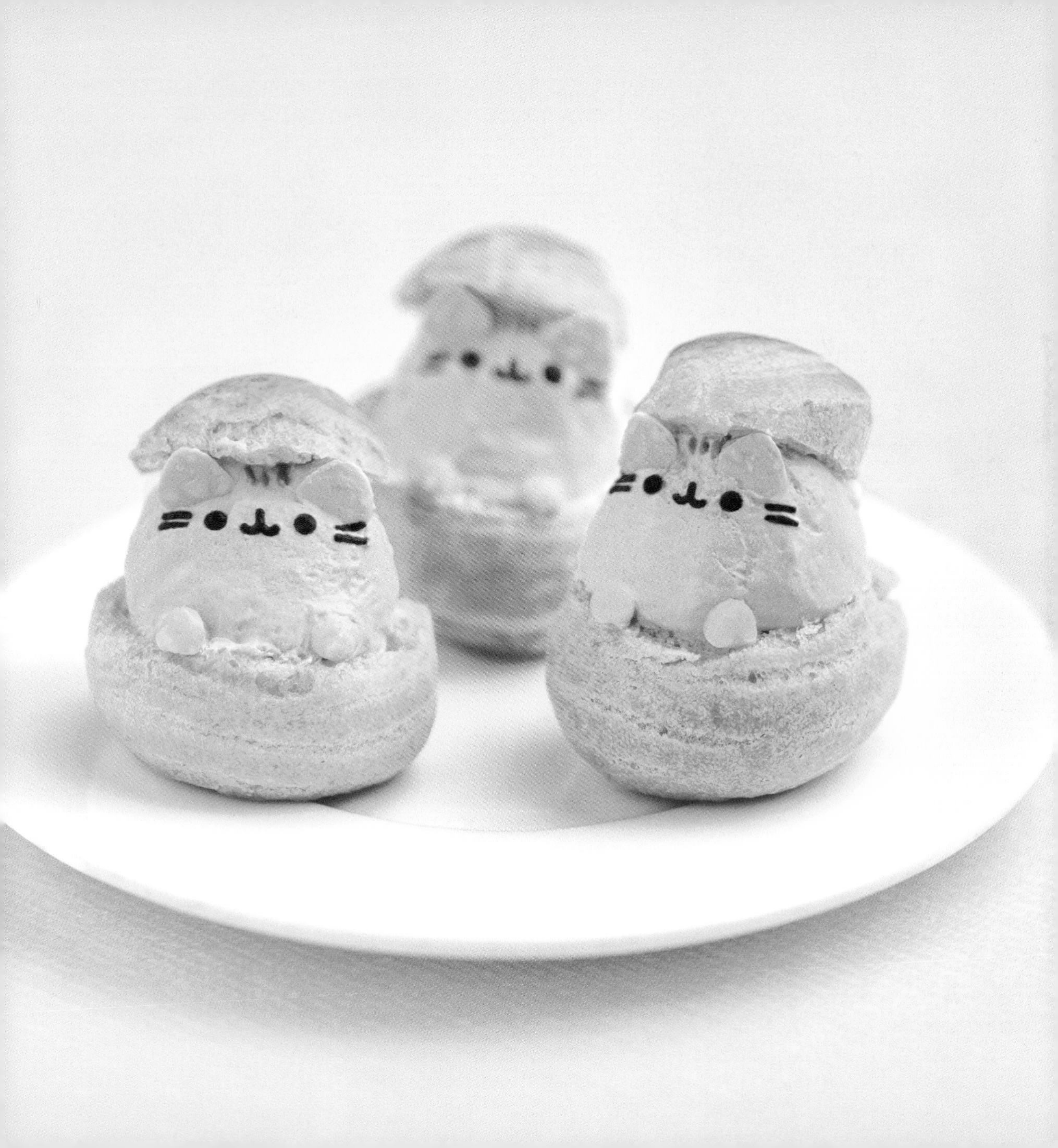

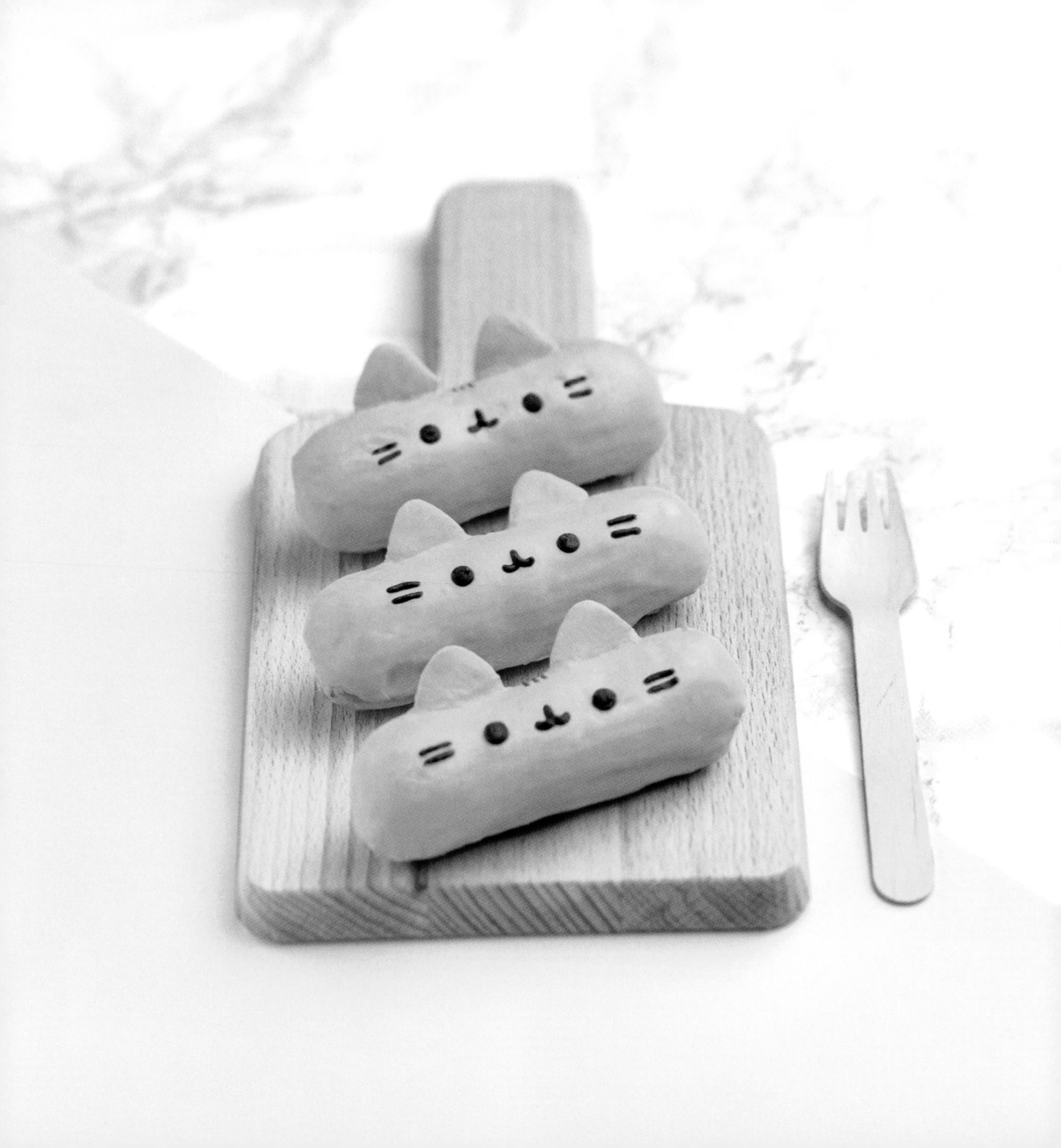

PUSHEEN ÉCLAIRS

MAKES 16 ÉCLAIRS · LEVEL OF DIFFICULTY: MEDIUM

Double the goodness, the deliciously crisp and puffy choux pastry shells used for Pusheen Cream Puffs (page 85) are now elongated and filled to the brim with lots of luscious whipped cream, then coated with rich chocolate and decorated to look like endearing Pusheen faces. Too good to be true!

. . . .

INGREDIENTS

Choux Pastry

½ cup (60g) bread flour*

½ cup (60g) all-purpose flour*

1 cup (240g) water

8 tablespoons (1 stick/115g) unsalted butter, cut into cubes and slightly softened but still cold

1½ teaspoons superfine sugar

½ teaspoon salt

3 large eggs

Egg Wash

1 large egg

1½ tablespoons water

Chantilly Cream Filling*

1 cup (240g) heavy cream

1 teaspoon pure vanilla extract or vanilla bean paste

3 tablespoons confectioners' sugar

Chocolate Coating

10½ ounces (300g) white coating/compound chocolate, chopped, or melting wafers

2 tablespoons coconut oil, plus more if needed

Black oil-based food coloring or unsweetened black cocoa powder

Decorations

3 ounces (80g) dark coating/compound chocolate, chopped, or melting wafers

3 ounces (80g) white coating/compound chocolate, chopped, or melting wafers

Black oil-based food coloring or unsweetened black cocoa powder

. . . .

*Tips: You can also use only bread flour, or only all-purpose flour, depending on the texture you like. Bread flour produces superior structure, while all-purpose flour gives a more melt-in-your-mouth quality.

You can replace the Chantilly cream filling with pastry cream filling (see page 75), if you like.

1 MAKE THE CHOUX PASTRY: Preheat the oven to 355°F (180°C). Line a baking sheet with parchment paper or a silicone baking mat.

2 Sift the bread flour and all-purpose flour together into a small bowl.

3 In a medium saucepan, combine the water, butter, superfine sugar, and salt. Bring to a boil over medium heat, stirring continuously, then remove from the heat and pour the flours into the mixture. Using a wooden spatula, mix well until a ball of dough forms, about 2 minutes. Reduce the heat to low and cook the dough for 3 minutes, stirring continuously. (This ensures that more moisture is removed from the dough.) Remove from the heat and let the dough cool for about 10 minutes, pressing it against the side of the pan to cool and remove bubbles.

4 Add 2 of the eggs, one at a time, mixing well with each addition. In small bowl, lightly beat the last egg and add it little by little, testing the consistency as you add it (you may not need to add the entire egg); the dough should form a V at the tip of the spatula when you lift it. (Another sign is that when you pull the spatula through the dough, it leaves a streak in the dough that doesn't collapse on itself.)

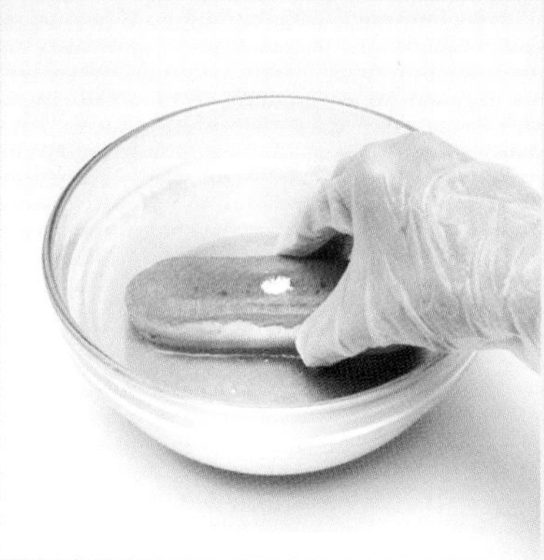

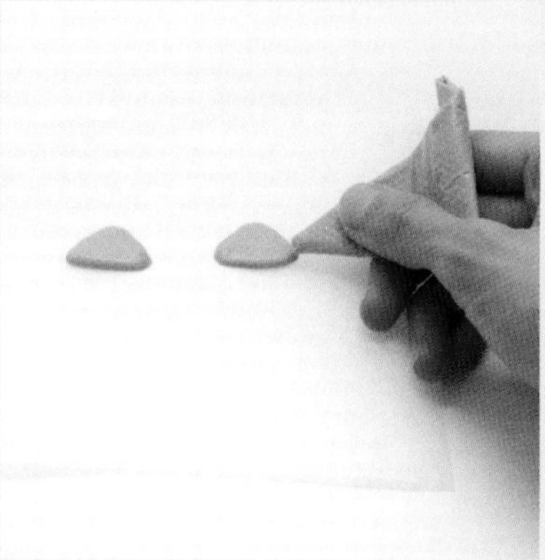

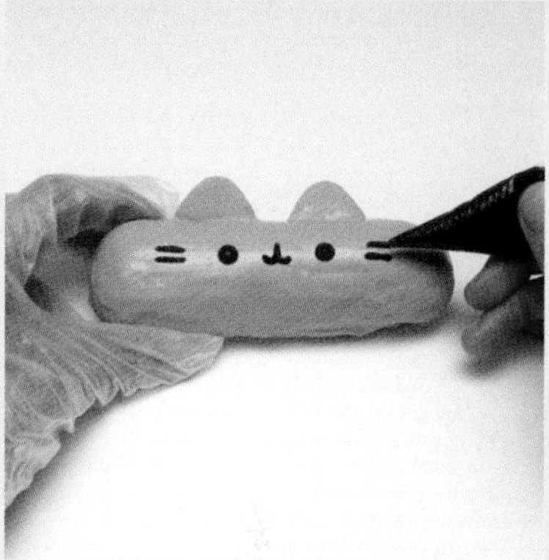

5 Transfer the dough to a piping bag fitted with a ½-inch (1.5cm) French star tip. Press the air out of the dough by flattening the dough in the piping bag. Gather the dough in the bag and pipe straight lines that are 5 inches (12.5cm) long by 1 inch (2.5cm) wide onto the prepared pan, leaving 2 inches (5cm) between the éclairs to allow space for expansion. As you pipe, hold the piping bag at a 45-degree angle to the pan and release the pressure at the end of each éclair.

6 MAKE THE OPTIONAL EGG WASH: In a small bowl, whisk together the egg and water, if desired. Using a pastry brush, flatten the tips at the ends of the éclairs using the egg wash (or just water). Use a clean pastry brush to dot water onto the parchment paper or silicone baking mat around the dough (not touching the dough; this will create steam that will help cause expansion as the éclairs bake).

7 Bake the éclairs for 20 minutes, then reduce the oven temperature to 320°F (160°C) and bake for 20 minutes more, until crisp and golden brown. While they are still hot, use a skewer or toothpick to pierce the side or bottom of the éclairs to release any steam. Let cool completely.

8 MAKE THE CHANTILLY CREAM FILLING: In a chilled large bowl, combine the cream, vanilla, and confectioners' sugar. Whisk until the cream holds stiff peaks.

⑨ Transfer the Chantilly cream to a piping bag fitted with a Bismarck tip. Insert the tip into each éclair and fill them with the Chantilly cream. Place the filled éclairs on a baking sheet and refrigerate while you prepare the chocolate decorations.

⑩ MAKE THE DECORATIONS AND ASSEMBLE THE ÉCLAIRS: To make the chocolate coating, place the white chocolate and 2 tablespoons coconut oil in a medium microwave-safe bowl and microwave in 30-second intervals, stirring after each to prevent burning. If needed, add more coconut oil, 1 teaspoon at a time, until the chocolate is melted and has a dipping or pouring consistency. (Alternatively, use a double boiler to melt the chocolate and coconut oil.) Add drops of black food coloring or pinches of black cocoa powder and stir until smooth and evenly tinted the desired shade of gray.

⑪ Dip the tops of the éclairs into the melted gray chocolate. Tap off or wipe off the excess and place the éclairs on a baking sheet or wire rack to set.

⑫ Set aside a small amount of the remaining gray chocolate for Pusheen's head stripes, then transfer the rest to a small piping bag. Snip a ⅛-inch (3mm) hole in the tip and pipe triangles for Pusheen's ears onto a piece of parchment paper, making one pair for each éclair and reserving a bit of the chocolate to use as "glue." Set aside to harden.

⑬ Stick the ears to the éclairs, using the reserved melted chocolate "glue." To make the decorations, melt the dark chocolate as you did the white chocolate, transfer it to a small piping bag, snip a small hole in the tip, and use it to pipe Pusheen's facial features onto the éclairs. Add a drop of black food coloring or a pinch of black cocoa powder to the reserved gray chocolate, transfer it to a small piping bag, snip a scant 1mm hole in the tip, and use it to pipe Pusheen's head stripes onto the éclairs.

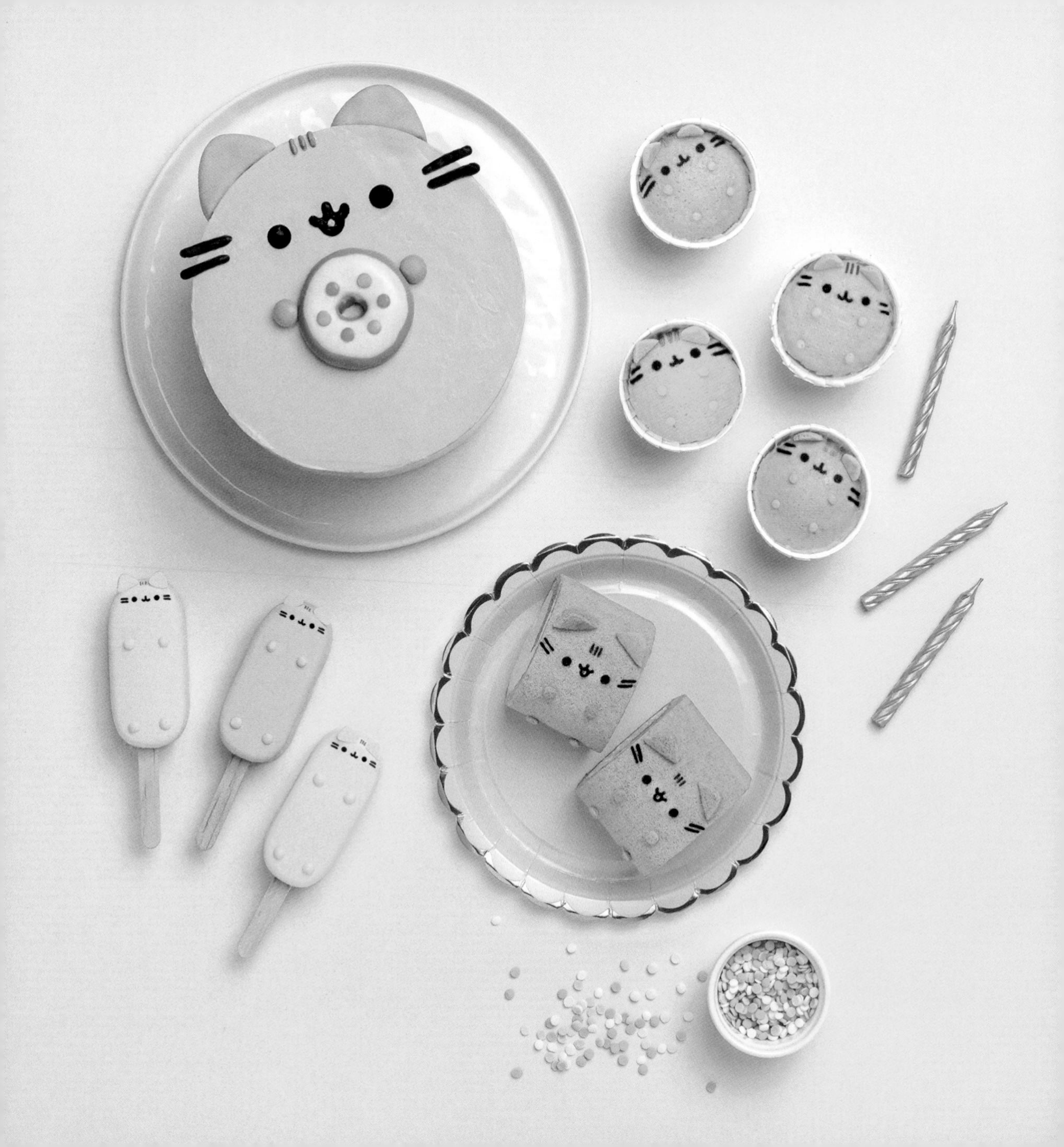

Cakes

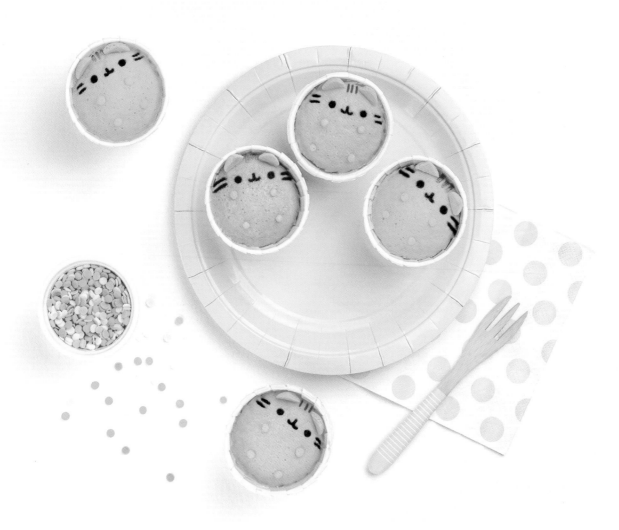

PASTEL PUSHEEN STEAMED CUPCAKES

MAKES SIX 2-INCH (5CM) CUPCAKES • LEVEL OF DIFFICULTY: MEDIUM

Moist and spongy, with a slightly heavier crumb than baked versions, these make a quick and tasty snack without an oven, and are most enjoyable right out of the steamer. Care has to be taken for the steam not to drip onto these adorable Pusheen cupcakes, which could cause them to wrinkle!

1 In a large bowl, using an electric mixer, combine the eggs, oil, superfine sugar, and vanilla and beat on medium-high speed for 6 minutes, or until the mixture falls in ribbons when you lift the beater out.

2 Sift the flour and baking powder together into a small bowl. Add the flour mixture to the egg mixture in two additions, alternating with the milk, and mix until combined.

3 Transfer 1 teaspoon of the batter to a small bowl, add a pinch of cocoa powder, and stir until evenly tinted gray. Transfer 2 teaspoons of the batter to a separate small bowl, add ½ teaspoon cocoa powder and a drop of purple food coloring,* and stir until evenly tinted dark purple. Transfer the tinted batters to separate small piping bags. Divide the remaining batter among three small bowls and tint with pink, purple, and green food coloring, using a different color for each portion.

*Tip: If you are using natural food coloring powder, dissolve it in an equal quantity of hot water before adding it to the batter to prevent uneven spots.

INGREDIENTS

- 2 large eggs
- 2 teaspoons vegetable oil
- ⅔ cup (133g) superfine sugar
- 1 teaspoon pure vanilla extract
- 1½ cups (180g) cake flour
- 2 teaspoons baking powder
- 6½ tablespoons (100g) whole milk
- Unsweetened black cocoa powder
- Food coloring: pink, purple, and green (or use natural food colorings: beet, purple sweet potato, and matcha powders)
- 1 tablespoon chopped white coating/compound chocolate

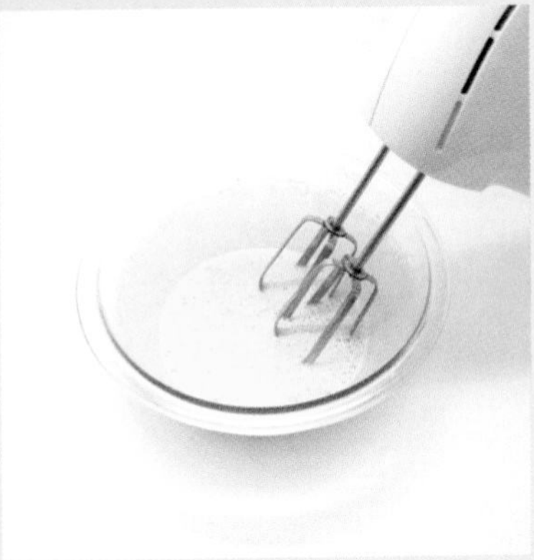

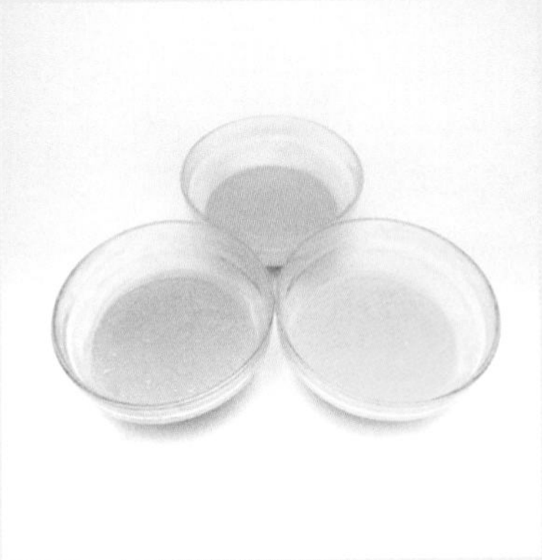

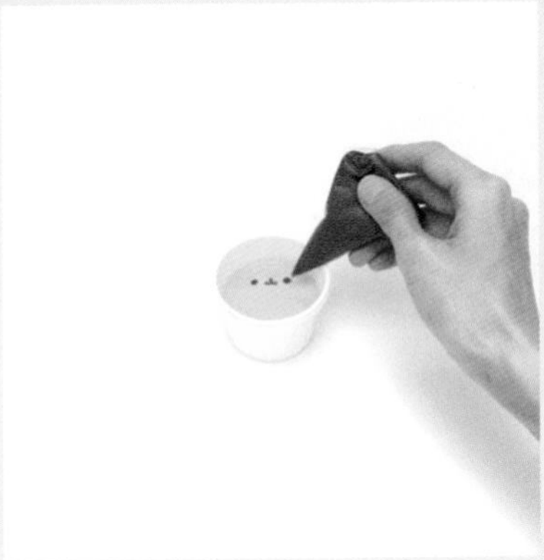

4 For each cupcake, stack two rigid paper cupcake liners together to prevent too much expansion during steaming. (You can also place paper cupcake liners into six ramekins or silicone cupcake liners that are slightly bigger than the paper liners to prevent too much side expansion.)

5 Fill the six cups with the pink, purple, and green batters two-thirds of the way (two cups of each color). Reserve the leftover batter for the ears, hands, and feet. Pipe Pusheen's facial features into the cups using the dark purple batter. Pipe Pusheen's head stripes using the gray batter.

6 Fill a large saucepan with 1 to 2 inches (2.5 to 5cm) of water and bring it to a boil over high heat, then reduce the heat to medium-low. Place a bamboo steamer basket in the pan, add the cupcakes, cover, and steam for 12 minutes. If you are using an electric steamer, fill the reservoir over the minimum mark, place the cupcakes into the steaming compartment, and steam for 12 minutes. Remove the cupcakes from the steamer basket or electric steamer* and let cool.

**Very important note:* Prevent water from dripping onto the cupcakes by either propping the lid of the electric steamer up slightly on one side with a bamboo skewer or wrapping the underside of the lid in a clean kitchen towel (to absorb the steam). When you open the steamer, always quickly tilt the lid

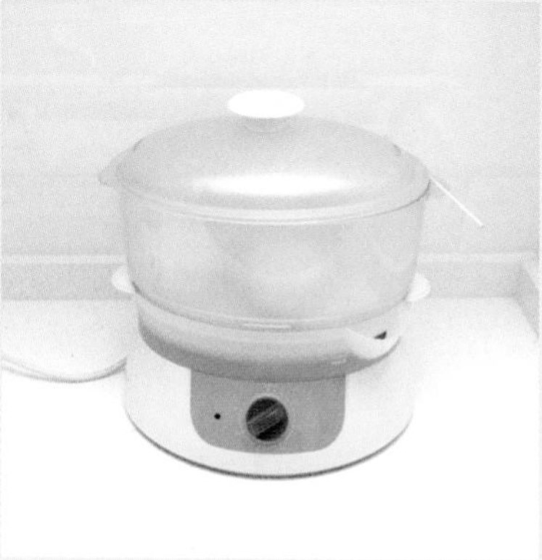
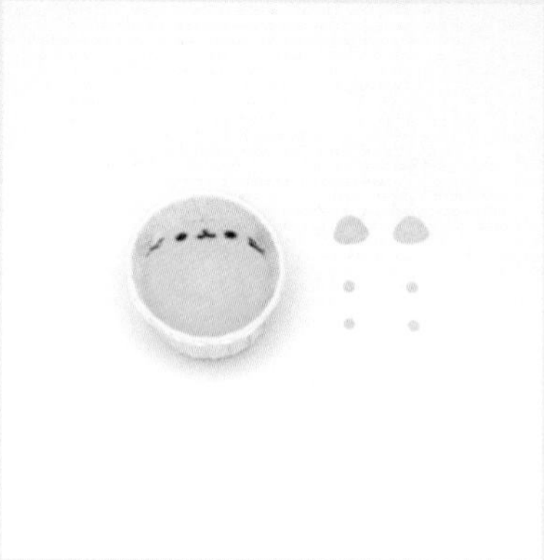
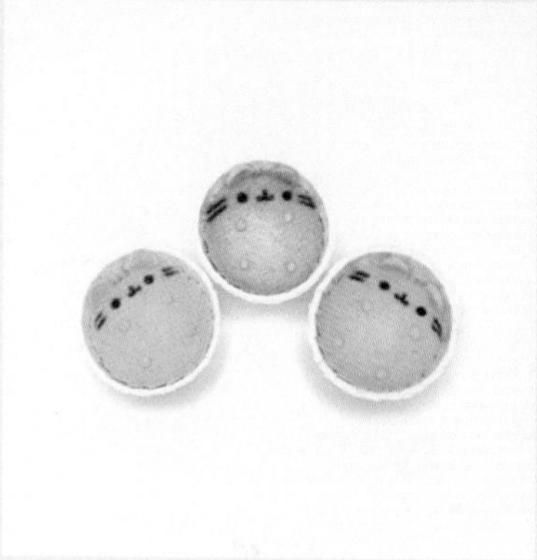

sideways to prevent any water that has condensed on its surface from falling onto your cupcakes. (This is not a problem if you are using a bamboo steamer.)

7 Transfer the remaining pink, purple, and green batters into separate small piping bags and snip a scant 1mm hole in the tips. Pipe 2 ears, 2 hands, and 2 feet for each cupcake onto a piece of parchment paper. Steam the small features for 3 minutes.

8 Place the white chocolate in a very small microwave-safe bowl and microwave in 30-second intervals, stirring after each to prevent burning, until melted and smooth. (Alternatively, use a double boiler to melt the chocolate.) Use the melted chocolate to attach the ears, feet, and hands to the cupcakes, and let the chocolate set for a few minutes before serving.

PUSHEEN ROLL CAKE

MAKES ONE 10-INCH (25CM) ROLL CAKE · LEVEL OF DIFFICULTY: MEDIUM

Soft and fluffy vanilla cake coupled with a sweet fresh cream filling make this roll cake extremely light, cottony, dreamy, and delectable. The Pusheens piped onto this treat create a fabric-print look that adds to its ethereal quality!

INGREDIENTS

Piping Batter

4½ teaspoons (20g) unsalted butter, cut into cubes and slightly softened but still cold

2½ tablespoons cake flour

2½ tablespoons confectioners' sugar

½ large egg white

Unsweetened dark cocoa powder

Black food coloring or unsweetened black cocoa powder

Vanilla Roll Cake

2 large egg yolks

3 tablespoons superfine sugar

2 tablespoons vegetable oil

2 tablespoons water

1 teaspoon pure vanilla extract

⅓ cup (40g) cake flour

Pink food coloring (optional)

3 large egg whites

¼ teaspoon cream of tartar

Chantilly Cream Filling

¾ cup (180g) heavy cream

2 tablespoons confectioners' sugar

Decorations

1 tablespoon chopped white coating/compound chocolate

Pink oil-based food coloring

1 Photocopy or scan and print the Roll Cake template on page 207 (template 13). Line a 10-inch (25cm) square baking pan with parchment paper. Place the template under the parchment paper and lightly grease the paper with some butter or nonstick spray.

2 MAKE THE PIPING BATTER: In a medium bowl, combine the butter, flour, confectioners' sugar, and egg white and mix well with a spoon.

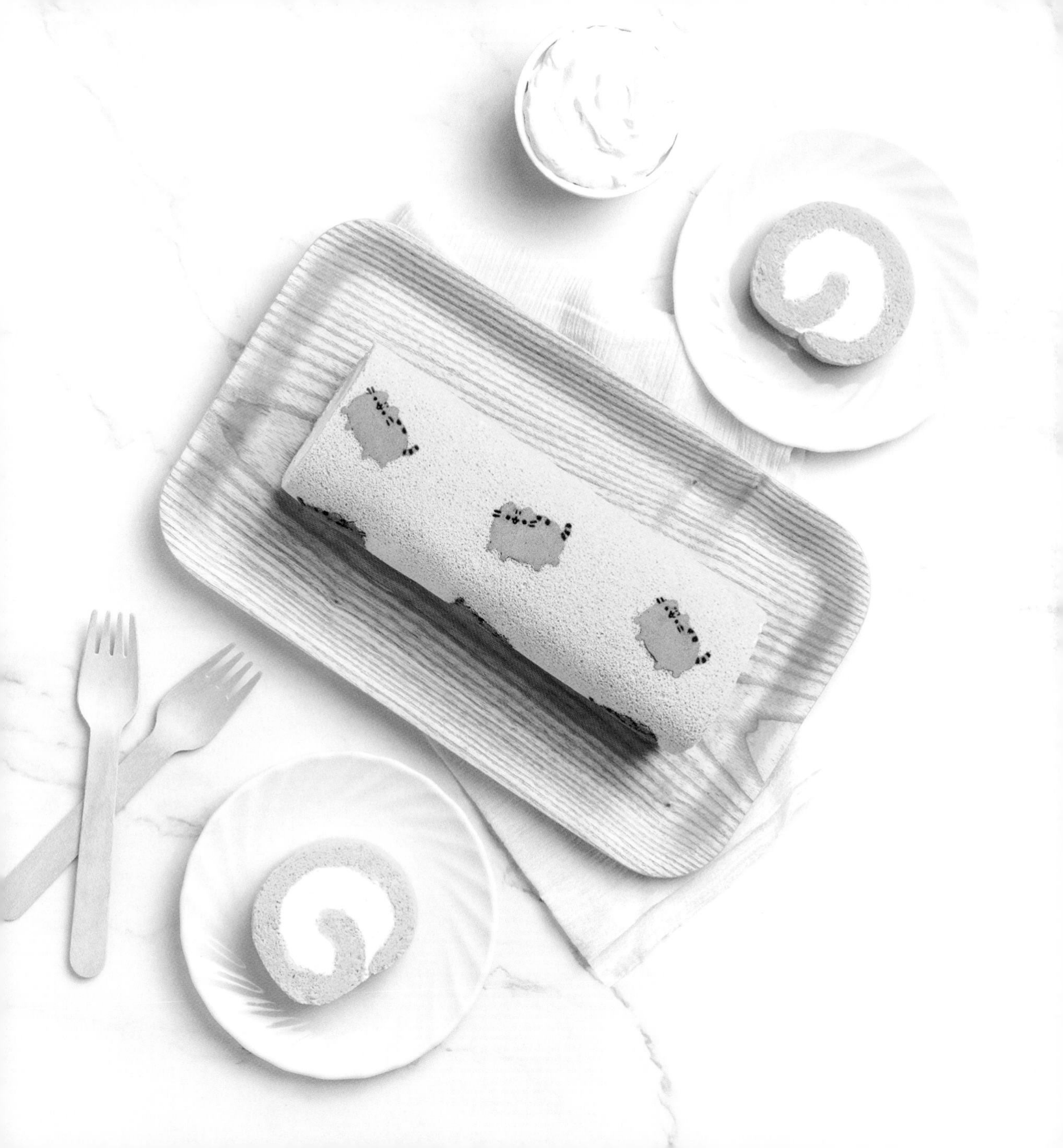

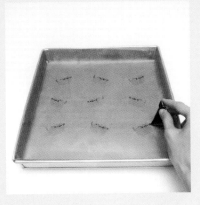  

3 Spoon 1 teaspoon of the batter into a small bowl, add a pinch of dark cocoa powder and a pinch of black cocoa powder or a drop of black food coloring, and stir until evenly tinted dark brown. Spoon another 1 teaspoon of the batter into a separate small bowl, add a drop of black food coloring or a pinch of black cocoa powder, and stir until evenly tinted dark gray. To the remaining batter, add 1 to 2 drops of black food coloring or a pinch of black cocoa powder and stir until evenly tinted light gray. Transfer the batters to separate small piping bags and snip a 1mm hole in the tips.

4 Following the template, pipe the small features onto the prepared pan using the dark brown batter for the face and whiskers and the dark gray batter for the head stripes. Refrigerate for 5 minutes.

5 Remove the pan from the fridge and, following the template, pipe the body onto the prepared pan, over the small features, using the light gray batter. Refrigerate for at least 30 minutes while you prepare the batter for the roll cake.

6 MAKE THE VANILLA ROLL CAKE: Preheat the oven to 320°F (160°C).

7 In a large bowl, using an electric mixer, whisk together the egg yolks and 1 tablespoon of the superfine sugar until pale and light. Add the oil, water, and vanilla and whisk until well combined. Sift

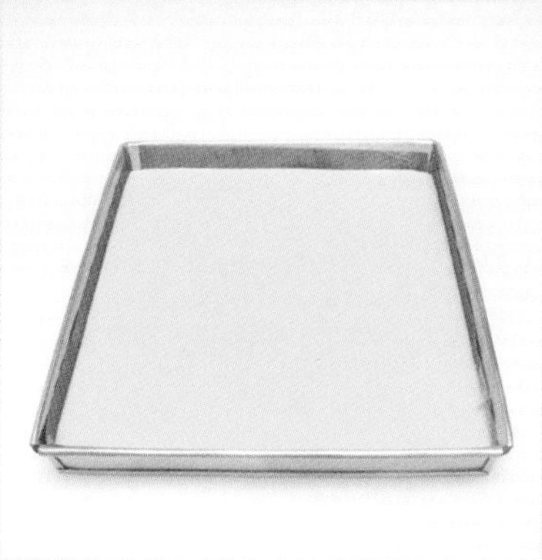
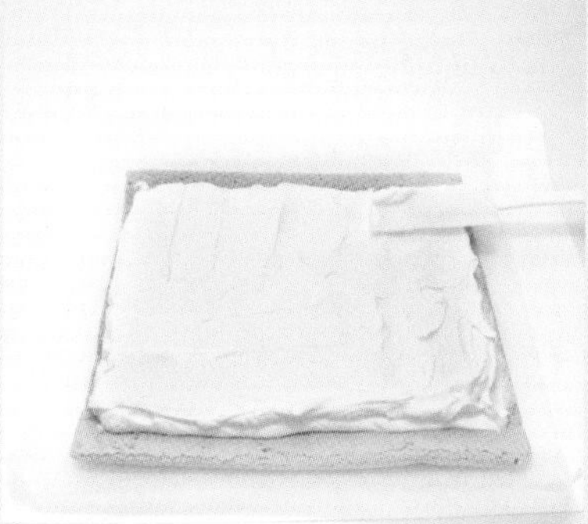
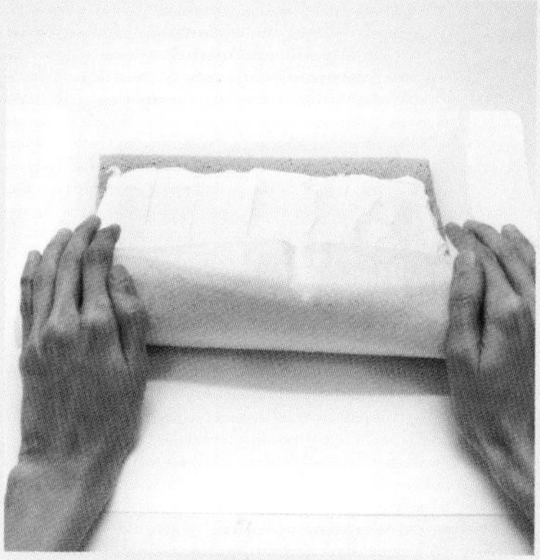

in the flour and whisk until no lumps are found. If desired, add a few drops of pink food coloring to tint the batter pink (you can leave the roll cake plain, if you like).

8 In another large bowl, using an electric mixer, combine the egg whites and cream of tartar and whisk until foamy. While whisking continuously, gradually add the remaining 2 tablespoons superfine sugar and whip until the meringue holds firm peaks. Gently fold the meringue into the batter in three additions with a spatula.

9 Transfer the batter to a large piping bag and snip a ⅜-inch (1cm) hole in the tip. Pipe the roll cake batter gently over the chilled Pusheen pattern to avoid disrupting it, covering the pattern evenly and filling the pan. Tap the pan against the counter to remove any bubbles and bake the cake for 25 minutes, or until a skewer inserted into the center comes out clean.

10 Remove from the oven and immediately flip the cake onto a silicone baking mat. Remove the template and peel off the parchment paper from the bottom and replace it with another baking mat. While the cake is still warm, roll it up in the two baking mats and let cool while you prepare the filling.

11 MAKE THE CHANTILLY CREAM FILLING: In a chilled large bowl, using an electric mixer, combine the cream and confectioners' sugar and whip until the cream holds stiff peaks. Refrigerate the Chantilly cream until you're ready to use it.

12 Once the roll cake has cooled, unroll it, remove the top baking mat, and spread the Chantilly cream over the surface of the cake, leaving ⅜ to ¾ inch (1 to 2cm) uncovered around the edges. Roll up the cake around the Chantilly cream and wrap in plastic wrap. Refrigerate for at least 2 hours and up to overnight before decorating and slicing.

13 DECORATE THE CAKE: Place the white chocolate in a very small microwave-safe bowl and microwave in 30-second intervals, stirring after each to prevent burning, until melted and smooth. (Alternatively, use a double boiler to melt the chocolate.) Add a drop of pink food coloring and mix well to evenly tint the chocolate pink.

14 Dot the melted pink chocolate onto the cake with a toothpick to fill the tongues. Using a serrated knife, slice crosswise into 8 pieces and serve.

PUSHEEN BLACK SESAME TEA CAKES

MAKES FOUR 2-INCH (5CM) CAKES · LEVEL OF DIFFICULTY: MEDIUM

Nutty, rich, and fragrant, black sesame whipped cream together with black sesame sponge cake pack a flavorful punch in these charming Pusheen tea cakes.

. . . .

INGREDIENTS

Piping Batter

2¼ teaspoons (10g) unsalted butter, softened

3¾ teaspoons cake flour

3¾ teaspoons confectioners' sugar

¼ large egg white

Unsweetened dark cocoa powder

Black food coloring or unsweetened black cocoa powder

Pink gel food coloring

Black Sesame Roll Cake

2 large egg yolks

1 teaspoon plus 2 tablespoons superfine sugar

2 tablespoons vegetable oil

2 tablespoons water

1 teaspoon pure vanilla extract

⅓ cup (40g) cake flour

Pinch of baking powder

1 tablespoon sweetened black sesame paste

1½ teaspoons whole milk

3 large egg whites

¼ teaspoon cream of tartar

Black Sesame Whipped Cream Filling

1 tablespoon sweetened black sesame paste

1½ teaspoons whole milk

¾ cup (180g) heavy cream

1 tablespoon confectioners' sugar

. . . .

1 Photocopy or scan and print the Tea Cakes template on page 203 (template 9). Line a 10-inch (25cm) square baking pan with parchment paper. Place the template under the parchment paper and lightly grease the paper with some butter or nonstick spray.

2 MAKE THE PIPING BATTER: In a medium bowl, combine the butter, flour, confectioners' sugar, and egg white and mix well with a spoon.

③ Spoon 1 teaspoon of the batter into a small bowl, add a pinch of dark cocoa powder and a pinch of black cocoa powder or a drop of black food coloring, and stir until evenly tinted dark brown. Spoon another 1 teaspoon of the batter into a separate small bowl, add a drop of black food coloring or a pinch of black cocoa powder, and stir until evenly tinted gray. Spoon another 1 teaspoon of the batter into a third small bowl, add a drop of pink food coloring, and stir until evenly tinted pink. Transfer the batters to separate small piping bags and snip a 1mm hole in the tips.

④ Following the template, pipe the facial features of 4 big Pusheens in a row into the prepared pan using the dark brown batter for the Pusheen features, the gray batter for the head stripes, and the pink batter for the mouth fill. Refrigerate for at least 30 minutes while you prepare the batter for the black sesame roll cake.

⑤ MAKE THE BLACK SESAME ROLL CAKE: Preheat the oven to 320°F (160°C).

⑥ In a large bowl, using an electric mixer, whisk together the egg yolks and 1 teaspoon of the superfine sugar until pale and light. Add the oil, water, and vanilla and whisk until well combined. Sift in the flour and baking powder and whisk until no lumps remain.

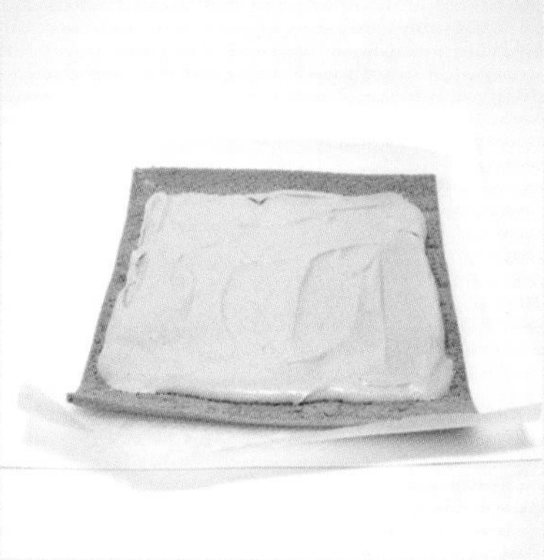

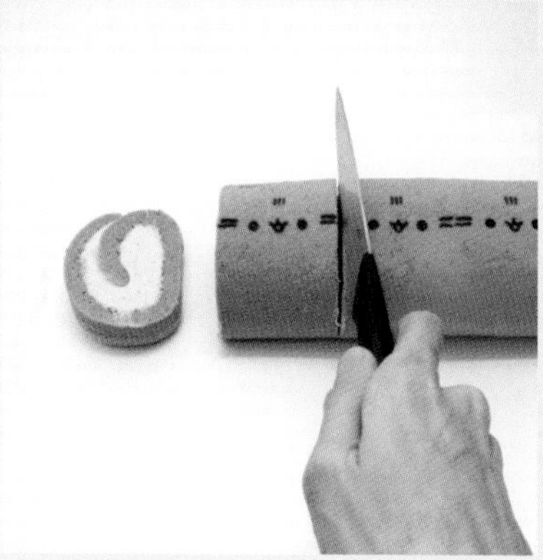

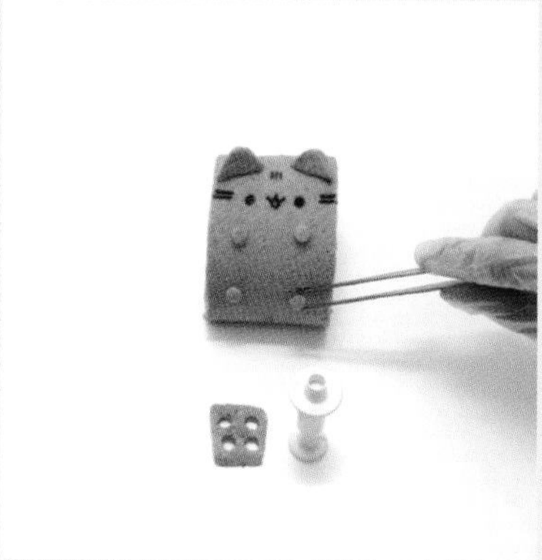

7 In a small bowl, stir together the black sesame paste and milk to soften the sesame paste. Add this mixture to the batter and mix well.

8 In a large bowl, using an electric mixer, combine the egg whites and cream of tartar and whisk until foamy. While whisking continuously, gradually add the remaining 2 tablespoons superfine sugar and whip until the meringue holds firm peaks. Gently fold the meringue into the batter in three additions with a spatula.

9 Transfer the batter to a large piping bag and snip a ⅜-inch (1cm) hole in the tip. Pipe the roll cake batter over the chilled Pusheen patterns, covering the patterns evenly and filling the pan. Tap the pan against the counter to remove any bubbles and bake the cake for 25 minutes, or until a skewer inserted into the center comes out clean.

10 Remove from the oven and flip the cake onto a silicone baking mat. Remove the template and peel off the parchment paper from the bottom and replace it with a another baking mat. While the cake is still warm, roll it up in the two baking mats and let cool while you prepare the filling.

11 MAKE THE BLACK SESAME WHIPPED CREAM FILLING: In a small bowl, stir together the black sesame paste and the milk to soften the sesame paste.

12 In a chilled large bowl, using an electric mixer, combine the cream and confectioners' sugar and whip until the cream holds stiff peaks. Fold in the softened black sesame paste with a spatula. Refrigerate the whipped cream until you're ready to use it.

13 Once the roll cake has cooled, unroll it and remove the top baking mat. Reserve some of the whipped cream to use to attach the ears, hands, and feet later and spread the remainder over the surface of the cake, leaving ⅜ to ¾ inch (1 to 2cm) uncovered around the edges. Roll up the cake around the whipped cream, wrap in plastic wrap, and refrigerate for at least 2 hours and up to overnight before slicing.

14 Remove from the fridge and discard the plastic wrap. Slice off about ⅜ inch (1cm) from both ends of the roll cake and reserve the scraps for the decorations. Slice the roll cake crosswise into 4 pieces, with the Pusheen faces in the center of each piece.

15 Cut out triangles for the ears and rounds for the hands and feet of the Pusheens from the reserved cake scraps. Attach the ears, hands, and feet using the reserved whipped cream.

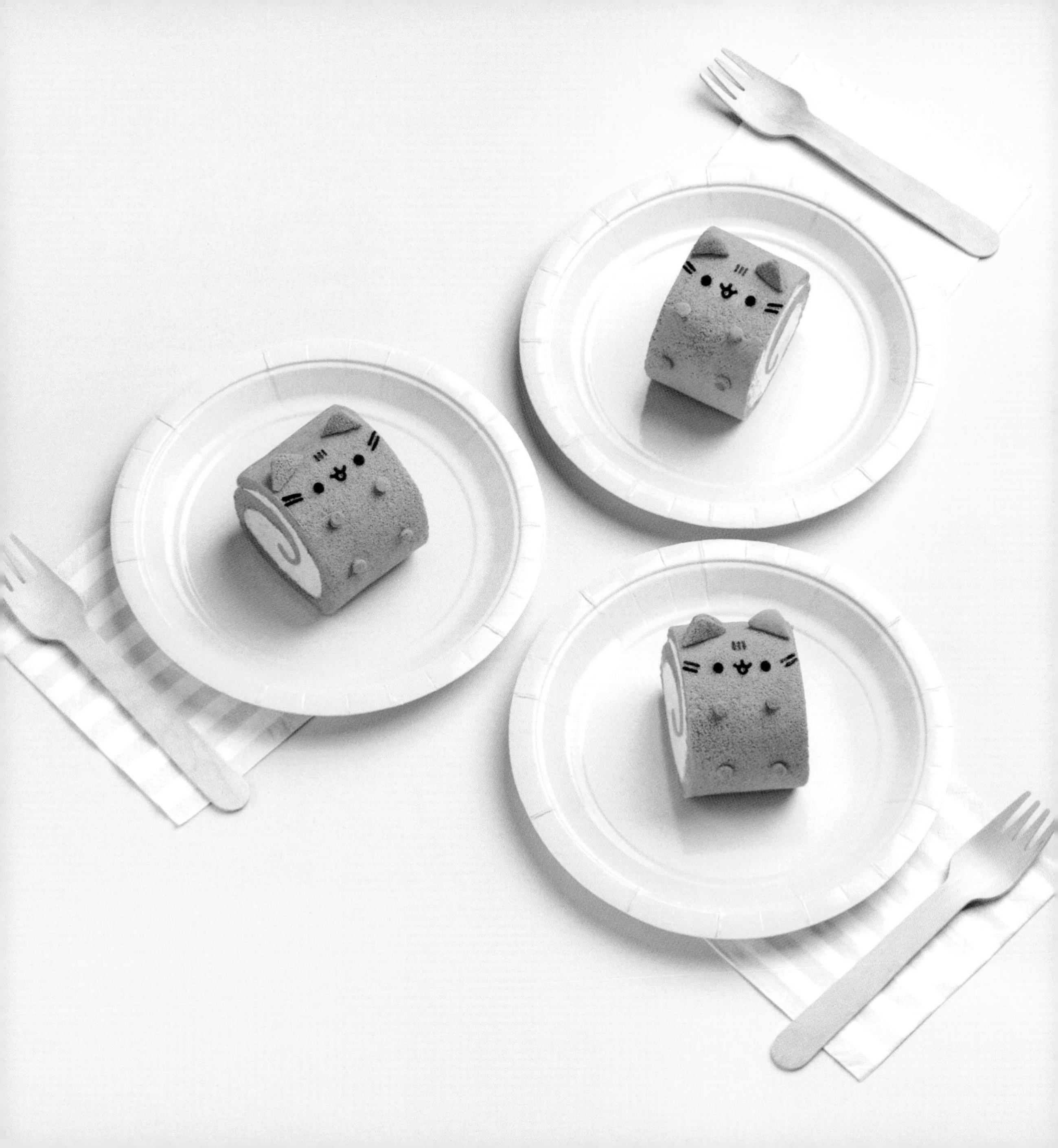

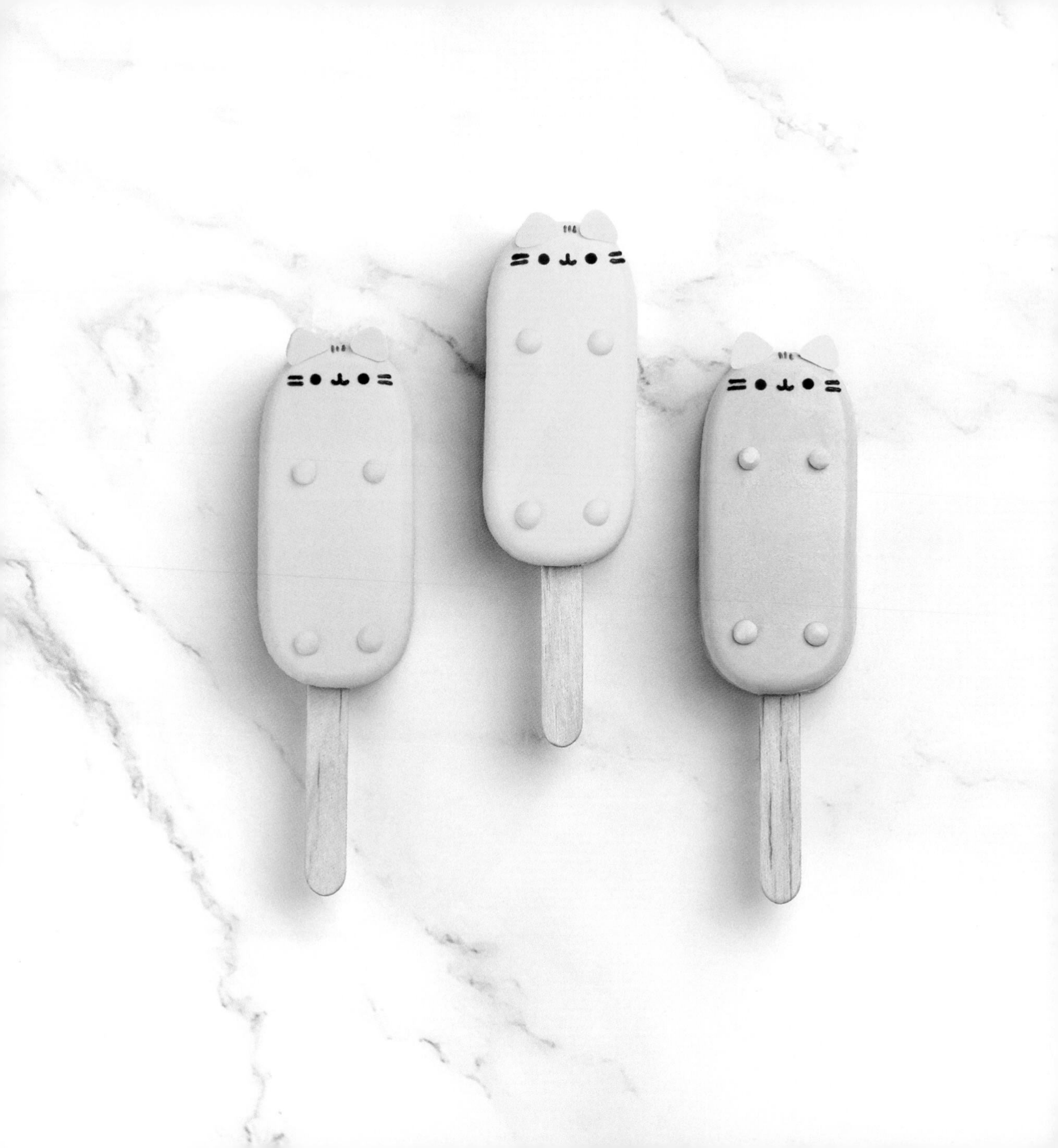

PASTEL PUSHEEN CAKESICLES

MAKES TWELVE 3 × 1½–INCH (7.5 × 4CM) CAKESICLES · LEVEL OF DIFFICULTY: EASY TO MEDIUM

Fun ice-pop versions of classic cake pops, the interior of these cakesicles consists of a sweet concoction of cake crumbs and frosting, while the exterior is a yummy chocolate coating. The pretty pastel cakesicles are easy to make and ideal for any Pusheen-themed celebration!

· ·

INGREDIENTS

Vanilla Cupcakes*

1 cup (120g) cake flour

2 teaspoons baking powder

8 tablespoons (1 stick/115g) unsalted butter, cut into cubes and slightly softened but still cold

⅔ cup (133g) superfine sugar

2 large eggs

1 teaspoon pure vanilla extract

2 tablespoons whole milk

Chocolate Coating

12 ounces (340g) white coating/ compound chocolate, chopped, or melting wafers

2 tablespoons plus ¾ teaspoon coconut oil, plus more if needed

Pink, purple, and green oil-based food coloring

Vanilla Buttercream

8 tablespoons (1 stick/115g) unsalted butter, cut into cubes and slightly softened but still cold

2 cups (250g) confectioners' sugar

1 tablespoon pure vanilla extract

Decorations

3 tablespoons chopped dark coating/ compound chocolate

1 tablespoon chopped white coating/ compound chocolate

Black oil-based food coloring or unsweetened black cocoa powder

· ·

*Note: This recipe makes 16 cupcakes, which you'll use to make the 12 cakesicles.

1 MAKE THE VANILLA CUPCAKES: Preheat the oven to 340°F (170°C). Line 16 cups of two muffin pans with cupcake liners.

2 Sift the flour and baking powder together into a medium bowl and set aside.

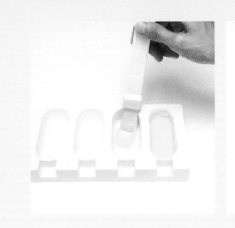

3 In a large bowl, using an electric mixer, cream the butter and superfine sugar until pale and fluffy. Add the eggs one at a time, followed by the vanilla.

4 Fold in the flour mixture in two additions, alternating with the milk, using a spatula. (You can beat in the flour mixture and the milk with the mixer instead, but do not overbeat.)

5 Scrape the batter into the prepared muffin pans. Bake for 20 minutes, or until a skewer inserted into the center of a cupcake comes out clean. Remove from the oven and let the cupcakes cool completely while you prepare the chocolate coating and buttercream.

6 MAKE THE CHOCOLATE COATING: Place the white chocolate and coconut oil in a medium microwave-safe bowl and microwave in 30-second intervals, stirring after each to prevent burning. If needed, add more coconut oil, 1 teaspoon at a time, until the chocolate is melted and has a dipping consistency. (Alternatively, use a double boiler to melt the chocolate and coconut oil.)

7 Divide the chocolate into three small bowls and tint it with pink, purple, and green food coloring, using a different color for each portion.

8 Using a pastry brush, coat 12 wells of a cakesicle or ice cream cake pop mold with a thin layer of the colored chocolate coating (you will coat 4 wells with each color of chocolate). While the chocolate is still wet, gently push ice cream sticks into the bottom of the mold and remove them, leaving holes where you'll insert the ice cream sticks into the cakesicles later.

9 Refrigerate the mold for 5 minutes to set the chocolate, then repeat the process twice to add 2 more layers of the coating, inserting and removing the ice cream sticks and refrigerating to set for 5 minutes each time.

10 Transfer a portion of each colored chocolate to separate small piping bags, reserving some chocolate to cover the tops of the cakesicles. Snip a small hole in the tips and pipe Pusheen's ears, hands, and feet onto a piece of parchment paper, making one set of the same color for each cakesicle. Refrigerate for at least 5 minutes to harden and set.

11 MAKE THE VANILLA BUTTERCREAM: In a large bowl, using an electric mixer, cream the butter until soft, then sift in the confectioners' sugar and add the vanilla. Beat until the mixture is light and fluffy.

12

ASSEMBLE THE CAKESICLES: Peel the liners off the cupcakes and place the cupcakes in a large bowl. Using a fork or wearing kitchen gloves and using your hands, break the cupcakes into fine crumbs. Add the buttercream tablespoon by tablespoon until you can form the dough into a ball.

13 Spoon the cake pop dough into the wells of the prepared mold and press to smooth and level the dough, filling the wells 90 percent of the way and leaving some space to cover the tops of the cakesicles with more chocolate. Insert the ice cream sticks.

14 Spoon 2 layers of the reserved melted chocolate over the cake pop dough, using the color that corresponds with the color on the bottom of each mold. Scrape off any excess and refrigerate to harden and set for 5 to 10 minutes.

15 DECORATE THE CAKESICLES: Carefully remove the cakesicles from the mold and place them on a sheet of parchment paper for the final assembly.

16 Place the dark chocolate and reserved colored chocolate in separate small microwave-safe bowls and microwave in 30-second intervals, stirring after each to prevent burning, until melted and smooth. Using some melted colored chocolate as "glue," stick on the ears, hands, and feet. Using a toothpick, draw on the Pusheen facial features with the melted dark chocolate. Melt the white chocolate as you did the dark chocolate. Add a drop of black food coloring or a pinch of black cocoa powder and stir until evenly tinted gray. Use the gray chocolate to draw on the head stripes.

PASTEL PUSHEEN BOMBE DOME CAKES

MAKES SIX 3-INCH (7.5CM) INDIVIDUAL CAKES · LEVEL OF DIFFICULTY: MEDIUM

With the most delicious white chocolate–cream cheese mousse and a raspberry surprise center, combined with a moist crumbly cake base and tasty chocolate coating modeled into Pusheen's face, this frozen bombe cake dessert is truly a feast for the senses, be it taste, texture, or looks!

· ·

INGREDIENTS

Vanilla Cake

1 cup (120g) cake flour

2 teaspoons baking powder

8 tablespoons (1 stick/115g) unsalted butter, cut into cubes and slightly softened but still cold

⅔ cup (135g) superfine sugar

2 large eggs

1 teaspoon pure vanilla extract

2 tablespoons whole milk

Chocolate Shell

10½ ounces (300g) white coating/compound chocolate, chopped, or melting wafers

2 tablespoons coconut oil, plus more if needed

Pink, purple, and green oil-based food coloring

White Chocolate–Cream Cheese Mousse

2 gold gelatin sheets (2g each), cut into quarters

2 tablespoons cold water, plus more if needed to soak the gelatin

7 ounces (200g) white couverture chocolate, chopped

5 ounces (150g) cream cheese, at room temperature

6½ tablespoons (100g) heavy cream

Assembly and Decorations

Fresh raspberries or other "surprise" of your choice, such as chocolate nibs

3 tablespoons chopped dark coating/compound chocolate

1 tablespoon chopped white coating/compound chocolate

Black oil-based food coloring or unsweetened black cocoa powder

· ·

1 MAKE THE VANILLA CAKE: Preheat the oven to 340°F (170°C). Line a 10-inch (25cm) square baking pan with parchment paper.

2 Sift the flour and baking powder together into a medium bowl and set aside.

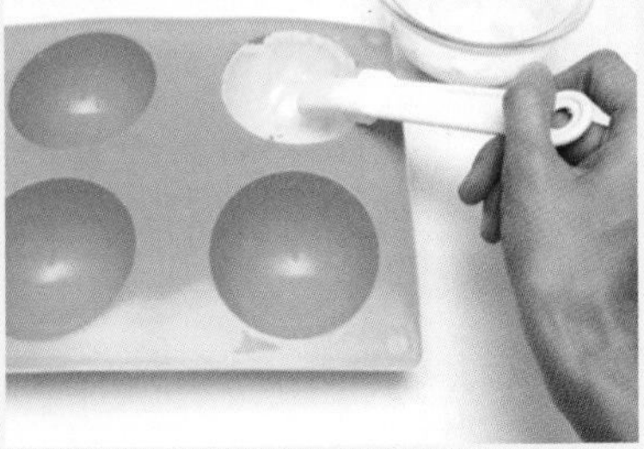
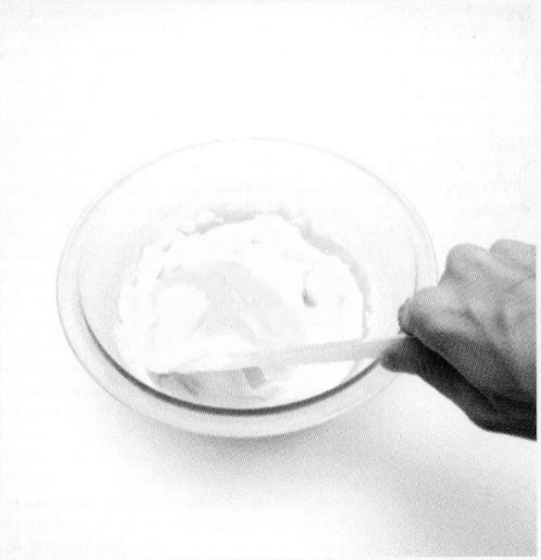
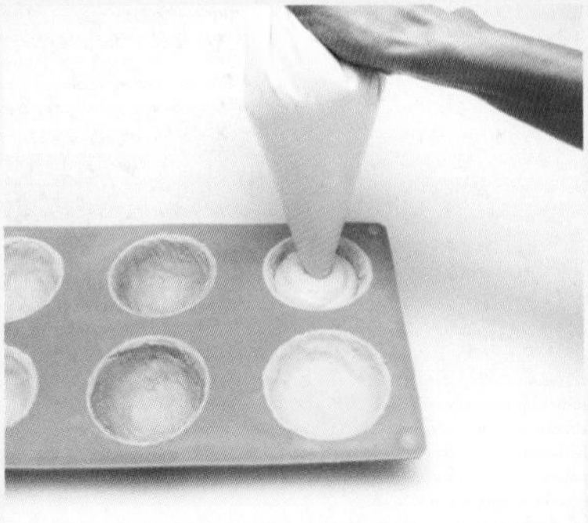

3 In a large bowl, using an electric mixer, cream the butter and superfine sugar until pale and fluffy. Add the eggs one at a time, followed by the vanilla. Fold in the flour mixture in two additions, alternating with the milk, using a spatula. (You can beat in the flour mixture and the milk with the mixer instead, but do not overbeat.)

4 Scrape the batter into the prepared pan. Bake for 14 to 16 minutes, until a skewer inserted into the center of the cake comes out clean.

5 Flip the cake out of the pan onto a new piece of parchment paper and peel off the parchment from the bottom. Cover with another new sheet of parchment paper and let cool.

6 MAKE THE CHOCOLATE SHELL: Place the white chocolate and coconut oil in a medium microwave-safe bowl and microwave in 30-second intervals, stirring after each to prevent burning. If needed, add more coconut oil, 1 teaspoon at a time, until the chocolate is melted and has a dipping consistency. (Alternatively, use a double boiler to melt the chocolate and coconut oil.)

7 Divide the chocolate among three small bowls and tint it with pink, purple, and green food coloring, using a different color for each portion.

8 Using a pastry brush, coat six 3-inch (7.5cm) domed silicone molds with a thin layer of the colored chocolate coating (you will coat 2 wells with each color of chocolate). Refrigerate the molds for 5 minutes to set the chocolate, then repeat to add 2 more layers of the coating to each well, refrigerating to set for 5 minutes after each coating.

9 Transfer the leftover chocolate to separate small piping bags and snip a small hole in the tips. Pipe Pusheen's ears and hands onto a piece of parchment paper, making one set for each bombe. Refrigerate the chocolate to harden and set.

10 MAKE THE WHITE CHOCOLATE–CREAM CHEESE MOUSSE: Place the gelatin in the bottom of a small bowl and add the cold water. The amount should be sufficient to bloom the gelatin without needing to drain excess water. If it isn't, add more cold water, 1 teaspoon at a time. (See page 191.) Set aside to bloom for 5 to 10 minutes.

11 Place the white couverture chocolate in a medium microwave-safe bowl and microwave in 30-second intervals, stirring after each to prevent burning, until melted and smooth. (Alternatively, use a double boiler to melt the chocolate.) Let cool for 10 minutes.

12 Transfer the gelatin to a small saucepan and melt it over low heat, or microwave it briefly, less than 10 seconds. Stir until all the gelatin has dissolved.

13 In a large bowl, using an electric mixer, beat the cream cheese until light and fluffy. Add the melted gelatin and chocolate and beat until smooth and well combined.

14 Clean the beaters for the mixer. In a separate large bowl, beat the cream until it holds stiff peaks. Fold the cream cheese mixture into the whipped cream with a spatula until uniformly incorporated.

15 ASSEMBLE AND DECORATE THE DOME CAKES: Transfer the mousse to a large piping bag and snip a ½-inch (1.5cm) hole in the tip. Fill the chocolate shells just under three-quarters full with the mousse.

16 Insert a raspberry (or surprise of your choice) into the center of the mousse in each mold and push it in about halfway. Cover with more mousse, filling the shell 90 percent of the way.

17 Using a 3-inch (7.5cm) round cutter, cut out rounds of the vanilla cake (they should match the size of the silicone molds). Place a cake round over the mousse in each mold. Cover with plastic wrap and freeze for at least 4 hours.

18 Photocopy or scan and print the Bombe Dome Cakes template on page 203 (template 9) and place the template under a piece of parchment paper. Place the dark chocolate in a small microwave-safe bowl and microwave in 30-second intervals, stirring after each to prevent burning, until melted and smooth. (Alternatively, use a double boiler to melt the chocolate.) Melt the white chocolate as you did the dark chocolate, add a drop of black food coloring or a pinch of black cocoa powder, and stir until smooth and evenly tinted gray. Transfer the melted chocolates to separate small piping bags, snip a small hole in the tips, and pipe Pusheen features onto the parchment paper. Set aside to harden.

19 Gently pop the domed cakes out of the molds. Attach the ears, hands, and facial features using some melted colored chocolate. Refrigerate for 5 to 10 minutes to set the chocolate before serving.

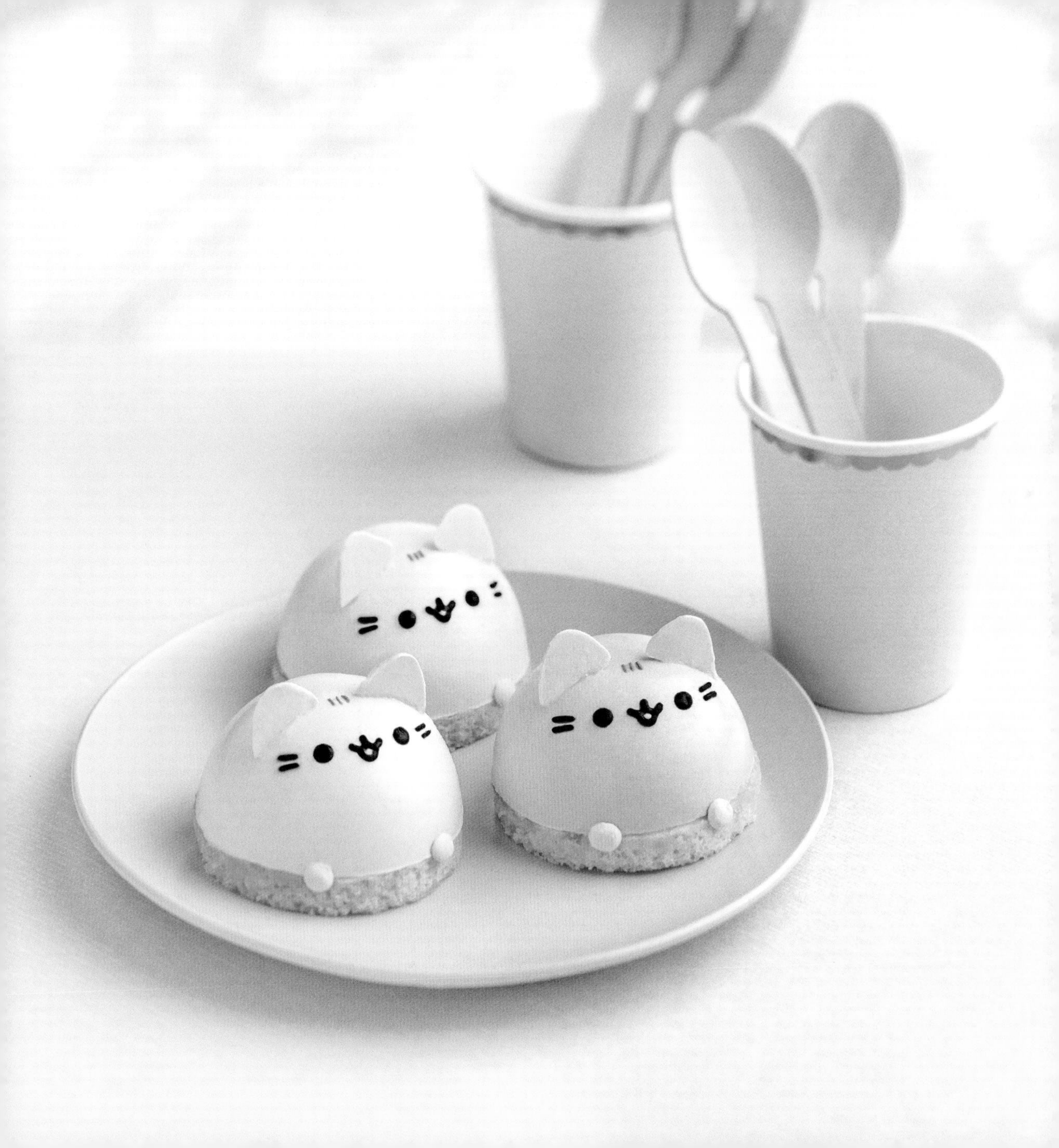

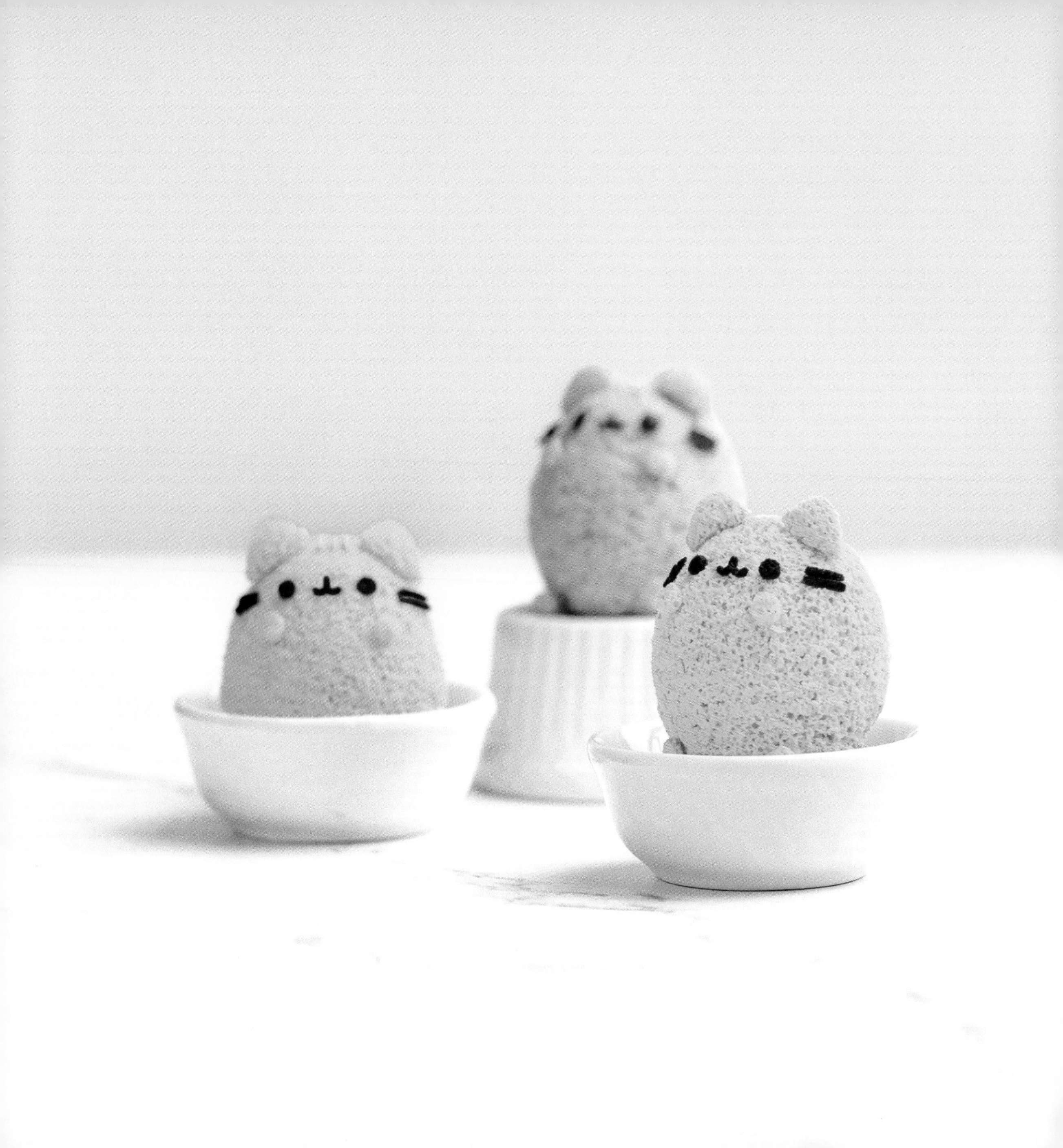

PASTEL PUSHEEN CHIFFON EGG CAKES

MAKES 6 EGG CAKES · LEVEL OF DIFFICULTY: MEDIUM

Fluffy egg-size Pusheen cakes that look like cuddly toys, made from soft, tasty chiffon cake? What's not to love!

1. Using a pointed chopstick or bamboo skewer, make a 1-inch (2.5cm) hole at the narrow tip of each egg and drain the contents from the shells, reserving 1 yolk and 1 white for the cake. Wash the eggshells and peel off the internal membrane. Allow to dry, then place each eggshell in a mini baking cup or the wells of a muffin pan.

2. MAKE THE CHIFFON CAKES: Preheat the oven to 285°F (140°C). In a large bowl, whisk together the egg yolk and 1 teaspoon of the superfine sugar. Add the oil, milk, and vanilla and whisk well. Sift in the cake flour and whisk until no lumps remain.

3. Spoon 1 teaspoon of the batter into a small bowl, add a pinch of dark cocoa powder and a pinch of black cocoa powder, and stir until evenly tinted dark brown. Spoon another 1 teaspoon of the batter into a separate small bowl, add a pinch of black cocoa powder, and stir until evenly tinted gray. Divide the remaining batter among three small bowls and tint it with pink, purple, and green food coloring,* using a different color for each portion.

*Tip: If you are using natural food coloring powder, dissolve it in an equal quantity of hot water before adding it to the batter to prevent uneven spots.

INGREDIENTS

Chiffon Cakes

6 large eggs

1 large egg yolk

1 teaspoon plus 1 tablespoon superfine sugar

1 tablespoon coconut oil or vegetable oil

1 tablespoon whole milk

½ teaspoon pure vanilla extract

1¾ tablespoons cake flour

Unsweetened dark cocoa powder

Unsweetened black cocoa powder

Food coloring: pink, purple, and green (or use natural food colorings: beet, purple sweet potato, and matcha powders)

1 large egg white

¼ teaspoon cream of tartar

Assembly

¼ cup (18g) mini marshmallows

½ teaspoon water

4 In a large bowl, whip the egg white with the cream of tartar until foamy. Add the remaining 1 tablespoon superfine sugar and whisk until it holds firm peaks.

5 Add 1 tablespoon of the meringue to the dark brown batter and 1 tablespoon to the gray batter and gently fold in the meringue with a spatula. Divide the remaining meringue among the colored batters and gently fold it in.

6 Fill the eggshells two-thirds full with the pink, purple, and green batter (you will fill 2 shells with each color). Bake for 30 to 35 minutes, until a skewer inserted into the center of a cake comes out clean. Remove from the oven and let the cakes cool completely on a wire rack.

7 Pour the leftover colored batter into mini baking cups, one for each colored batter, to be used for cutting out the ears, hands, and feet later. Pour the dark brown and gray batters into separate baking cups as well.* Bake for 18 minutes, or until a skewer inserted into the center of a cake comes out clean. Remove from the oven and let the cakes cool completely on a wire rack.

*Optional: You will use these cakes for Pusheen's facial features. If desired, you can just pipe on features with melted chocolate and skip baking the dark brown and gray cakes.

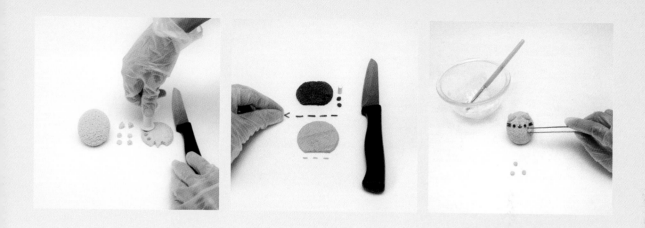

8 ASSEMBLE THE CAKES: To unmold the egg cakes, crack the eggshells into small pieces using the back of a teaspoon and peel the pieces off. Peel off the baking cups to unmold the mini round cakes and place the cakes on a cutting board. Cut out triangles and small rounds from the pastel rounds for the ears, hands, and feet. Cut out facial features from the dark brown cake; cut small strips for the head stripes from the gray cake.

9 Place the mini marshmallows and water in a medium microwave-safe bowl and toss to coat the marshmallows. Microwave for 30 seconds to melt them. Stir until smooth. Using the melted marshmallows as "glue," attach the facial features, head stripes, ears, hands, and feet to the egg cakes using a pair of forceps or tweezers.

SMALL PUSHEEN FONDANT CAKE

MAKES ONE 4½–INCH (11.5CM) CAKE · LEVEL OF DIFFICULTY: DIFFICULT

This Pusheen fondant cake is a definite showstopper at any party! Both beautiful and delicious, it consists of moist vanilla sponge cake coated with white chocolate ganache and then covered with delightful homemade marshmallow fondant. Swap vanilla for your favorite flavor (variations are provided).

INGREDIENTS

Vanilla Cake

1 cup (120g) cake flour

1½ teaspoons baking powder

8 tablespoons (1 stick/115g) unsalted butter, cut into cubes and slightly softened but still cold

⅔ cup (135g) superfine sugar

2 large eggs

1 teaspoon pure vanilla extract

¼ cup (60g) whole milk

Glazing Syrup

3 tablespoons superfine sugar

3 tablespoons water

1 teaspoon liqueur of your choice or pure vanilla extract

White Chocolate Ganache Coating

10½ ounces (300g) white couverture chocolate, chopped

6½ tablespoons (100g) heavy cream

Fondant*

3½ cups (250g) mini marshmallows

2½ tablespoons water

½ cup (75g) white chocolate chips

4 cups (500g) confectioners' sugar

Shortening, for greasing

Food coloring: black, brown, and pink (or use natural food colorings: unsweetened black cocoa, unsweetened dark cocoa, and beet powders)

Cornstarch, for dusting (optional)

*Optional: Instead of making homemade fondant, you can use 1 pound store-bought fondant if you prefer.

1 MAKE THE VANILLA CAKE: Preheat the oven to 355°F (180°C). Prepare a mini doll cake pan with 4-inch (10cm) dome cavities and a silicone cake pop mold with 1-inch (2.5cm) wells. Lightly grease the doll cake pan with some butter or nonstick spray.

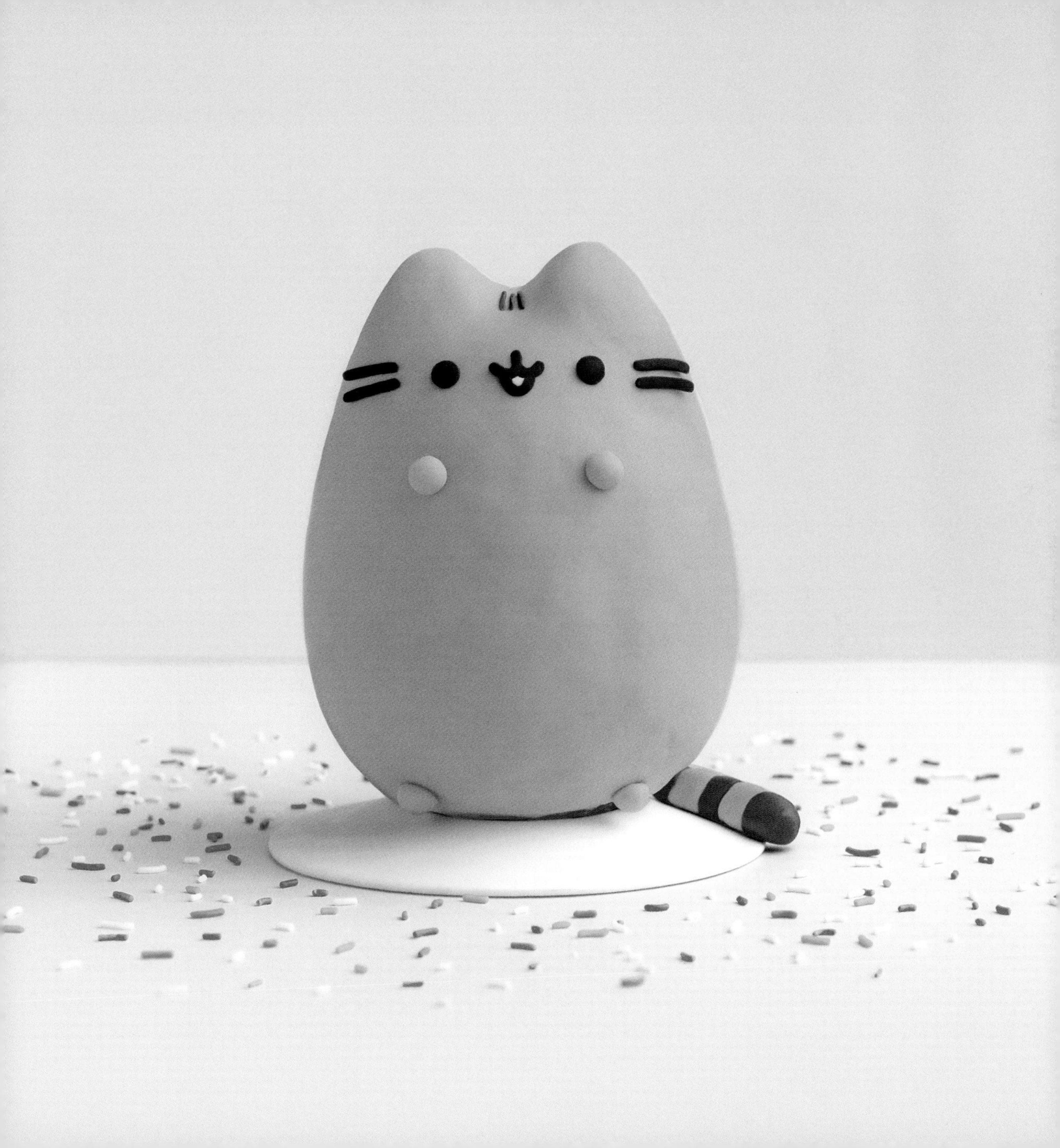

2 Sift the flour and baking powder together into a medium bowl and set aside.

3 In a large bowl, using an electric mixer, cream the butter with the superfine sugar until pale and fluffy. Add the eggs one at a time, followed by the vanilla.

4 Fold in the flour mixture in two additions, alternating with the milk, using a spatula. (You can beat the flour and milk into the mixture with the mixer, but do not overbeat.)

5 Divide the batter among two 4-inch (10cm) dome cavities and two 1-inch (2.5cm) cake pop wells. Bake the cake pops for 14 minutes and the dome cakes for 25 minutes, or until a skewer inserted into the center of a cake pop or dome cake comes out clean. Remove from the oven and allow the cakes to cool completely before unmolding the cakes.

6 MAKE THE GLAZING SYRUP: In a small saucepan, combine the superfine sugar and water and heat over medium heat until the sugar has dissolved. Remove from the heat and let cool. Add the liqueur and stir to flavor the syrup.

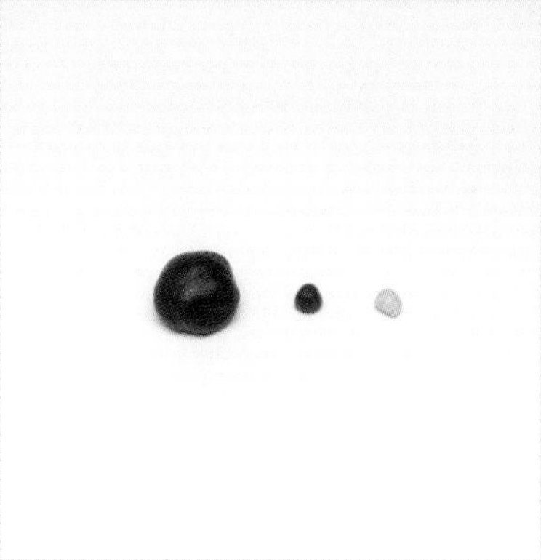

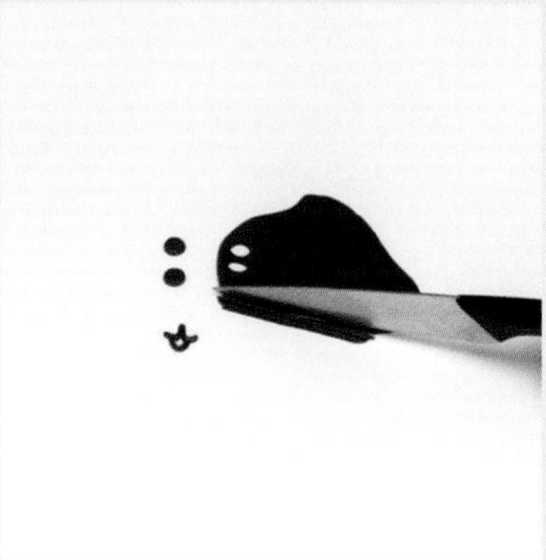

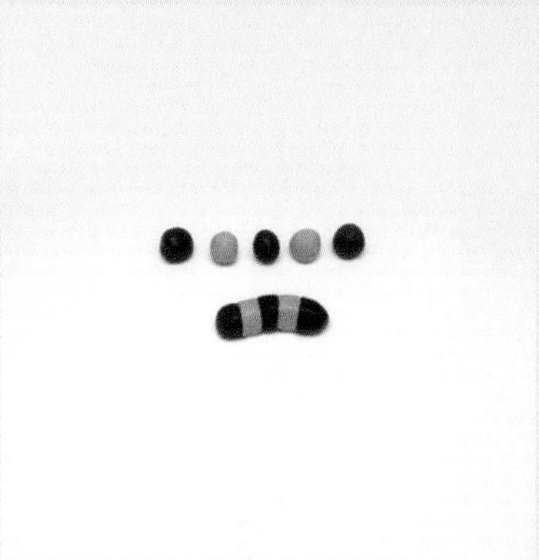

7 MAKE THE WHITE CHOCOLATE GANACHE COATING: Place the chocolate in a medium microwave-safe bowl and microwave on medium power in 30-second intervals, stirring after each to prevent burning, until melted and smooth.

8 Place the cream in a small microwave-safe bowl and microwave on medium power in 30-second intervals, checking after each, until it starts to bubble. Pour the cream over the melted chocolate and stir with a spatula in one direction until smooth and well combined. Refrigerate the ganache for at least 1 hour, until thickened slightly. Using an electric mixer, beat the ganache until it is pale and fluffy and has a spreadable consistency.

9 ASSEMBLE THE CAKE: Level the base of the dome cakes with a knife to make them flat, if needed. Spread some ganache onto a cake board. Trim a little off the top of one dome cake, place the cake on the cake board flat side up, and brush on the syrup. Spread some ganache over the top of the dome cake and place the second dome cake on top, flat side down.

10 Cut triangles from the cake pops for Pusheen's ears. Using some ganache as "glue," attach them to the top of the stacked dome cakes.

11 Coat the cake, including the ears, with ganache and refrigerate for a few hours to set.

Note: If using store-bought fondant, skip to step 15.

12 MAKE THE FONDANT: Place the mini marshmallows and water in a large microwave-safe bowl and toss to coat the marshmallows. Microwave in 30-second intervals, stirring after each, until all the marshmallows have melted and the mixture is smooth, about 2 minutes. Add the white chocolate chips and stir until melted and smooth.

13 Sift the confectioners' sugar over the melted marshmallow mixture. Fold in the confectioners' sugar using a wooden spatula until the mixture comes together.

14 Put on gloves and grease your hands and a clean work surface generously with shortening. Turn the fondant out onto the greased surface and knead until it forms a smooth and elastic ball that will stretch without tearing, about 8 minutes. (Alternatively, transfer the melted marshmallow mixture to the bowl of a stand mixer fitted with the dough hook, sift over the sugar, and mix on low speed until the mixture comes together. Then knead with the dough hook for about 8 minutes, until smooth and elastic.)

15 Add black food coloring drop by drop or black cocoa powder pinch by pinch and knead it into the fondant until evenly tinted the desired shade of gray. Pinch off a 1-inch (2.5cm) ball of fondant for making the decorations and facial features later. (If you're not using the fondant right away, grease the surface of the fondant ball, wrap it in plastic wrap, and keep it at room temperature.)

16 DECORATE THE CAKE: Put on a new pair of gloves and dust your hands and a clean work surface generously with cornstarch (if you live in a humid climate) or grease them with shortening (if you live in a dry climate). Using a silicone rolling pin, roll out the fondant to about ¼ inch (6mm) thick and slightly larger (by about 1 inch) than the surface you want to cover.

17 Lay the fondant over the cake and gently smooth it outward and down. Trim off the excess fondant at the bottom of the cake with a sharp knife. Use a fondant smoother to further smooth the fondant over the cake.

18 Divide the reserved ball of fondant into 1 large and 2 smaller balls. Using food coloring, tint the large ball of fondant dark brown (for the facial features), one smaller ball dark gray (for the head stripes), and the other smaller ball pink (for the mouth fill). Knead each portion until the fondant is uniformly tinted the desired color.

19 Roll out the dark brown fondant and cut out thin strips and small rounds to make Pusheen's facial features, and attach them to the cake using a little water. Fill the mouth with some of the pink fondant, using some water to adhere it. Roll out the dark gray fondant and cut out thin strips for Pusheen's head stripes, and adhere them to the cake similarly. Join alternating dark brown and light gray fondant balls (5 altogether), roll them into a log to form Pusheen's tail, and join the tail to the body.

NOTES

CAKE FLAVOR VARIATIONS

- CHOCOLATE: In the vanilla cake batter, replace 1 tablespoon of the cake flour with unsweetened dark cocoa powder and add an extra ¼ teaspoon baking powder.

- ORANGE: In the vanilla cake batter, replace the milk and vanilla extract with fresh orange juice and add 1 tablespoon grated orange zest.

- LEMON: In the vanilla cake batter, replace half the milk and all the vanilla with fresh lemon juice and add 1 tablespoon grated lemon zest.

- To make a 6-inch (15cm) Pusheen cake, triple the recipe and use two 6-inch-wide (15cm) deep ball pans.

- Do not refrigerate fondant cakes, or the fondant will sweat.

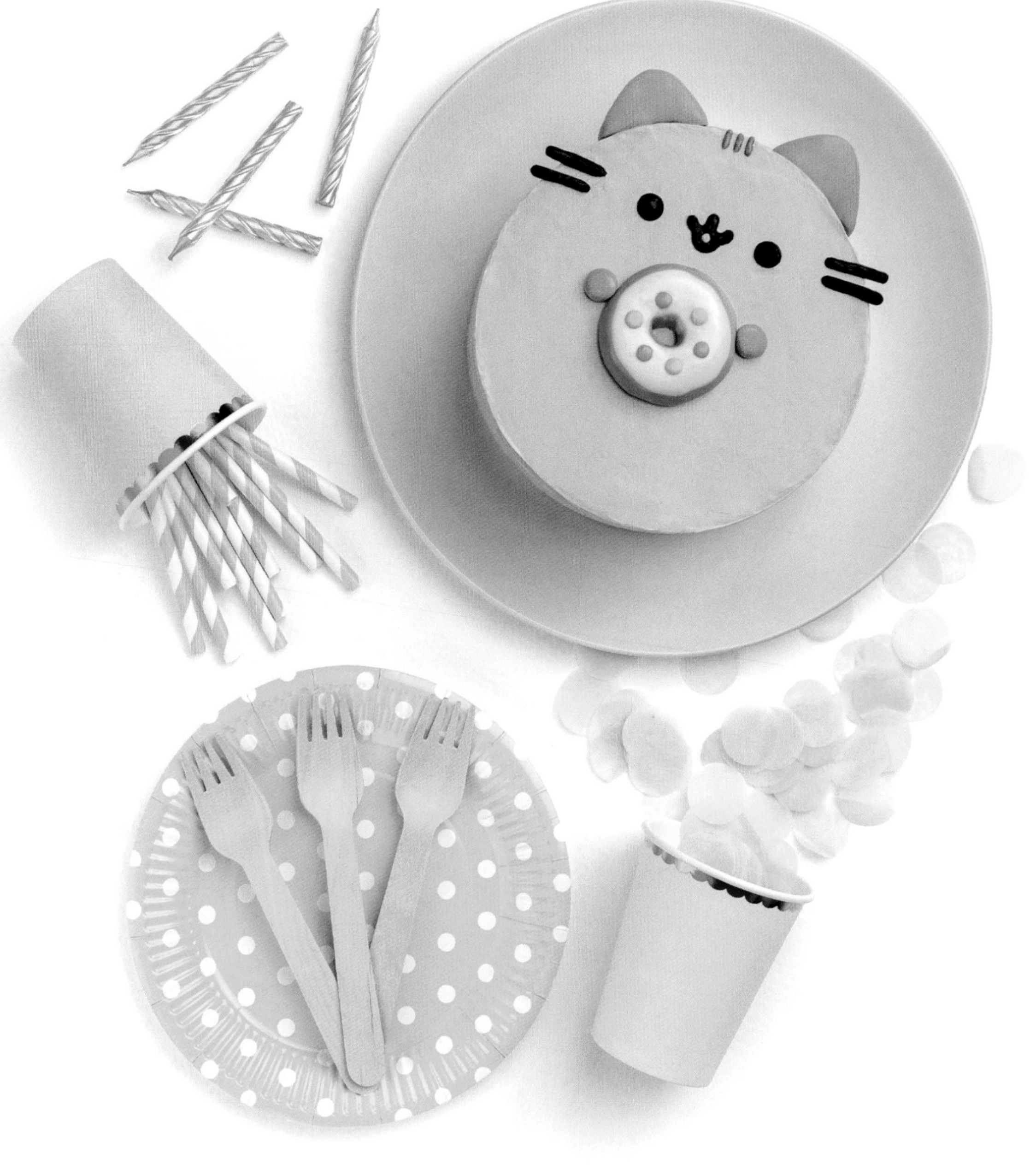

PUSHEEN BIRTHDAY CAKE WITH WHITE CHOCOLATE SWISS MERINGUE BUTTERCREAM

MAKES ONE 6-INCH (15CM) TRIPLE-LAYER CAKE • LEVEL OF DIFFICULTY: MEDIUM TO DIFFICULT

An easy-to-make, versatile birthday cake recipe that features a cute Pusheen holding a donut! Tender vanilla sponge cake filled and covered with white chocolate Swiss meringue buttercream—simply yum, and cute to boot!

INGREDIENTS

Vanilla Cake

2½ cups (300g) cake flour

1 tablespoon baking powder

2½ sticks (10 ounces/285g) unsalted butter, melted and cooled

1¼ cups (300g) whole milk

1 tablespoon pure vanilla extract

5 large eggs

1⅔ cups (335g) superfine sugar

White Chocolate Swiss Meringue Buttercream

8 ounces (225g) couverture white chocolate, chopped

6 large egg whites

2 cups (400g) superfine sugar

4 sticks (1 pound/455g) unsalted butter, cut into cubes and slightly softened but still cold

Black food coloring or unsweetened black cocoa

Glazing Syrup

3 tablespoons superfine sugar

3 tablespoons water

1 teaspoon liqueur of your choice or pure vanilla extract

Decorations

4 ounces (114g) fondant, store-bought or homemade using the recipe on page 126

Food coloring: black, brown, pink, blue, and yellow (or use natural food colorings: unsweetened black cocoa, unsweetened dark cocoa, beet, butterfly blue pea flower, and turmeric powders)

1 tablespoon chopped dark coating/compound chocolate, optional

1. **MAKE THE VANILLA CAKE:** Preheat the oven to 350°F (175°C). Line the bottoms of three 6-inch (15cm) cake pans with parchment paper cut to fit.

2. Sift the flour and baking powder together into a medium bowl and set aside.

③ In a medium bowl, stir together the melted butter, milk, and vanilla. Set aside.

④ Bring a medium saucepan filled with about 1½ inches of water to a simmer over low heat. Combine the eggs and superfine sugar in a medium heatproof bowl. Place the bowl on top of the saucepan (make sure the bottom of the bowl does not touch the water).* Beat the eggs and superfine sugar with an electric mixer until pale and fluffy and remove the bowl from the heat.

*Optional: You can use slightly warm eggs instead of beating the eggs and sugar over simmering water, if you prefer.

⑤ Fold the flour mixture into the egg mixture in two additions, alternating with the butter mixture, using a spatula. (You can beat the flour and butter mixtures into the egg mixture with the mixer, but do not overbeat.)

⑥ Divide the batter evenly among the prepared pans. Bake for 20 to 22 minutes, until a skewer inserted into the center of a cake comes out clean. Remove from the oven and let cool in the pans on a wire rack.

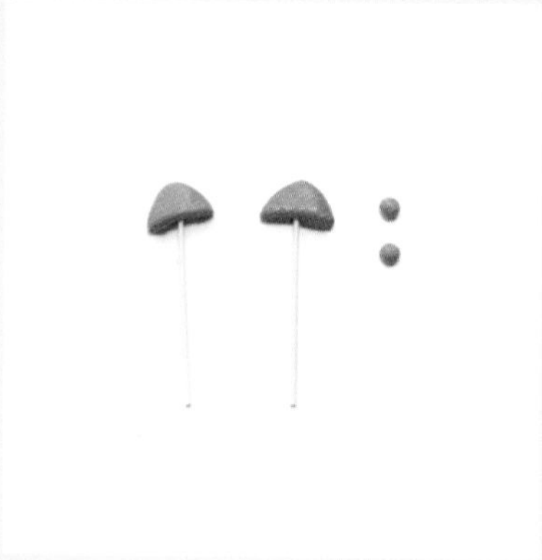
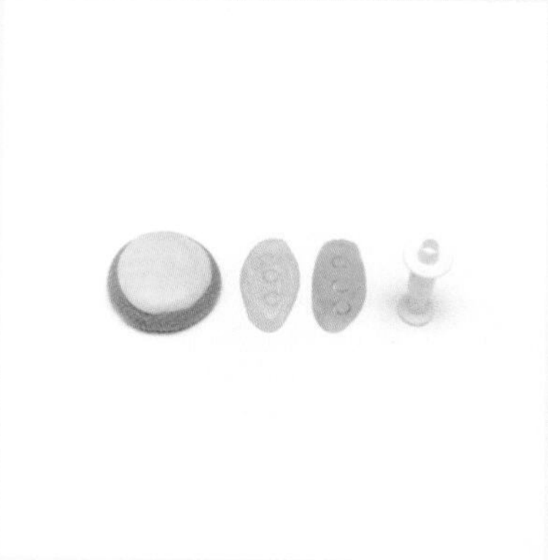
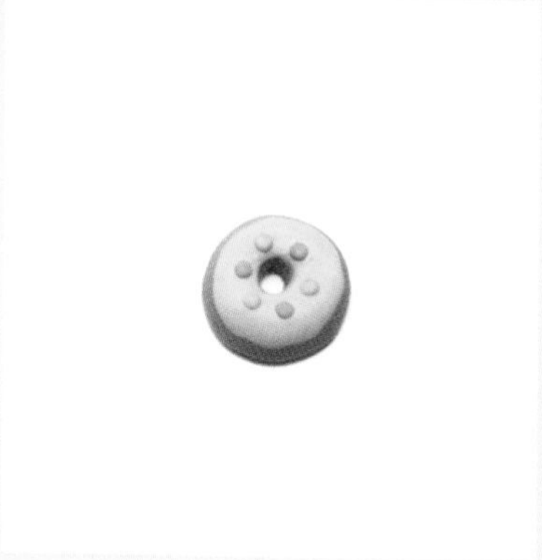

7 MAKE THE WHITE CHOCOLATE SWISS MERINGUE BUTTERCREAM: Place the white chocolate in a medum microwave-safe bowl and microwave on medium power in 30-second intervals, stirring after each to prevent burning, until melted and smooth. (Alternatively, use a double boiler to melt the chocolate.)

8 Bring a medium saucepan filled with about 1½ inches of water to a simmer over low heat. Combine the egg whites and sugar in a heatproof bowl. Place the bowl on top of the saucepan (make sure the bottom of the bowl does not touch the water). Whisk continuously until the sugar has dissolved completely and the mixture is warm to the touch, 160°F (71°C) on a candy thermometer. Do not allow the egg whites to scramble/coagulate. To test, rub a bit of the egg white mixture between your fingers; if it is still gritty, the sugar has not fully dissolved. Remove the bowl from the heat.

9 Using an electric mixer, beat the egg white mixture on medium-high speed until stiff and glossy. The mixture should be cool to the touch at this point.

10 With the mixer running on medium speed, add the butter to the egg whites in three additions and beat until fluffy and firm, like shaving cream. The mixture may initially become watery as the butter is being incorporated, but just continue beating; it will firm up again. Add the melted chocolate and beat until smooth.

⑪ Divide the Swiss meringue buttercream between two medium bowls. To one portion, add black food coloring drop by drop or black cocoa powder pinch by pinch until the buttercream is evenly tinted light gray. Leave the other portion plain.

⑫ MAKE THE GLAZING SYRUP: In a small saucepan, combine the superfine sugar and water and heat over medium heat until the sugar has dissolved. Remove from the heat and let cool. Add the liqueur and stir to flavor the syrup.

⑬ ASSEMBLE THE CAKE: Flip the cooled cakes out of their pans and remove the parchment paper. Flip the cakes again so they're right-side up. Level the tops of the vanilla cakes with a cake leveler or serrated knife.

⑭ Spread some buttercream on a cake board and place 1 cake layer on the board, untrimmed side down. Brush the cake with glazing syrup, then spread buttercream over the top. Place a second cake layer on top of the first, untrimmed side down, brush it with syrup, and spread buttercream over the top. Repeat with the final cake layer, flipping it over so the untrimmed side is facing up.

⑮ Using an offset spatula, spread a thin layer of the plain buttercream over the entire cake.* Use a bench scraper to clean up the sides. Refrigerate the cake in a covered container for at least 1 to 2 hours to set the buttercream.

*Note: This is called a crumb coat—it traps any loose crumbs so they don't mar the surface of the finished cake.

⑯ Remove the cake from the fridge and, using a clean offset spatula, spread a layer of the light gray buttercream over the entire cake. Refrigerate the cake in a covered container while you're working on the decorations.

17 MAKE THE DECORATIONS: For the Pusheen features, melt 1 tablespoon chopped dark coating/compound chocolate, transfer it to a small piping bag, and snip a small hole in the tip. Pipe the features onto a piece of parchment paper and let set before transferring them to the cake.

18 Tint some fondant gray using black food coloring. Mold some of the gray fondant into 2 rounded triangles for the ears. Insert 2 dowels or cake pop sticks into the ears to attach them onto the cake. Mold some gray fondant into 2 small balls for the hands.

19 Tint separate portions of the fondant brown, pink, blue, and yellow. Mold the brown fondant into a 2-inch (5cm) flattened dome. Roll the pink fondant into a thin sheet. Cut a 1.5-inch (3.8cm) round from the pink fondant and stick it on top of the dome. Use a straw or ring cutter to punch out a hole in the center of the dome to make a donut shape. Roll the blue and yellow fondant into thin sheets and use a pastry tip, straw, or round fondant plunger to cut out mini rounds for the "sprinkles." Stick the mini blue and yellow sprinkles onto the donut. Place the donut and Pusheen's hands onto the cake.

NOTES

· Fondant should not be refrigerated, so when decorating the cake, add the fondant decorations as the last step, just before serving.

CAKE FLAVOR VARIATIONS

· CHOCOLATE: In the vanilla cake batter, replace 3 tablespoons of the cake flour with unsweetened dark cocoa powder and add an extra ½ teaspoon baking powder.

· ORANGE: In the vanilla cake batter, replace the milk and vanilla extract with fresh orange juice and add 2 tablespoons grated orange zest.

· LEMON: In the vanilla cake batter, replace half the milk and all the vanilla with fresh lemon juice and add 2 tablespoons grated lemon zest.

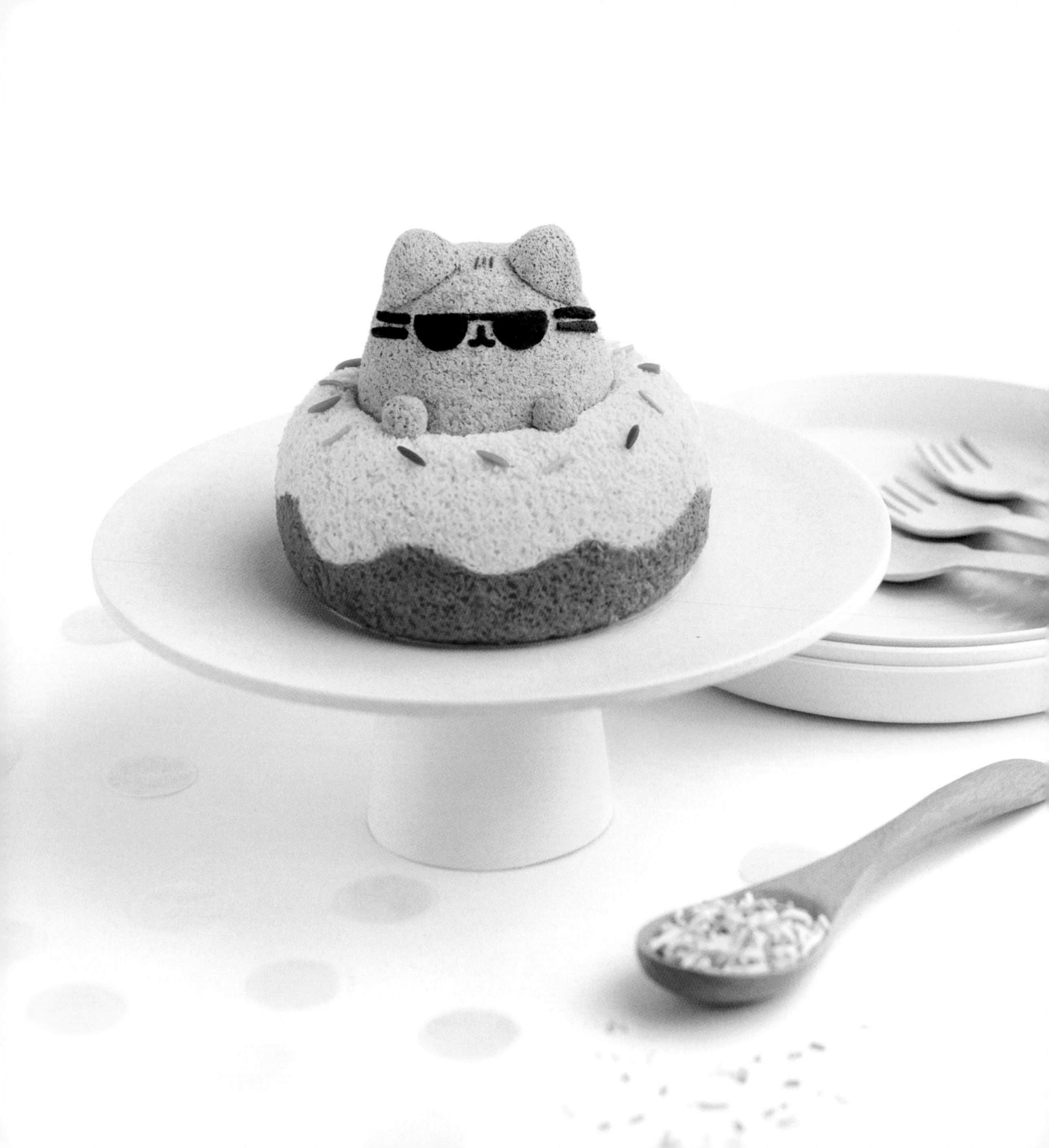

PUSHEEN DONUT CHIFFON CAKE

MAKES ONE 6-INCH (15CM) NEAPOLITAN-FLAVORED CAKE • LEVEL OF DIFFICULTY: DIFFICULT

A 3D cake that looks amazingly like a plush toy. This Pusheen donut cake, made from soft, flavorful Neapolitan chiffon cake, is certain to be the talking point and centerpiece of any party!

Tip: If you're not using marshmallows for the "surprise," make sure you use a sweet that does not melt easily, as chiffon cakes absorb moisture.

1 MAKE THE NEAPOLITAN CHIFFON CAKE: Preheat the oven to 285°F (140°C). Have a 6-inch (15cm) donut tube pan, a 4-inch (10cm) ball pan or mini doll pan, a silicone cake pop mold (with 1-inch/2.5cm wells), and a 6-inch (15cm) rimmed square baking sheet lined with parchment paper on hand.

2 In a large bowl, whisk the egg yolks and 1 tablespoon of the superfine sugar until pale and light. Whisk in the oil, water, and vanilla until well combined. Sift in the flour and whisk until no lumps remain.

3 Portion 3 tablespoons of the batter into each of three small bowls. Stir the strawberry paste into one bowl, add 1 to 2 drops of pink food coloring (or until desired shade), and stir until evenly tinted pink. Add a generous ¼ teaspoon dark cocoa powder to the second bowl and stir until evenly tinted brown. Add a drop of black food coloring or a pinch of black cocoa powder to the third bowl and stir until evenly tinted gray. *

*Tip: The colors will lighten after the meringue is incorporated, so these batters should be darker than you'd like the final product to be. Depending on the brand of food coloring you use, you may need to adjust the amounts slightly to achieve the desired shades.

INGREDIENTS

Neapolitan Chiffon Cake

2 large egg yolks

3½ tablespoons superfine sugar

2 tablespoons vegetable oil

2 tablespoons water

1 teaspoon pure vanilla extract

⅓ cup (40g) cake flour

¼ teaspoon strawberry paste or pure strawberry extract

Pink food coloring

Unsweetened dark cocoa powder

Black food coloring or unsweetened black cocoa powder

3 large egg whites

¼ teaspoon cream of tartar

Assembly

¼ cup (18g) mini marshmallows, plus more for the "surprise"

½ teaspoon water

Rainbow-colored sprinkles

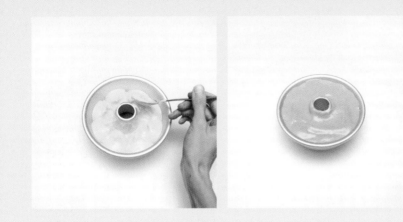

4 Spoon 2 tablespoons of the plain batter into a separate small bowl, add 1 teaspoon dark cocoa powder and ½ teaspoon black food coloring or black cocoa powder, and stir until evenly tinted dark brown.*

*Optional: You will use this dark brown batter to make a cake for Pusheen's facial features. Alternatively, you can omit steps 4 and 9 and just pipe on the features with melted chocolate in step 12.

5 In a large bowl, combine the egg whites and cream of tartar and whisk until foamy. While whisking continuously, gradually add the remaining 2½ tablespoons superfine sugar and whisk until the meringue holds firm peaks.

6 Fold the meringue into the tinted batters with a spatula in three additions: add 6 tablespoons each to the pink, brown, and gray batters, and the remaining meringue to the dark brown batter.

7 Spoon the pink batter into the tube pan in mounds, then fill the "valleys" between each mound with brown batter. Top with more brown batter and tap the pan against the counter to remove any bubbles. Bake for 35 to 40 minutes, until a skewer inserted into the cake comes out clean.

8 Divide the gray batter among the 4-inch (10cm) ball pan and 4 wells of the cake pop mold. Bake the cake pops for 16 to 18 minutes and the ball cake for 30 minutes.

9 Pour the dark brown batter into the prepared baking sheet. Bake for 14 to 16 minutes.

10 Remove the cakes from the oven as they are done and let cool completely in the pans. Gently unmold each cake shape.

11 ASSEMBLE THE CAKE: Place the tube cake on a cake round, brown side down, and fill the hole with mini marshmallows or the "surprise" of your choice. Place the ball cake over the center of the tube cake.

12 Cut cake pops into 2 triangles for the ears. Flip the dark brown sheet cake onto a cutting mat and remove the parchment paper. Cut the cake into strips and rounds for Pusheen's facial features and head stripes.

13 Place the ¼ cup mini marshmallows and the water in a small microwave-safe bowl and toss to coat the marshmallows. Microwave in 30-second intervals, stirring after each, until all the marshmallows have melted and the mixture is smooth.

14 Using the melted marshmallows as "glue," stick on Pusheen's ears and facial features and decorate the donut with some sprinkles. Use a large straw (⅜-inch/1cm diameter) to cut out balls from the remaining cake pops for the hands and attach them to the cake, using the melted marshmallows as "glue."

PUSHEEN VANILLA-LEMON SWISS MERINGUE BUTTERCREAM CUPCAKES

MAKES SIXTEEN 2-INCH (5CM) CUPCAKES · LEVEL OF DIFFICULTY: EASY TO MEDIUM

Swiss meringue buttercream gets a Pusheen makeover in these cheerful, moist vanilla-lemon cupcakes with vanilla-lemon Swiss meringue buttercream topping. Every bite bursts with lemon flavor!

· ·

INGREDIENTS

Vanilla-Lemon Cupcakes

1 cup (120g) cake flour

2 teaspoons baking powder

8 tablespoons (1 stick/115g) unsalted butter, cut into cubes and slightly softened but still cold

⅔ cup (135g) superfine sugar

1 tablespoon grated lemon zest

2 large eggs

1 teaspoon pure vanilla extract

1 tablespoon plus 2 teaspoons whole milk

1 teaspoon fresh lemon juice

Vanilla-Lemon Swiss Meringue Buttercream

4 large egg whites

¾ cup (150g) superfine sugar

3 sticks (12 ounces/345g) unsalted butter, cut into cubes and slightly softened but still cold

2 tablespoons fresh lemon juice

1 teaspoon pure vanilla extract

Black oil-based food coloring or unsweetened black cocoa powder

Decorations

5 tablespoons chopped dark coating/compound chocolate

2 tablespoons chopped white coating/compound chocolate

Black oil-based food coloring or unsweetened black cocoa powder

· ·

1 MAKE THE VANILLA-LEMON CUPCAKES: Preheat the oven to 340°F (170°C). Place sixteen 2-inch (5cm) baking cups on a sheet pan.

2 Sift the flour and baking powder together into a medium bowl and set aside.

3 In a large bowl, using an electric mixer, cream the butter, superfine sugar, and lemon zest until pale and fluffy. Add the eggs one at a time, followed by the vanilla.

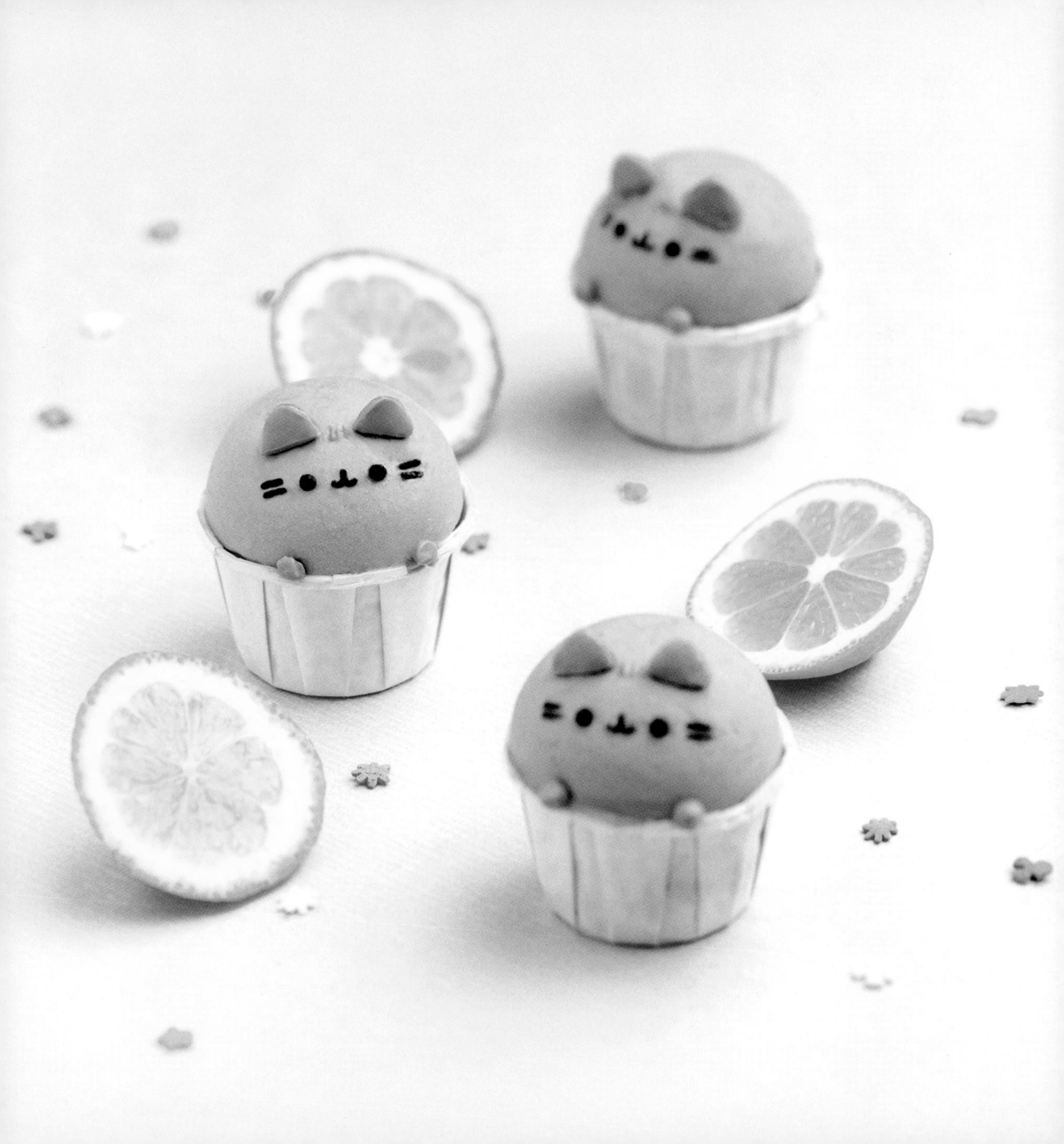

4 In a spouted measuring cup or small bowl, stir together the milk and lemon juice.

5 Fold the flour mixture into the butter mixture in two additions, alternating with the milk mixture. (You can beat the flour and milk mixtures into the butter mixture with the mixer instead, but do not overbeat.)

6 Scrape the batter into the prepared baking cups. Bake for 20 minutes, or until a skewer inserted into the center of a cupcake comes out clean. Remove the cupcakes from the oven and let them cool completely.

7 MAKE THE VANILLA-LEMON SWISS MERINGUE BUTTERCREAM: Bring about 1½ inches of water to a simmer in a medium saucepan over low heat. Place the egg whites and sugar in a heatproof bowl and place it on the saucepan (make sure the bottom of the bowl does not touch the water). Whisk continuously until the sugar dissolves completely and the mixture is warm to the touch, 160°F (71°C) on a candy thermometer. Do not allow the egg whites to scramble/coagulate. To test, rub a bit of the egg white mixture between your fingers; if it is still gritty, the sugar has not fully dissolved. Remove the bowl from the heat.

8 Using an electric mixer, beat the egg white mixture on medium-high speed until very stiff and glossy. The mixture should be cool to the touch at this point.

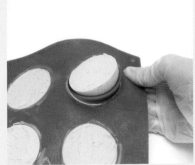

9 With the mixer running on medium speed, add the butter to the egg whites in three additions and beat until fluffy and firm, like shaving cream. The mixture may initially become watery as the butter is being incorporated, but just continue beating; it will firm up again.

10 Add the lemon juice and vanilla to the buttercream and beat well to combine. Add black food coloring drop by drop or black cocoa powder pinch by pinch until the buttercream is evenly tinted light gray.

11 Fill sixteen 2-inch (5cm) cake pop molds (or cake pop molds with a diameter that matches the top diameter of your cupcake liners) with the buttercream and freeze for at least 2 hours, until the buttercream hardens and is fully frozen. This helps create perfect domes. Reserve the remaining buttercream.

12 ASSEMBLE AND DECORATE THE CUPCAKES: Trim the tops of the cupcakes so they're level. Unmold the frozen buttercream domes and place them on top of the cupcakes.

13 Transfer half of the remaining buttercream to a small piping bag fitted with a ⅜-inch (1cm) petal piping tip. Pipe triangular ears onto the buttercream domes.

(14) Place the dark chocolate in a small microwave-safe bowl and microwave in 30-second intervals, stirring after each to prevent burning, until melted and smooth. (Alternatively, use a double boiler to melt the chocolate.) Melt the white chocolate as you did the dark chocolate, add a drop of black food coloring or a pinch of black cocoa powder, and stir until smooth and evenly tinted gray.

(15) Draw on Pusheen features using a toothpick dipped in the melted chocolate. Use the dark chocolate for the facial features and the gray chocolate for the head stripes.

(16) Transfer the remaining buttercream to a small piping bag fitted with a ⅛-inch (3mm) round tip and pipe on small Pusheen hands.

PUSHEEN SURPRISE CAKE

MAKES ONE 5-INCH (13CM) CAKE • LEVEL OF DIFFICULTY: DIFFICULT

A strawberry yogurt sponge cake that slices to unveil a lovable Pusheen design is a great-tasting and memorable way to surprise your loved one!

- -

INGREDIENTS

Pusheen Surprise Sponge Cake

8 tablespoons (1 stick/115g) unsalted butter, cut into cubes and slightly softened but still cold

1 cup (125g) confectioners' sugar

1 cup (120g) cake flour

4 large egg whites

Unsweetened dark cocoa powder

Black food coloring or unsweetened black cocoa powder

Pink food coloring

Strawberry Yogurt Chiffon Sponge Cake

2 large egg yolks

3 tablespoons superfine sugar

2 tablespoons vegetable oil

3 tablespoons strawberry yogurt drink

1 teaspoon pure vanilla extract

1 teaspoon pure strawberry extract or strawberry paste

⅓ cup (40g) cake flour

Pink gel food coloring (optional)

2 large egg whites

¼ teaspoon cream of tartar

- -

1 Photocopy or scan and print the Surprise Cake template on page 209 (template 14). Line a 10-inch (25cm) square baking pan with a silicone baking mat that does not crease. Place a template under the baking mat and lightly grease the baking mat with some butter or nonstick spray.

2 MAKE THE PUSHEEN SURPRISE SPONGE CAKE: Preheat the oven to 285°F (140°C). In a large bowl, using an electric mixer, cream the butter and confectioners' sugar until pale and fluffy. Gently beat in the flour, alternating with the egg whites, until well combined.

3 Spoon 1 teaspoon of the batter into a small bowl, add a pinch of dark cocoa powder and a pinch of black cocoa powder or a drop of black food coloring, and stir until evenly tinted dark brown. Spoon

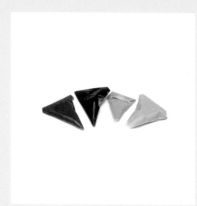  

1 teaspoon of the batter into a second small bowl, add a drop of black food coloring or a pinch of black cocoa powder, and stir until evenly tinted dark gray. Spoon ½ teaspoon of the batter into a third small bowl, dip a toothpick into pink food coloring, and stir it into the batter until evenly tinted pink. To the remaining batter, add black food coloring drop by drop or black cocoa powder pinch by pinch until the batter is evenly tinted light gray.

4 Transfer the dark brown, dark gray, and pink batters to separate small piping bags and snip a scant 1mm hole in the tip of each. Transfer 2 tablespoons of the light gray batter to a separate small piping bag and snip a scant 1mm hole in the tip.

5 Following the template, pipe the small Pusheen features into the prepared pan using the dark brown batter for the facial features, hands, and feet, dark gray batter for the head stripes, and pink batter for the mouth fill. Pipe in light gray batter to fill the spaces between the features. Repeat this for two or three layers, until the batter is a generous 2mm thick, so the Pusheen features are seen all the way through, from the baking mat to the top of the batter. Refrigerate for at least 5 minutes for the piped patterns to set.

6 Transfer the remaining light gray batter to a large piping bag and snip a ⅜-inch (1cm) hole in the tip. Fill the empty spaces in the pan with the light gray batter, but do not cover the piped designs. Bake

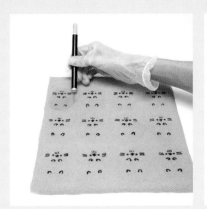

the sheet cake for 20 minutes, or until a skewer inserted into the center comes out clean. Remove from the oven and let cool completely in the pan, then flip the cake out onto a cutting board and remove the template and baking mat.

7 Cut out Pusheen shapes around the piped features using the same Surprise Cake template from page 209 (template 14) used earlier. There should be Pusheen features visible on both the front and back sides and all through the Pusheen cutouts. Stack the Pusheen cutouts together.

8 Preheat the oven to 285°F (140°C). Line the bottom of a 6-inch round cake pan 4 inches deep with parchment paper cut to fit.

9 MAKE THE STRAWBERRY YOGURT CHIFFON SPONGE CAKE: In a large bowl, whisk together the egg yolks and 1 tablespoon of the superfine sugar until pale and light. Add the oil, yogurt drink, vanilla, and strawberry extract and whisk until well combined. Sift in the flour and whisk until no lumps remain. Add a few drops of pink gel food coloring, if desired, and stir until the batter is evenly tinted pink. (You can leave the batter plain, if you like.)

10 In a large bowl, combine the egg whites and cream of tartar and whisk until foamy. While whisking continuously, gradually add the remaining 2 tablespoons superfine sugar and whisk until the meringue holds firm peaks. Fold the meringue into the batter with a spatula in three additions.

11 Pour the batter into the prepared round cake pan, filling it one-third of the way. Place the stack of Pusheen cutouts headfirst in the pan. Gently fill the spaces around the stack of Pusheen cutouts with the batter, ensuring that there are no air bubbles trapped around the cutouts. Gently pour in the remaining batter to cover the cutouts and fill the pan 80 percent of the way to the top.

12 Bake the cake for 50 to 60 minutes, until a skewer inserted into the center of the cake comes out clean. Remove from the oven and let cool completely in the pan. To remove the cake from the pan, gently press it away from the side of the pan, then invert the pan to release the cake. Peel off the parchment paper and serve.

Variation: You can use your favorite cake recipe in place of the strawberry yogurt chiffon sponge. If you prefer vanilla-flavored chiffon cake, use the recipe on page 102.

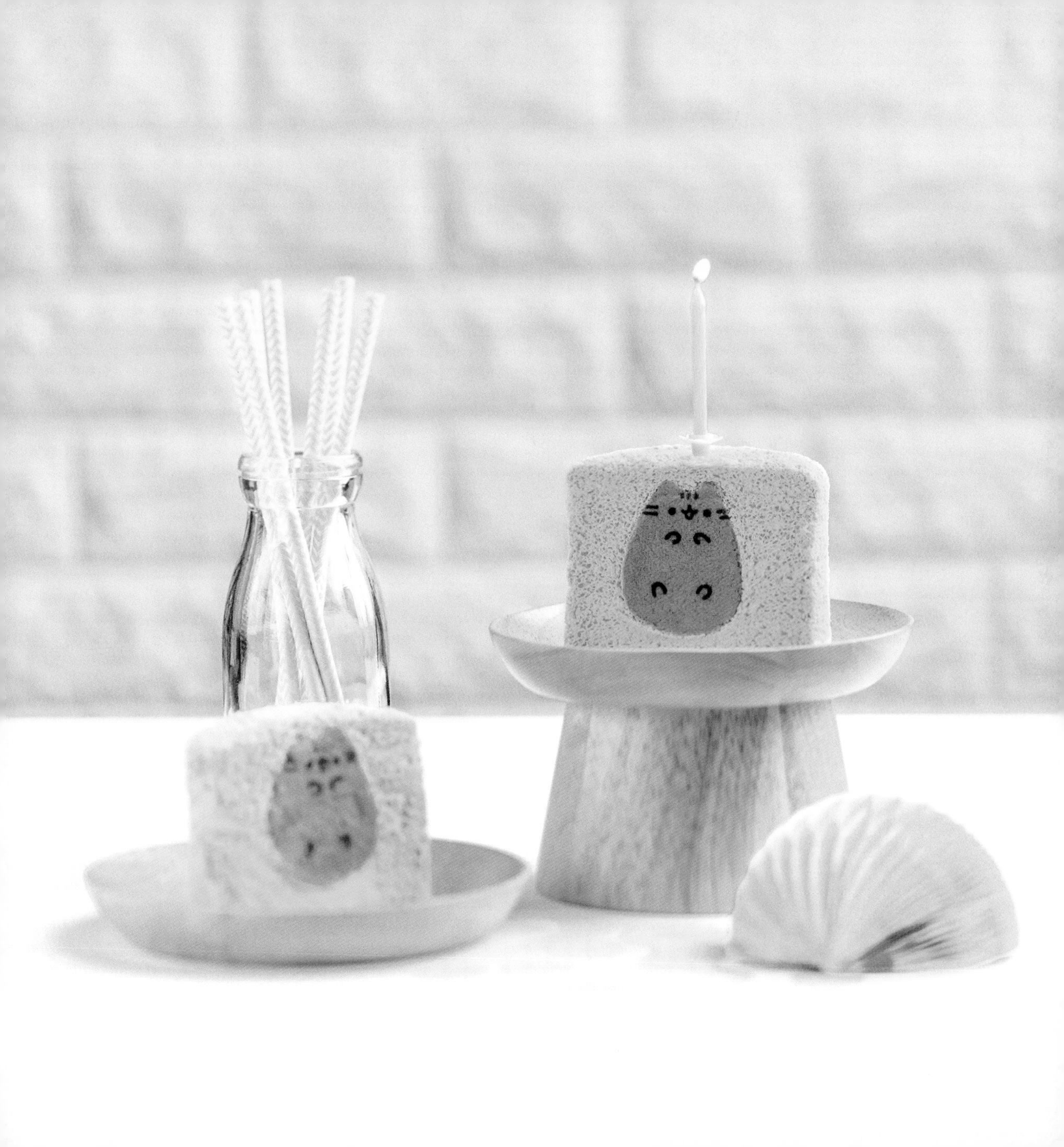

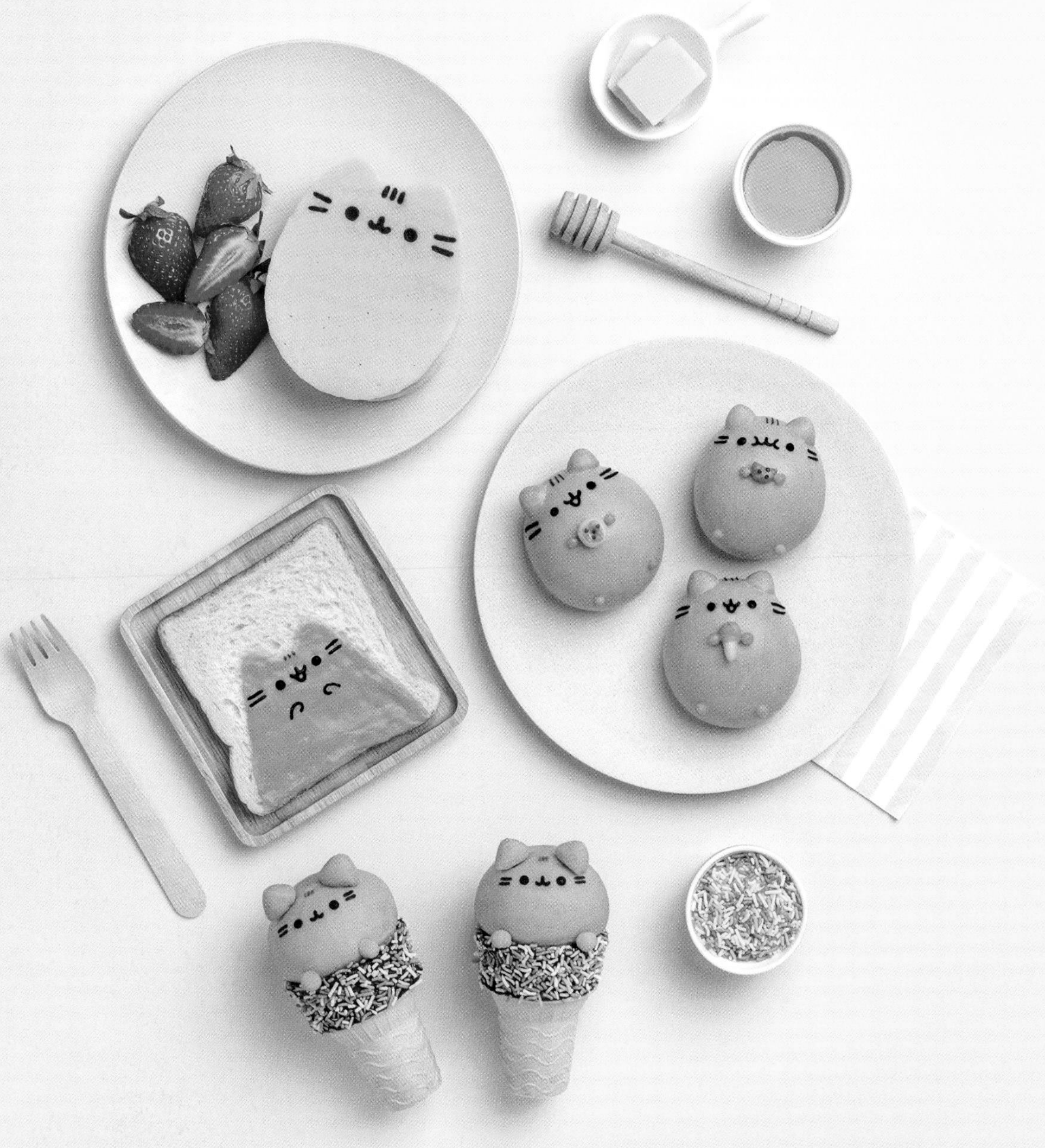

Breads & Breakfast

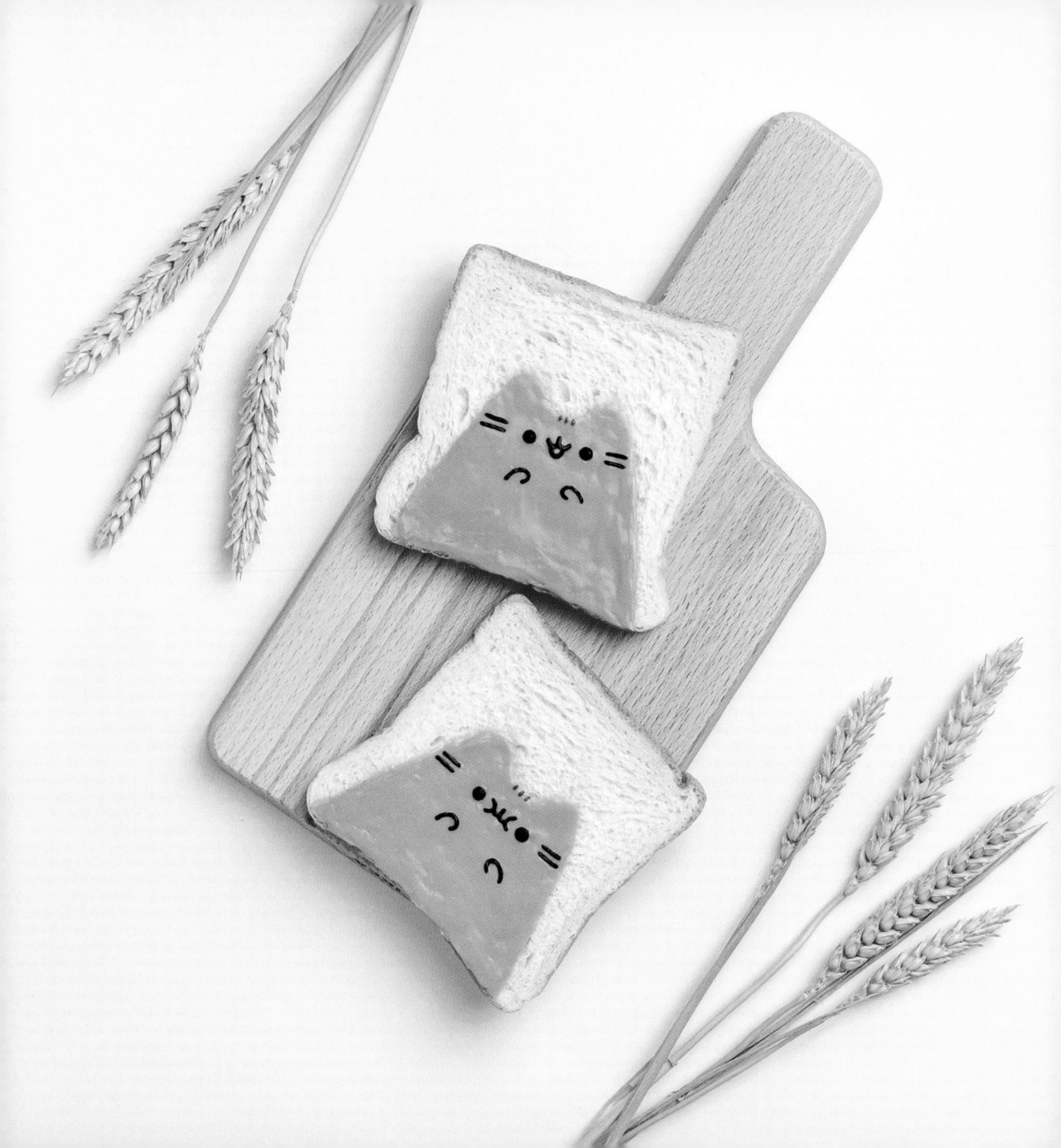

PUSHEEN BREAD
WITH BLACK SESAME–MILK SPREAD

SERVES 5 • LEVEL OF DIFFICULT: EASY

Milky, nutty, sweet, and creamy, the super-easy spread, shaped into Pusheen, is so good, it will cheer you up every morning.

. . . .

1 In a small saucepan, combine the black sesame paste and 3 tablespoons of the milk and heat over low heat, stirring, until smooth. Add the remaining 3½ tablespoons milk and the cream. Increase the heat to medium-low and cook, stirring, for 15 minutes, or until thickened. Remove from the heat. Let the paste cool slightly. Transfer to an airtight container and refrigerate overnight to further thicken to a spreadable consistency.

2 Spread the black sesame–milk spread on a slice of bread in a Pusheen shape. Repeat with the remaining bread slices. (Any leftover spread can be stored in the airtight container in the fridge for up to 1 week.)

3 DECORATE THE BREAD: Place the dark chocolate in a small microwave-safe bowl and microwave in 30-second intervals, stirring after each to prevent burning, until melted and smooth. Place 1 teaspoon of the white chocolate into each of two small bowls and melt as you did the dark chocolate. To one bowl, add a

INGREDIENTS

- 1½ teaspoons sweetened black sesame paste
- 6½ tablespoons (100g) whole milk
- ⅓ cup (80g) heavy cream
- 5 slices of bread

Decorations

- 1 tablespoon chopped dark coating/compound chocolate
- 2 teaspoons chopped white coating/compound chocolate
- Black oil-based food coloring or unsweetened black cocoa powder
- Beetroot powder or pink oil-based food coloring

drop of black food coloring or a pinch of black cocoa powder, and stir until evenly tinted gray. To the second bowl, add a pinch of beetroot powder or a drop of pink food coloring, and stir until evenly tinted pink.

4 Transfer the melted chocolates to separate small piping bags and snip a small hole in the tips. Use the dark chocolate to pipe Pusheen's features onto the slices of bread. Use the gray chocolate to pipe on Pusheen's head stripes. Use the pink chocolate to pipe on the mouth fill.

PUSHEEN STEAMED BUNS

MAKES 3 BUNS · LEVEL OF DIFFICULTY: MEDIUM TO DIFFICULT

These soft, fluffy steamed bread buns, shaped into full 3D versions of Pusheen, look too adorable to be eaten. Steamed buns are best consumed warm, right after steaming, when they are very fragrant and pillowy soft.

1 In a large bowl, combine the milk, superfine sugar, salt, and yeast. Mix with a wooden spatula until well combined, then add the flour and oil and mix until the dough comes together.

2 Turn the dough out onto a lightly floured surface and knead for 10 minutes, or until the dough is smooth. (Alternatively, prepare and knead the dough in the bowl of a stand mixer fitted with the dough hook.)

3 Set aside a small portion of the dough (about 1 ounce/28g) to use later for the decorations. To the remaining dough, add black food coloring drop by drop or black cocoa powder pinch by pinch and knead it in until the dough is evenly tinted gray. The easiest way to do this is to roll the dough into a long rope, fold it in thirds, then roll it into a long rope again. This also helps to expel trapped air bubbles.

4 Pull off three 2-ounce (57g) portions of the gray dough and roll into balls. Reserve any leftover gray dough to use later for ears, hands, and feet. Work with one portion of the dough at a time and keep the others wrapped in plastic wrap to prevent them from drying out. Roll each portion of the dough into a log,

INGREDIENTS

- ⅓ cup (80g) whole milk, plus more as needed
- 1 tablespoon superfine sugar
- Pinch of salt
- Generous ¼ teaspoon (1g) instant dry yeast
- 1 ¼ cups (150g) all-purpose flour, plus more for dusting
- 1 teaspoon liquid coconut oil
- Food coloring: black, brown, pink, yellow, and blue (or use natural food colorings: unsweetened black cocoa, unsweetened dark cocoa, beet, turmeric, and butterfly blue pea flower powders)

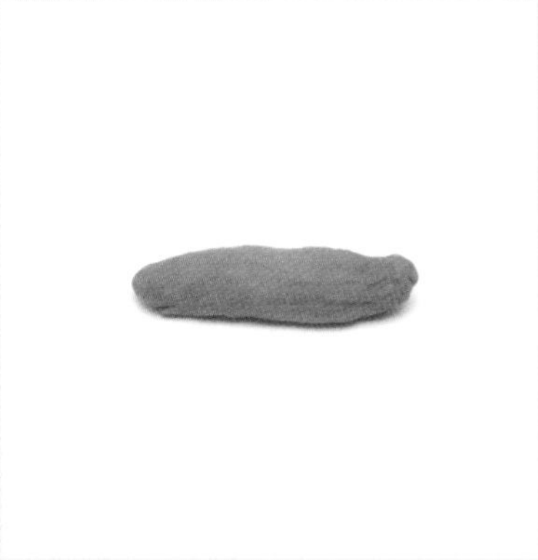
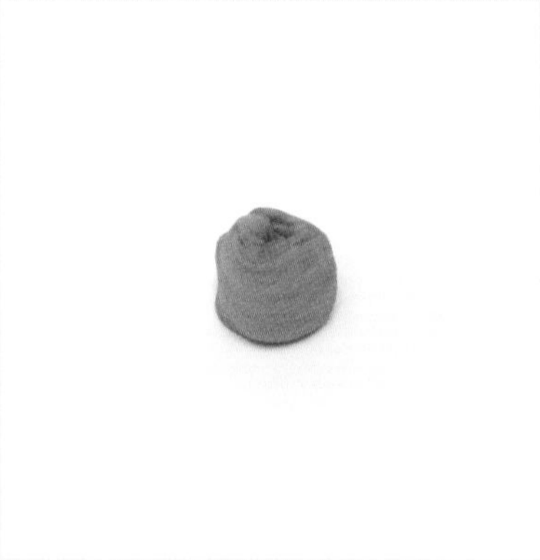
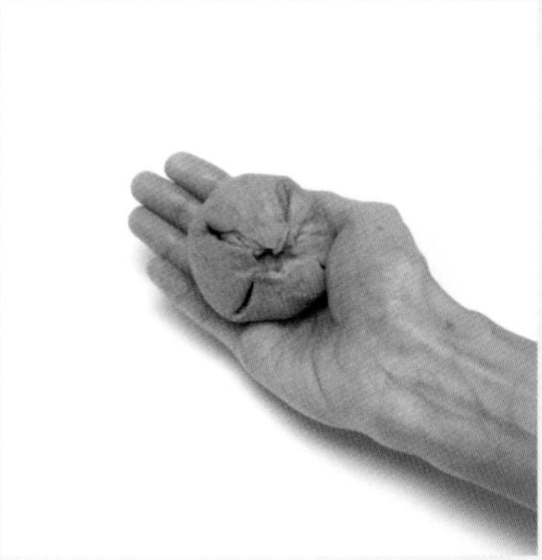

roll up the log into a snail, flatten the snail, gather the dough around the sides into the center, and pinch the dough at the center to seal. If you want to add any filling, place it within the flattened dough and pinch the dough at the center to seal it in. You can dab the dough with some milk to help seal it. Place the ball seam side down on your work surface, then roll it in a circular motion and gently shape it into a tall oval ball. Wrap the ball of dough in plastic wrap while you shape the remaining portions.

5 Shape 2 small rounded triangles for ears and 4 small balls for hands and feet from the reserved gray dough, making one set for each oval ball. Wrap these in plastic wrap to prevent them from drying out.

6 Divide the remaining gray dough in half. Knead ¼ teaspoon black cocoa powder and ¼ teaspoon dark cocoa powder or a few drops of black and brown food coloring into half of the dough until evenly tinted dark brown. Roll the dark brown dough into a thin strand and cut it into strips for the whiskers, nose, and mouth. Roll 2 small balls of dark brown dough for the eyes, making 3 pairs. Knead a pinch of black cocoa powder into the remaining gray dough until evenly tinted dark gray. Roll the dark gray dough into thin strips to make the head stripes.

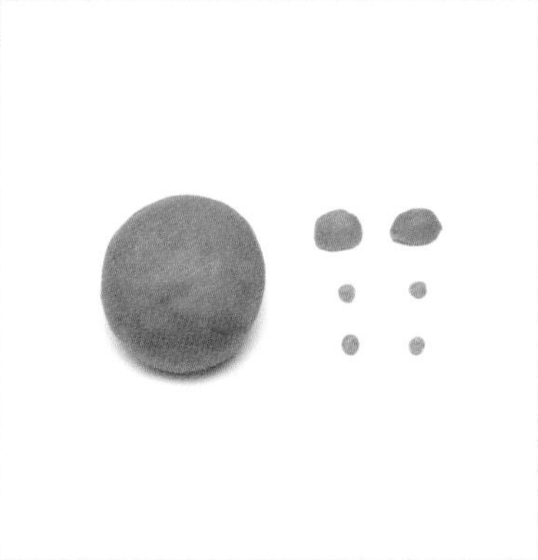
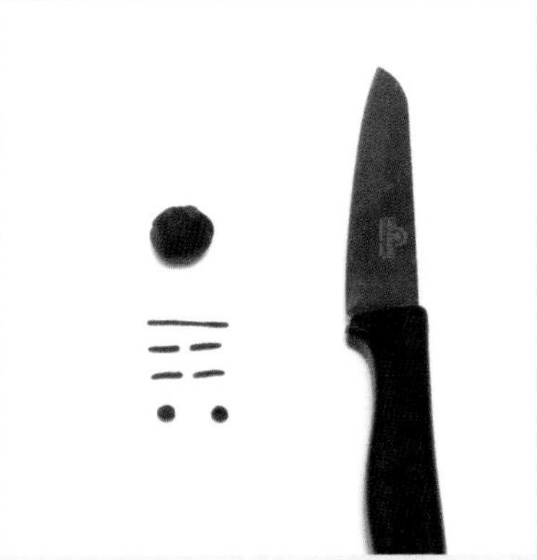
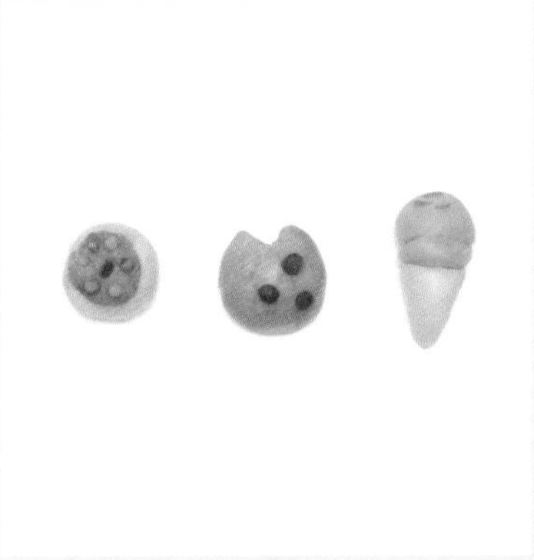

7 Using a bit of milk to help adhere them, add Pusheen's facial features and ears to each oval ball of dough. Make sure to seal the edges of the ears tightly against the head using a toothpick, to prevent bulging.

8 Using the reserved plain dough, form a mini donut, a chocolate chip cookie, and an ice cream cone, keeping the dough for the donut and ice cream plain and kneading in a pinch of dark cocoa powder for the light brown cookie and more dark cocoa powder for the darker brown chocolate chips. Knead small amounts of food coloring into bits of the remaining dough to evenly tint to the desired shades of pink, yellow, and blue for the toppings of the donut and ice cream. Shape and combine the different colored doughs to form the donut, cookie, and ice cream cone.

9 Attach the donut, cookie, ice cream cone, hands, and feet to the Pusheen bodies with a dab of milk. Place the Pusheen buns on a baking sheet, lightly cover with plastic wrap, and set in a warm spot* to proof for 30 to 45 minutes, until increased in volume by 50 percent.

*Tip: If your kitchen is cool, you can place the dough and cups of hot water in an enclosed space—for example, in the oven with the power switched off—to create a warm, humid environment to help the dough rise.

10 Bring a few inches of water to a boil in a large saucepan over high heat. Reduce the heat to medium-low when the water starts boiling. Place the buns in a bamboo steamer basket, leaving at least 1½ inches (4cm) between them to allow room for expansion. Set the bamboo steamer basket in the pan, cover, and steam over medium-high heat for 15 to 18 minutes, until puffy and smooth. Turn off the heat and wait 1 to 2 minutes before removing the cover to prevent sudden changes in temperature, which may cause wrinkling. (Alternatively, you can use an electric steamer: Fill the reservoir over the minimum mark, place the buns into the steaming compartment, leaving at least 1½ inches (3.8cm) between them, and steam for 15 minutes.*) The steamed buns are best eaten warm.

*_Very important note:_ If you are using an electric steamer instead of a bamboo steamer basket, prevent water from dripping onto the buns either by propping the steamer lid up slightly on one side with a bamboo skewer or wrapping the underside of the lid in a clean kitchen towel (to absorb the steam). When you open the lid, always quickly tilt it sideways to prevent any water that has condensed on its surface from falling onto the buns.

Optional: If you like, omit the donut/cookie/ice cream cone decorations and make plain gray Pusheens. In this case, add ¼ teaspoon black cocoa powder or 1 to 2 drops of black food coloring with the flour when you're preparing the dough and knead as directed, making sure the dough is evenly tinted gray.

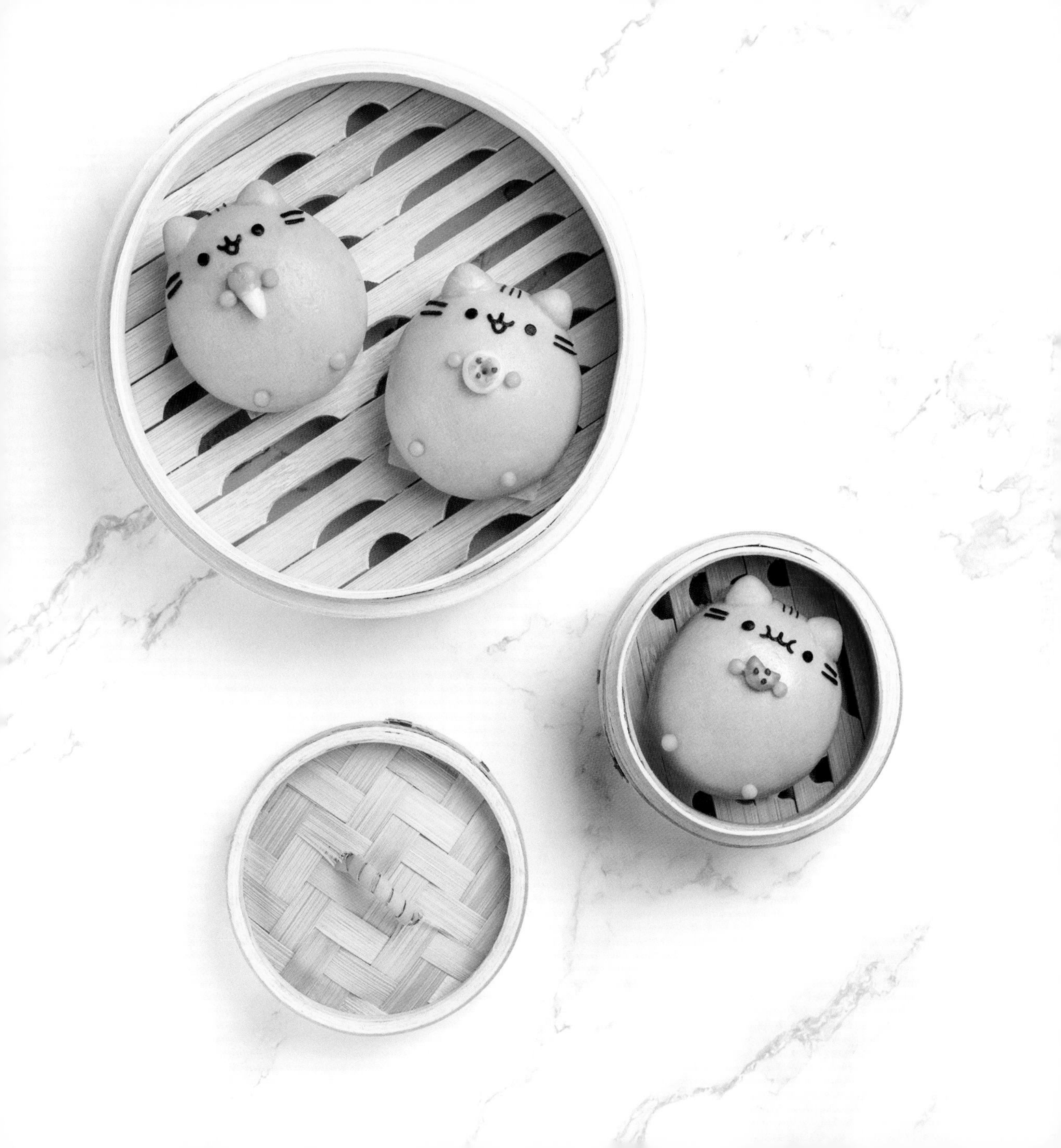

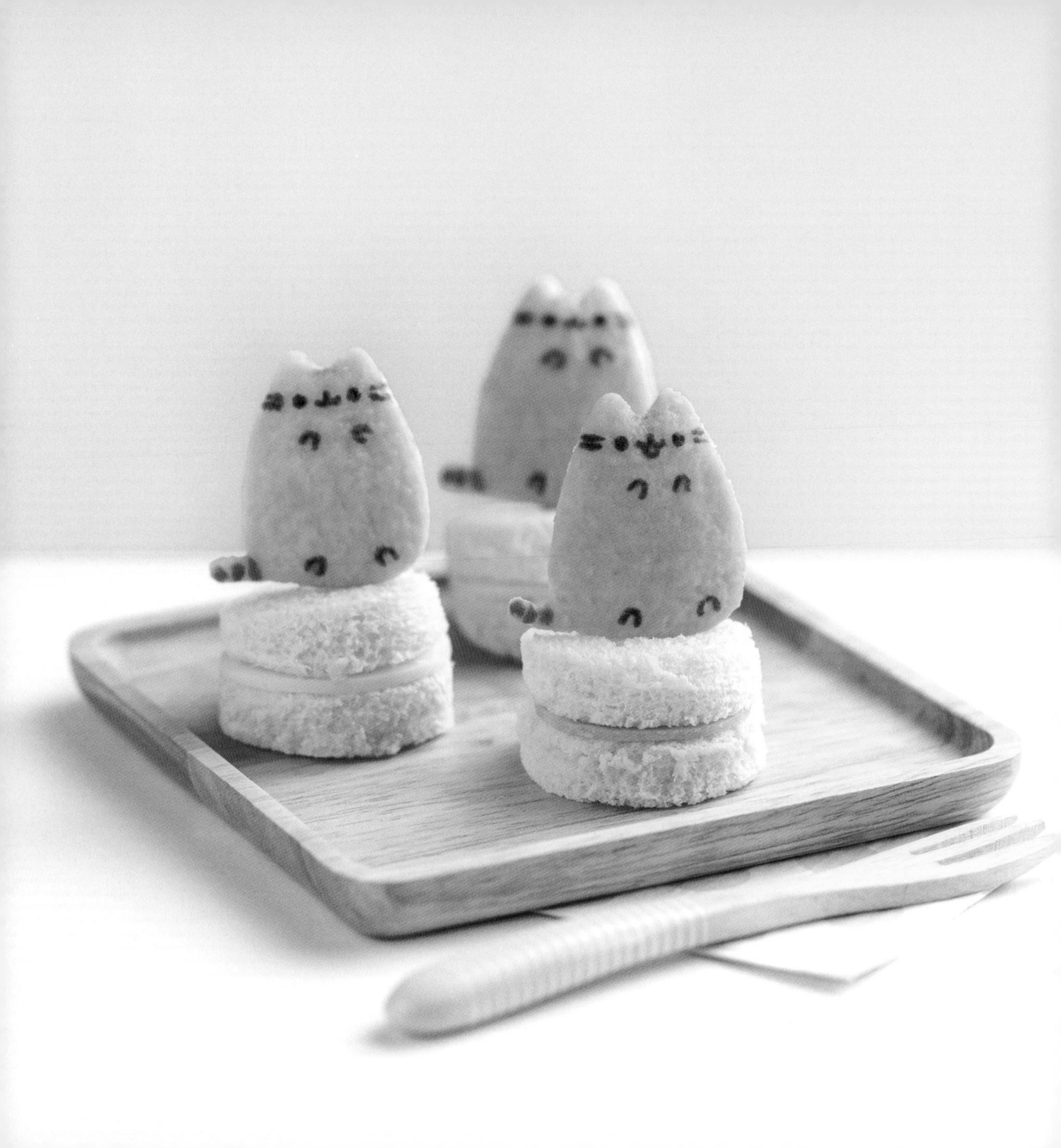

PUSHEEN DECO TOAST SANDWICHES

MAKES 20 MINI SANDWICHES • LEVEL OF DIFFICULTY: EASY TO MEDIUM

Sweet and slightly crusty on the surface, this Pusheen pop-up toast instantly brightens and ramps up a common sandwich, both in terms of the cute factor and the flavors!

1 Preheat the oven to 355°F (180°C).

2 Photocopy or scan and print the Deco Toast Sandwiches template on page 197 (template 4) and use it to cut Pusheen shapes from 5 of the bread slices. You should be able to cut 4 Pusheen shapes from each slice of bread.

3 Place the butter and sugar in a medium microwave-safe bowl and microwave in 15-second intervals, stirring after each, until all the sugar has dissolved. Whisk in the egg white, followed by the sifted cake flour, and whisk well to ensure that there are no lumps.

4 Spoon 2 teaspoons of the batter into a small bowl, add ¼ teaspoon of dark cocoa powder or 1 to 2 drops of dark brown food coloring, and stir until evenly tinted dark brown. Spoon 2 teaspoons of the batter into a second small bowl, add a pinch of black cocoa powder or a drop of black food coloring, and stir until evenly tinted dark gray. Spoon 1 teaspoon of the batter into a third small bowl, add ¼ teaspoon beet powder or a drop of pink food coloring, and stir until evenly tinted pink. To the remaining batter, add a pinch of black cocoa powder or a drop of black food coloring and stir until evenly tinted light gray.

INGREDIENTS

- 15 slices of bread
- 5½ teaspoons (⅕ stick/25g) unsalted butter, cut into cubes and slightly softened but still cold
- 2 tablespoons superfine sugar
- ½ large egg white
- 3½ tablespoons cake flour, sifted
- Food coloring: black, dark brown, and pink (or use natural food colorings: unsweetened black cocoa, unsweetened dark cocoa, and beet powders)
- 5 slices ham and/or cheese of your choice, for filling (each slice can be cut into rounds for 4 mini sandwiches)

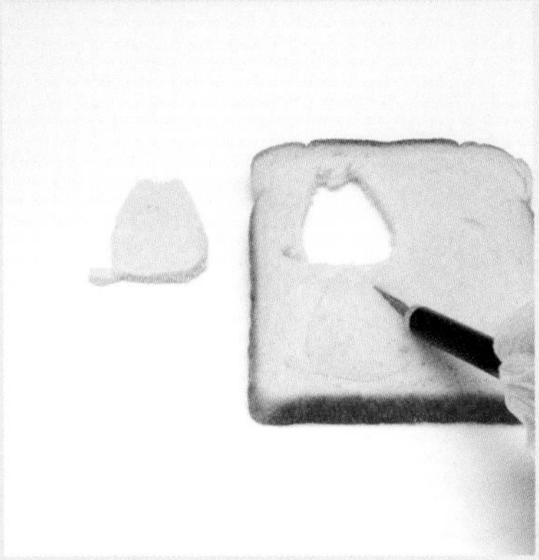

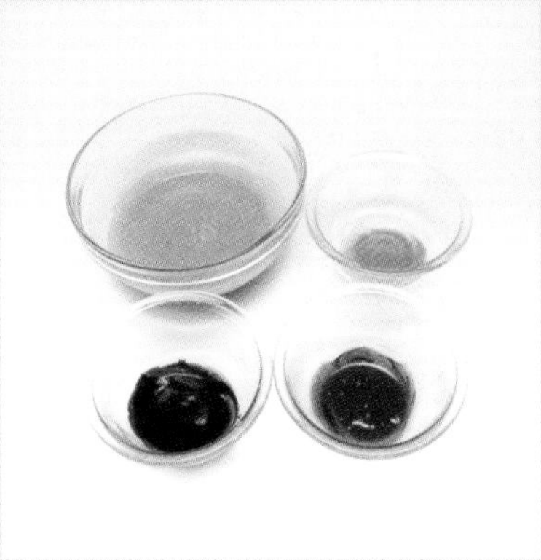

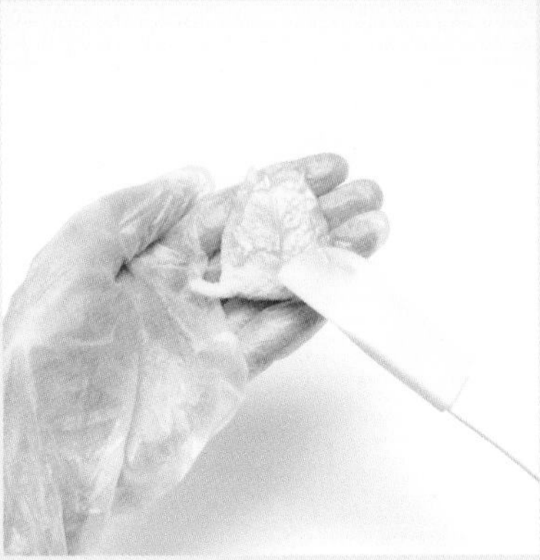

5 Spread the light gray batter over the Pusheen bread cutouts with a spatula and place them on a baking sheet.

6 Transfer the dark brown, dark gray, and pink batters to separate small piping bags, snip a small hole in the tips, and use them to pipe Pusheen's facial features, hands, feet, and tail stripes.

7 Toast for 4 to 5 minutes. Remove from the oven and allow to cool until the toast batter is dry.

8 Using a 2-inch (5cm) round cutter, cut a total of 40 rounds (for 20 sandwiches) from the remaining slices of bread. Each slice should yield 4 rounds. Use the same cutter to cut 1 round for each sandwich from the sliced ham or cheese for the filling.

9 Assemble each sandwich by topping a round of bread with a round of ham or cheese and then closing it with another round of bread. Insert a toothpick into the bottom of each toasted Pusheen cutout and stick the opposite end of the toothpick into a sandwich stack.

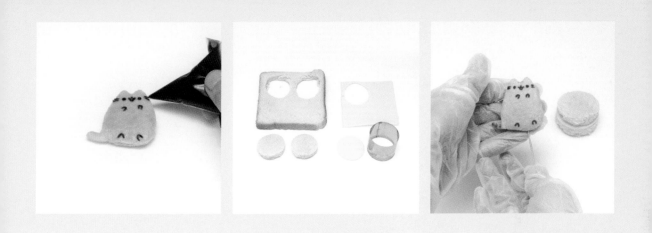

PUSHEEN BREAD BUNS-IN-CONES

MAKES 6 BREAD BUNS-IN-CONES · LEVEL OF DIFFICULTY: MEDIUM

The humble sweet-and-savory bread bun gets an endearing Pusheen spin, complemented by a crunchy ice cream cone, rich chocolate, and lots of sweet sprinkles! Such a delight!

. . . .

1 In a large bowl, combine half the bread flour, 1 to 2 drops of black food coloring or ¼ teaspoon black cocoa powder, sugar, and yeast. Add the warm milk and mix vigorously using a wooden spatula for a few minutes to activate the yeast. If you see tiny bubbles popping when you stop stirring, the yeast is activated and you can stop.

2 Add the remaining flour, the butter, and the salt and stir for a few minutes, until the mixture is combined and a dough forms. Turn the dough out onto a floured work surface and knead for 20 minutes. Check to see how thin you can stretch the dough without it tearing or breaking; if you can stretch it thin enough that you can almost see through it, it's ready. This is called the window pane test. (Alternatively, prepare and knead the dough in the bowl of a stand mixer fitted with the dough hook.)

3 Return the dough to the bowl, cover with plastic wrap or a damp kitchen towel, and set aside in a warm place for 30 minutes for the first rising. The dough should rise to 1½ to 2 times its size. Press a finger into the risen dough; if it has risen successfully, your finger should leave an indent. Turn the dough out of the bowl and punch it down.

INGREDIENTS

- 1½ cups plus 2 tablespoons (195g) bread flour, plus more for dusting
- Black food coloring or unsweetened black cocoa powder
- 2 tablespoons superfine sugar
- 1 teaspoon (3g) instant dry yeast
- ½ cup (120g) warm milk, plus more as needed
- 4 teaspoons (20g) unsalted butter, cut into cubes and slightly softened
- Generous ¼ teaspoon salt
- 6 ice cream wafer cup cones

Decorations

- 3 tablespoons chopped dark coating/compound chocolate, plus 3 ounces for coating, if desired
- 1 tablespoon chopped white coating/compound chocolate
- Black oil-based food coloring or unsweetened black cocoa powder
- 3 tablespoons rainbow-colored sprinkles (optional)

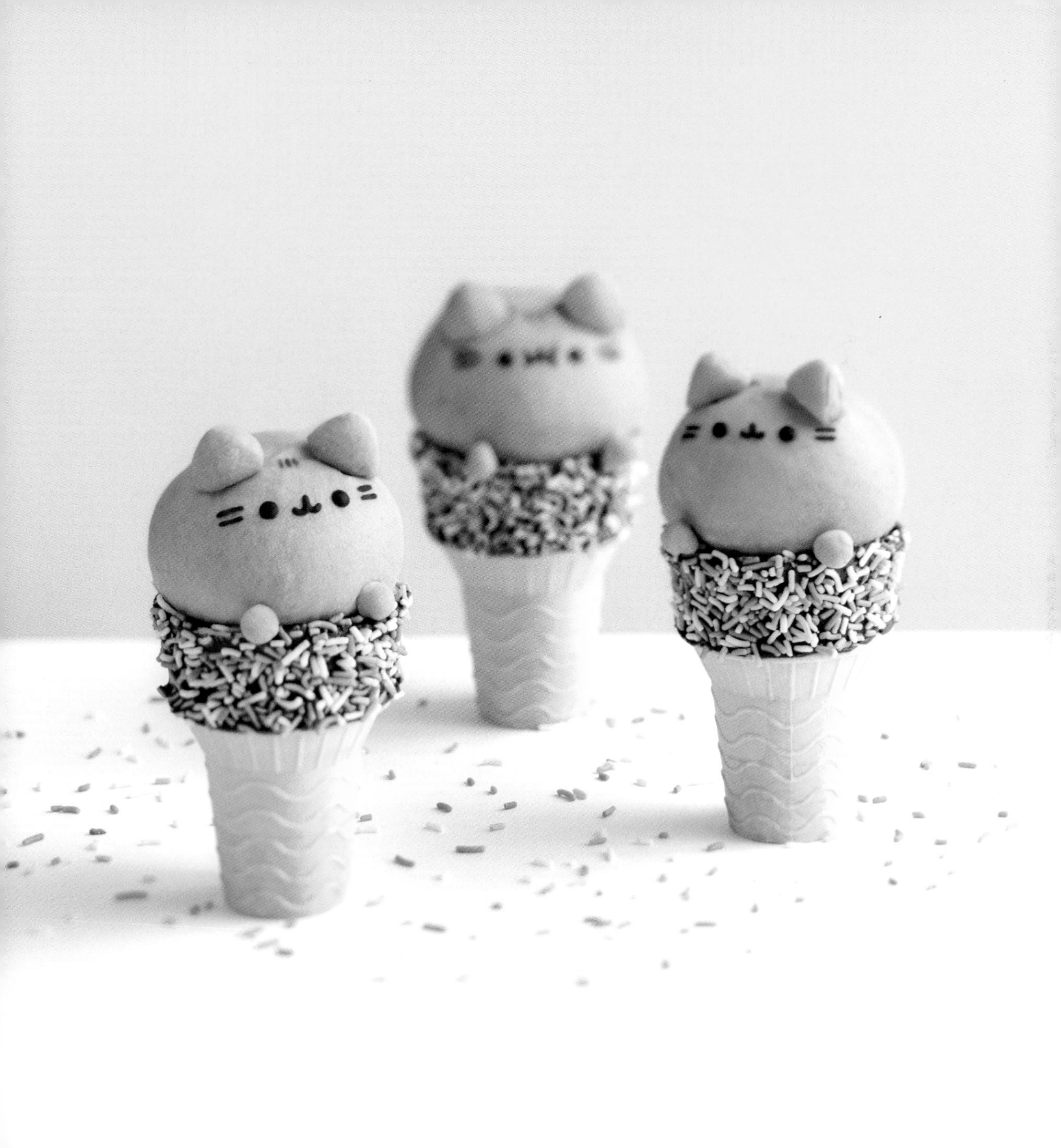

④ Pull off six 2-ounce (57g) portions of dough; set the small bit of remaining dough aside to use later for the ears and hands. Work with one portion of the dough at a time and keep the others wrapped in plastic wrap to prevent them from drying out. Roll each portion into a log, roll up the log into a snail, flatten the snail, gather the dough around the sides into the center, and pinch the dough at the center to seal. If you want to add any filling, place it within the flattened dough and pinch the dough at the center to seal it in. Place the ball seam side down on your work surface, then roll it in a circular motion and gently shape it into a tall, round ball. Wrap the ball of dough in plastic wrap while you shape the remaining portions.

⑤ Shape 2 small rounded triangles for ears and 2 small balls for hands from the extra portion of dough, making one set for each ball. Wrap these in plastic wrap to prevent them from drying out.

⑥ Set the dough balls and small parts in a warm spot* to proof for 30 minutes, until about doubled in size.

*Tip: If your kitchen is cool, you can place the dough and cups of hot water in an enclosed space—for example, in the oven with the power switched off—to create a warm, humid environment to help the dough rise.

⑦ Preheat the oven to 355°F (180°C).

8 Place each dough ball seam side down in an ice cream wafer cup cone. Using a bit of milk to help adhere them, attach the ears and hands to each dough ball. Make sure to seal the edges of the ears tightly against the head using a toothpick, to prevent bulging.

9 Place the cones in the wells of a popover pan to prevent the cones from toppling in the oven. Reduce the oven temperature to 300°F (150°C), place the cones in the oven, and bake for 25 to 30 minutes, until the tops of the buns are firm to the touch and sound hollow when tapped. Remove from the oven and let the cones cool completely.

10 DECORATE THE BUNS: Place the 3 tablespoons dark chocolate in a small microwave-safe bowl and microwave in 30-second intervals, stirring after each to prevent burning, until melted and smooth. Melt the white chocolate as you did the dark chocolate, add a drop of black food coloring or a pinch of black cocoa powder, and stir until evenly tinted gray. Using a toothpick, draw Pusheen's facial features onto each bun with the melted dark chocolate. Draw on Pusheen's head stripes using the gray chocolate.

11 If desired, melt the remaining 3 ounces dark chocolate. Using a pastry brush, brush the melted chocolate around the top of the cones and add some sprinkles. Let the chocolate set before serving.

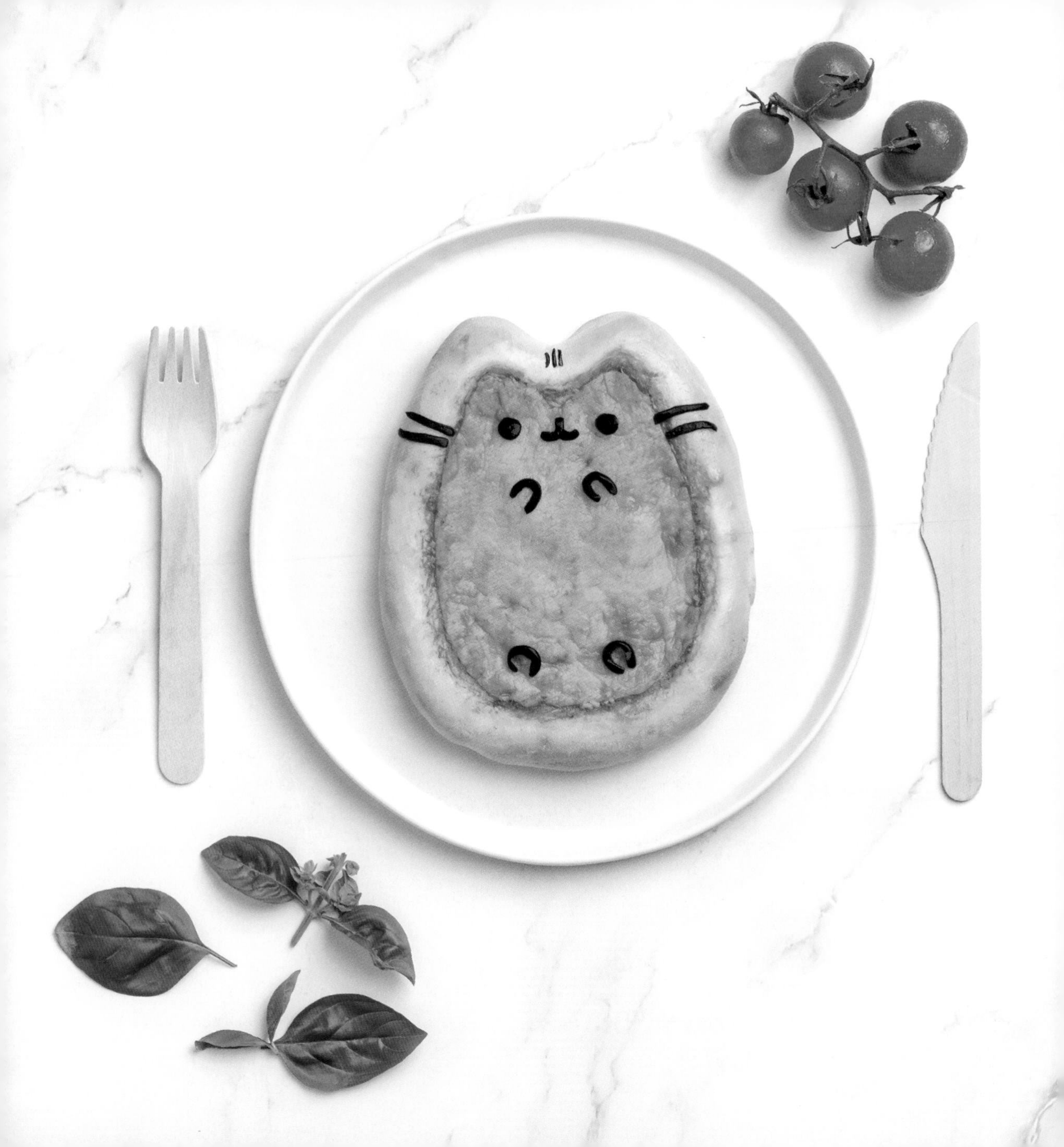

PUSHEEN PIZZA

MAKES THREE 6 × 7-INCH (15 × 18CM) PUSHEEN PIZZAS • **LEVEL OF DIFFICULTY: EASY TO MEDIUM**

Pizzas have never looked cuter than this! Use the template at the back of the book to create your own tasty, puffy, Pusheen-shaped crust. In addition to the wholesome homemade sauce, you can customize and add your own preferred toppings to this oozing cheese pizza, to create your very own masterpiece!

INGREDIENTS

Pizza Dough

1 cup (240g) warm water

1 teaspoon (3g) instant dry yeast

2 tablespoons superfine sugar

1 tablespoon olive oil, plus more for greasing

2½ cups (300g) all-purpose flour, plus more for dusting

1 teaspoon salt

Pizza Sauce

1 cup (240g) canned diced tomatoes

5 tablespoons (85g) tomato paste (half of a 6-ounce/170g can)

1 tablespoon dried oregano

1 tablespoon Italian seasoning

½ teaspoon garlic salt

Generous ¼ teaspoon garlic powder

1 teaspoon superfine sugar

Toppings

10 ounces mozzarella cheese, shredded

Other toppings of your choice

Pitted black olives

① **MAKE THE PIZZA DOUGH:** In a small bowl, combine the warm water, yeast, and superfine sugar and mix vigorously using a wooden spatula to activate the yeast. Set aside for 10 minutes, or until foamy.

② Stir the olive oil into the yeast mixture.

③ In a large bowl, combine the flour and salt and make a well in the center. Pour the yeast mixture into the well and stir to combine.

④ When the dough has pulled together, turn it out onto a flour-dusted work surface and knead until it is smooth and elastic, about 5 minutes. (Alternatively, prepare and knead the dough in the bowl of a stand mixer fitted with the dough hook.)

⑤ Lightly oil another large bowl. Shape the dough into a ball and place it in the bowl. Cover with plastic wrap or a damp kitchen towel and set aside in a warm spot* for 1 hour, or until the dough is doubled in size.

*Tip: If your kitchen is cool, you can place the dough and cups of hot water in an enclosed space—for example, in the oven with the power switched off—to create a warm, humid environment to help the dough rise.

⑥ Preheat the oven to 445°F (230°C). Photocopy or scan and print the Pizza template on page 211 (template 15).

⑦ MAKE THE PIZZA SAUCE: In a large bowl, combine the diced tomatoes and tomato paste and stir until well combined. Add the oregano, Italian seasoning, garlic salt, garlic powder, and sugar and mix well.

⑧ Turn the dough out onto a flour-dusted work surface and punch it down. Divide the dough into thirds. Use a rolling pin to roll each portion into a 6 × 7–inch (15 × 18cm) oval shape. Place the Pizza template under a piece of parchment paper, then transfer one dough oval onto the parchment. Shape the dough into a Pusheen shape, following the template beneath as a guide and folding in the edges to make a

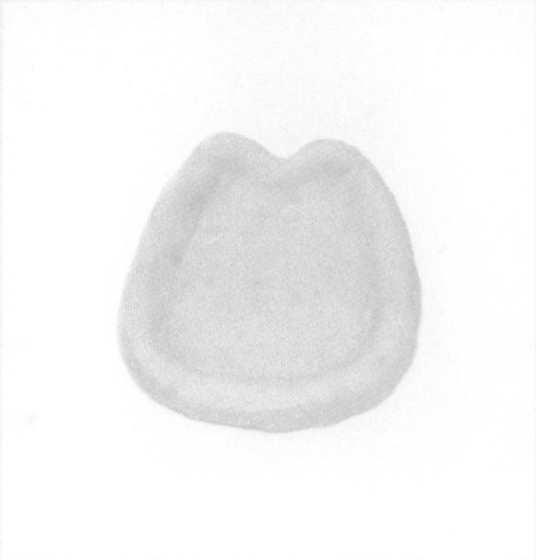
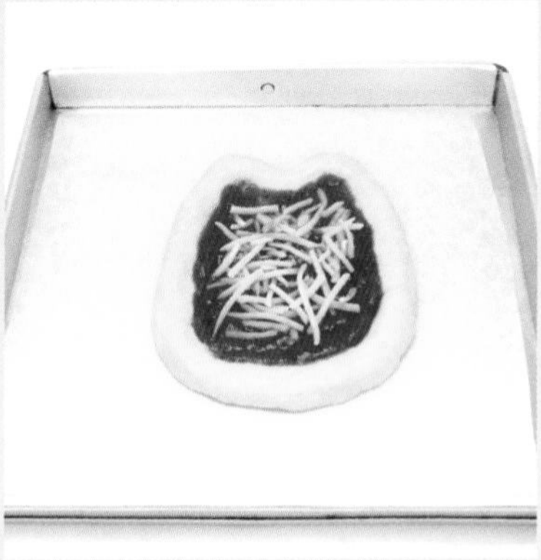
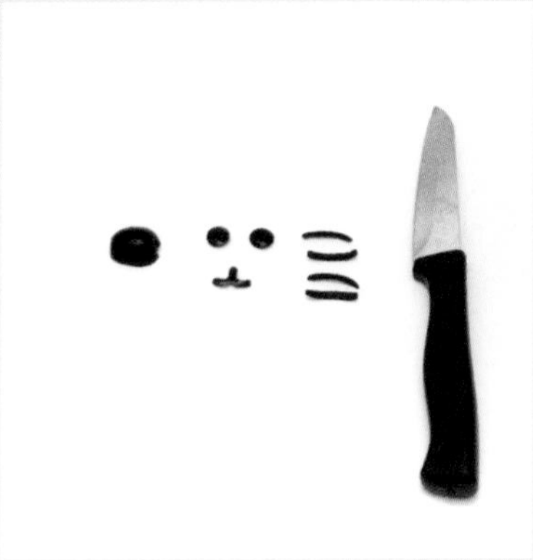

thicker border. Flip the dough over to hide the seams. Slightly reshape the dough if flipping it has affected the shape. Slide the Pusheen-shaped dough, still on the parchment, onto a baking sheet (this prevents the pizza from sticking to the baking sheet and changing shape). Repeat to shape the remaining dough.

Optional: If you like your pizza crust to have a deeper color, whisk together 1 egg and 1 tablespoon water and brush it onto the thicker portion of the crust around the edges.

9 ASSEMBLE THE PIZZAS: Spread a thin layer of pizza sauce over each piece of dough, keeping it within the thicker border. Top the pizzas evenly with the mozzarella cheese and your favorite toppings. Bake the pizzas for 12 to 14 minutes, or until the crust is brown and the cheese has melted.

10 Thinly slice some black olives and cut out Pusheen's facial features and head stripes. Add them to the pizzas. Use a fat straw to cut out half circles from the outer portion of a black olive to make Pusheen's hands and feet. Place them on the pizza to complete the Pusheen.

Variation: You can use mayonnaise tinted with black food coloring instead of black olives to draw on Pusheen's features.

PUSHEEN SMOOTHIE BOWL

SERVES 1 • LEVEL OF DIFFICULTY: EASY

Packed with lots of vitamins, antioxidants, and energy, this smooth and invigorating strawberry-banana-coconut smoothie, with a lovely Pusheen drawn on it, is sure to perk anyone up in the morning!

INGREDIENTS

Pink Smoothie

½ cup (80g) strawberries, frozen (about 9)

1 banana, sliced and frozen

1 tablespoon fresh lemon juice

2 tablespoons coconut cream

⅛ teaspoon beet powder

Gray Base

¼ teaspoon sweetened black sesame paste

Pinch of unsweetened black cocoa powder or ½ to 1 drop of black food coloring

4 tablespoons coconut cream

Dark Brown Base

½ teaspoon unsweetened black cocoa powder or 1 to 2 drops of black food coloring

1 teaspoon unsweetened dark cocoa powder or 1 to 2 drops of dark brown food coloring

2 tablespoons coconut cream

Banana Smoothie

1 banana, sliced and frozen

1 tablespoon fresh lemon juice

1 MAKE THE PINK SMOOTHIE: Place the frozen strawberries, frozen banana, lemon juice, coconut cream, and beet powder in a blender. Blend until smooth and creamy.

2 Pour the pink smoothie into a 6-inch (15cm) smoothie bowl, reserving a small bit for Pusheen's mouth fill.

3 MAKE THE GRAY BASE: In a small bowl, combine the black sesame paste, black cocoa powder or black food coloring, and 1 teaspoon of the coconut cream. Stir until the mixture forms a smooth paste. Put the remaining coconut cream in a separate small bowl and stir in the sesame paste mixture (this helps to prevent the black sesame paste from clumping).

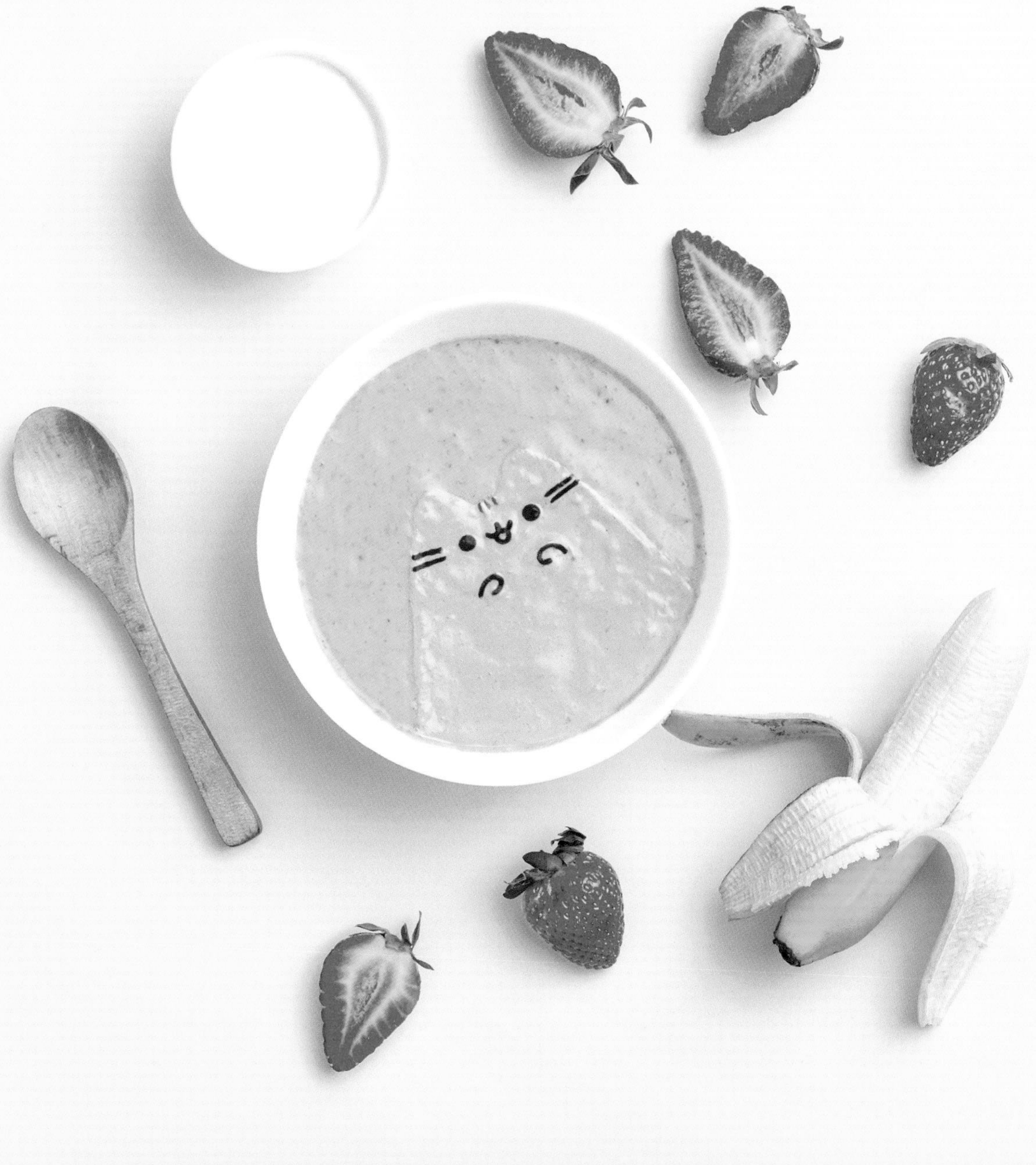

4 MAKE THE DARK BROWN BASE: In a small bowl, combine the black cocoa powder or black food coloring, dark cocoa powder or dark brown food coloring, and 1 teaspoon of the coconut cream. Stir until the mixture forms a smooth paste. Add the remaining coconut cream and mix well.

5 MAKE THE PUSHEEN SMOOTHIE: Put the frozen banana and lemon juice in a clean blender and blend until smooth. Divide this mixture between the gray and dark brown bases and mix well, until smooth and creamy.

6 ASSEMBLE THE SMOOTHIE: Transfer the gray smoothie to a squeeze bottle or small piping bag, snip a small hole in the tip, and pipe a Pusheen shape onto the pink smoothie.

7 Using a bamboo stick or toothpick, draw on Pusheen's facial features and hands with the dark brown smoothie.

8 In a small bowl, stir together 1 teaspoon of the dark brown smoothie and 1 teaspoon of the gray smoothie to make a dark gray smoothie. Using a bamboo stick or toothpick, draw on Pusheen's head stripes using the dark gray smoothie.

9 Use the reserved pink smoothie for the mouth fill and serve.

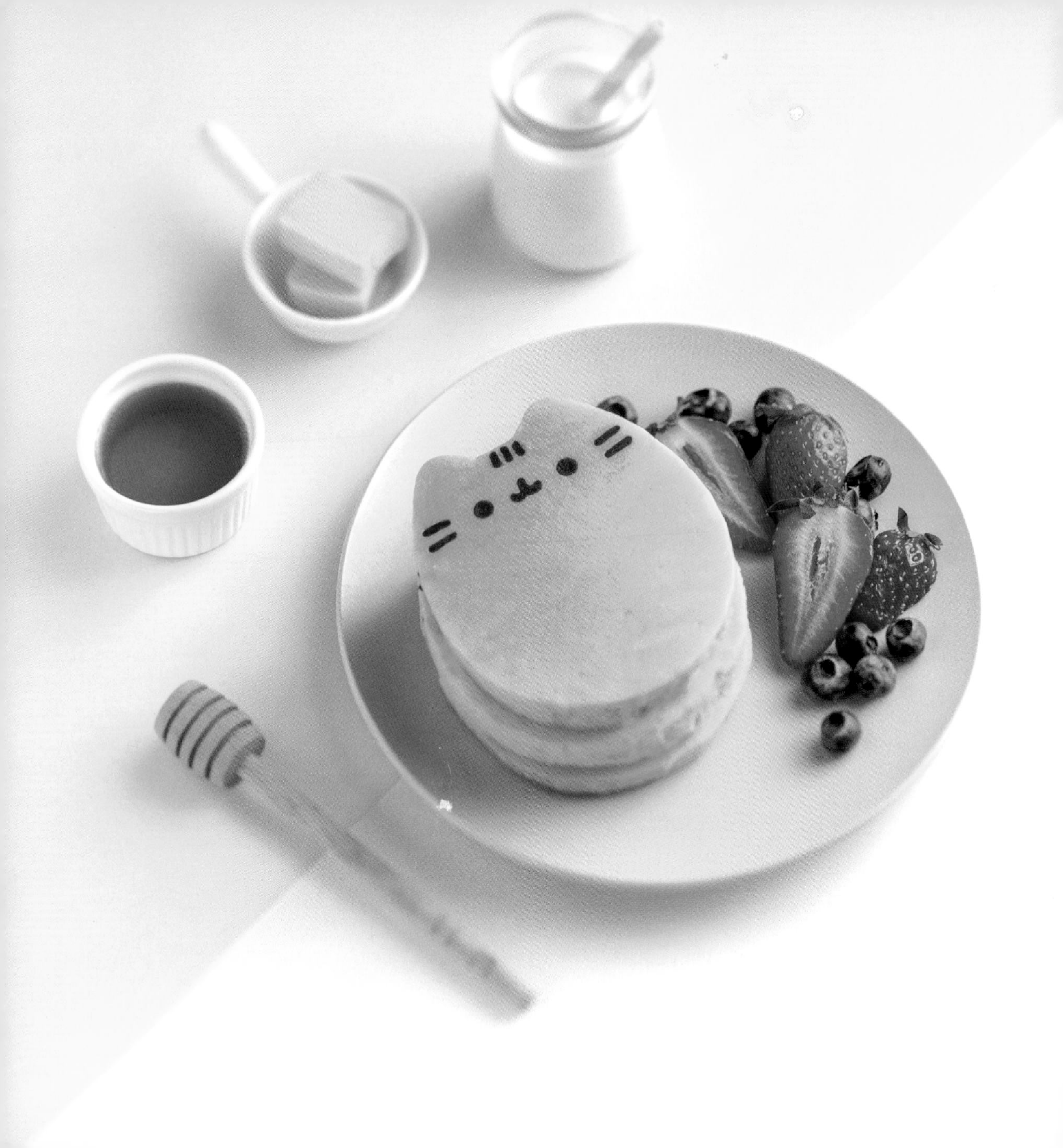

PUSHEEN PANCAKE STACK

MAKES 9 THICK PANCAKES · LEVEL OF DIFFICULTY: EASY

Fluffy, sweet-scented, and scrumptious, and fashioned into Pusheen with features drawn using basic pancake art, this pancake stack is certain to give you a great start to your day!

1 MAKE YOUR OWN PUSHEEN-SHAPED MOLD FROM ALUMINUM FOIL: Fold a piece of foil into a strip ½ inch (1.25cm) thick and 11 inches (28cm) long. Bend the strip into a Pusheen shape that is 5 inches (13cm) tall and 4 inches (10cm) wide following the Pancake Stack template on page 205 (template 12) as a guide. Staple the ends or fold them over each other to close the shape. It is good to prepare a few molds in case one becomes damaged during cooking.

2 Sift the flour, superfine sugar, baking powder, and salt together into a large bowl.

3 In a medium bowl, whisk together the milk, melted butter, vanilla, and egg. Whisk the wet ingredients into the dry ingredients until just combined.

4 Grease or butter the Pusheen mold and a griddle or large skillet. Place the Pusheen mold in the middle of the griddle or skillet and heat the pan over medium-low heat.

5 Transfer 1 tablespoon of the batter to a small bowl. Add ½ teaspoon dark cocoa powder and a pinch of black cocoa

INGREDIENTS

- 2 cups (240g) all-purpose flour
- ¼ cup (50g) superfine sugar
- 4 teaspoons baking powder
- ½ teaspoon salt
- 1½ cups (360g) whole milk
- 4 tablespoons (½ stick/60g) butter, melted and cooled
- 2 teaspoons pure vanilla extract
- 1 large egg
- Unsweetened dark cocoa powder or brown food coloring
- Unsweetened black cocoa powder or black food coloring

powder or 1 drop of brown food coloring and 1 drop of black food coloring. Mix well until evenly tinted dark brown.* Transfer the brown batter to a squeeze bottle or small piping bag and snip a 1mm hole in the tip. Pipe Pusheen's features in the mold on the hot griddle or pan and cook for 2 minutes.

*Optional: If desired, instead of tinting the batter dark brown, you can allow the plain batter to cook longer, 4 to 5 minutes, until it turns brown. The brown color will not be as dark.

6 Transfer the plain batter to a large piping bag and snip a ⅜-inch (1cm) hole in the tip. Gently pipe the plain batter over the Pusheen features first, then fill the entire mold with batter to your desired thickness.

7 Increase the heat to medium and cook for about 4 minutes, until the top starts to bubble. Remove the Pusheen mold gently with tongs, then use a spatula to flip the pancake and cook for 2 to 3 minutes more, until lightly browned on the bottom. Transfer the pancake to a plate.

8 Repeat with the remaining batter, greasing the Pusheen mold again after each pancake. The Pusheen mold can be reused; however, if it is damaged, use one of the extra molds prepared earlier.

Optional: Instead of making a mold with foil, you can use the plain batter to pipe a Pusheen outline directly onto the pan, over Pusheen's features. The pancake will not be as thick.

SLOTH CHOCOLATE-COATED BANANAS

MAKES 4 CHOCOLATE-COATED BANANAS · LEVEL OF DIFFICULTY: EASY

Chocolate-coated frozen bananas are turned into irresistibly adorable sloths. They taste amazing, are packed with nutrients, and are super simple to make!

· ·

1 Line a baking sheet with parchment paper. Peel the bananas and cut each banana into 2 pieces, one piece two-thirds long and the other one-third long. Discard the one-third-long portions. Insert an ice cream stick into the two-thirds portion of each banana. Place them on the prepared baking sheet. Wrap in plastic wrap and freeze until firm, at least 1 hour and up to overnight.

2 MAKE THE CHOCOLATE COATING: Combine the light cocoa or milk chocolate and white chocolate in a medium microwave-safe bowl and microwave in 30-second increments, stirring after each to prevent burning, until the chocolate is melted and smooth. (Alternatively, use a double boiler to melt the chocolate.) Add a drop of yellow food coloring to achieve the desired shade for the Pusheen sloth. Stir in the coconut oil until you get a dipping consistency.*

*Tip: You may want to adjust the amounts of light cocoa or milk chocolate and yellow food coloring to get the desired shade. You may need to adjust the amount of coconut oil as well, depending on the brand of white compound chocolate, to get the proper dipping consistency.

INGREDIENTS

4 ripe but firm bananas

Chocolate Coating

2 ounces (55g) light cocoa or milk chocolate coating/compound chocolate, chopped, or melting wafers

5 ounces (150g) white coating/compound chocolate, chopped, or melting wafers

Yellow oil-based food coloring

4 teaspoons coconut oil

Decorations

¼ cup chopped dark coating/compound chocolate or melting wafers

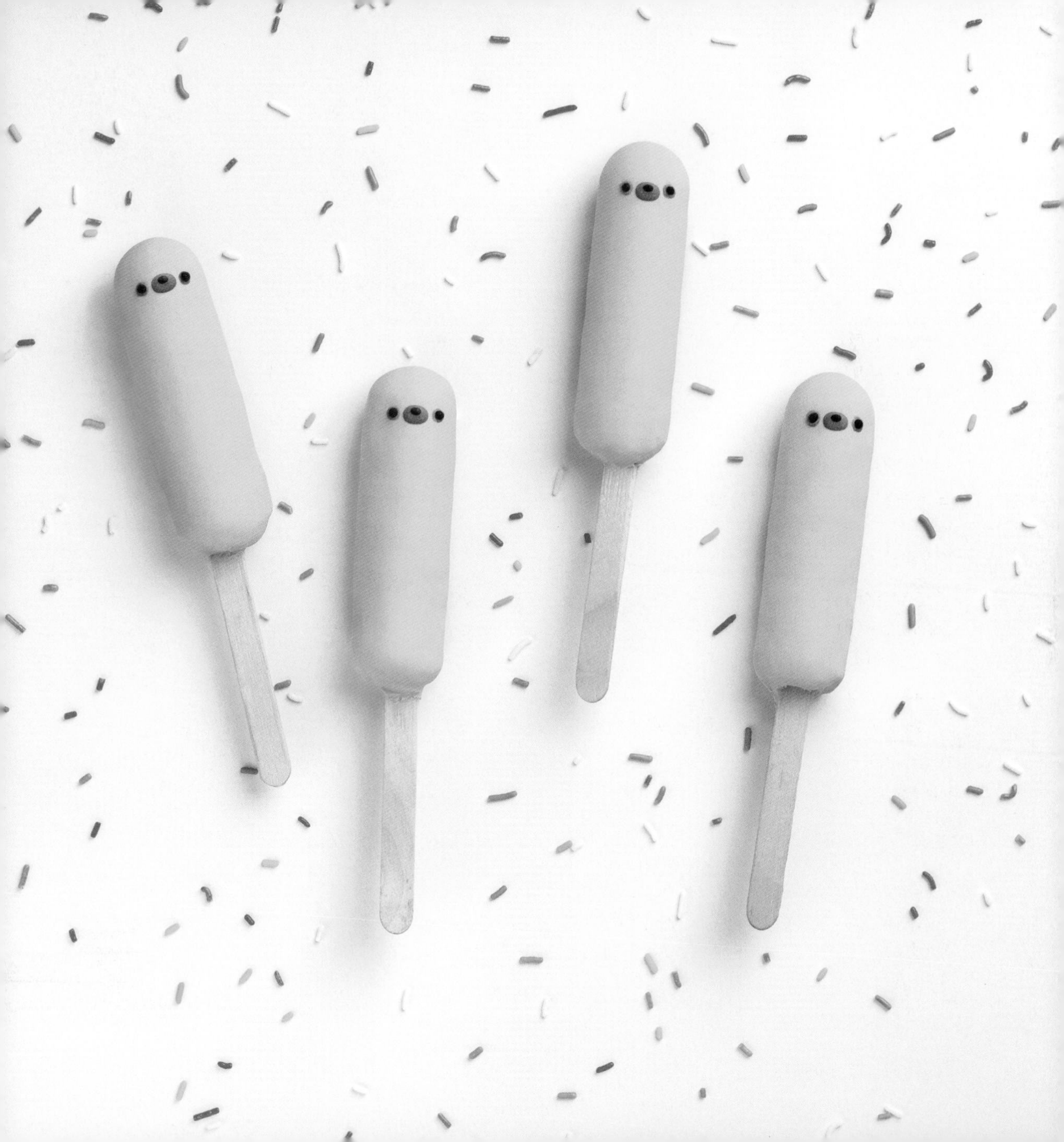

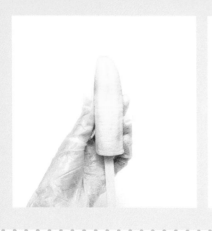  

③ One at a time, dip the frozen bananas into the chocolate coating, rotating them quickly and allowing the excess chocolate to drip off. The chocolate will set quickly, as the banana is cold. (Alternatively, hold a banana over the chocolate and use a large spoon to ladle the chocolate over the banana, rotating the banana at the same time.) Place the coated banana back on the baking sheet. Repeat to coat the remaining bananas. Freeze the chocolate-coated bananas to set while you prepare the decorations. Reserve the remaining chocolate coating.

④ MAKE THE DECORATIONS: Place the dark chocolate in a small microwave-safe bowl and microwave in 30-second increments, stirring after each to prevent burning, until melted and smooth. (Alternatively, use a double boiler to melt the chocolate.)

5 In a small bowl, combine 2 tablespoons of the melted dark chocolate and 2 tablespoons of the reserved chocolate coating to achieve a light brown shade for the fur around the Pusheen sloths' noses and eyes.

6 Remove the chocolate-coated bananas from the freezer. Working quickly, use a toothpick to draw on the muzzle and fur around the eyes with the light brown chocolate, then draw on the nose and eyes with the darker melted chocolate. Store the chocolate-coated bananas in the freezer in zip-top freezer bags until you are ready to eat them or up to 1 week.

Acknowledgments

We would like to express our utmost gratitude to the following people for making this book possible:

Our literary agent, Myrsini Stephanides, for her invaluable advice, support, and encouragement from the onset of the project.

Our editors at Simon & Schuster, Lauren Spiegel and Rebecca Strobel, for giving us the opportunity to publish this book, and for their endless guidance, insight, and support throughout the process of producing it.

The awesome Pusheen crew, Cassandra Lipin, Cate D'Allessandro, and the entire Pusheen art and design team, for their infectious enthusiasm, wonderful teamwork, management, and direction of the project.

The photographer and designer, Liu Hongde and Claire Chin, for making all the creations look so beautiful, and to Katie Belton for adding the finishing touches.

Last but not least, to the fans who have supported Pusheen and inspired us with their love and boundless creativity. Thank you so much!

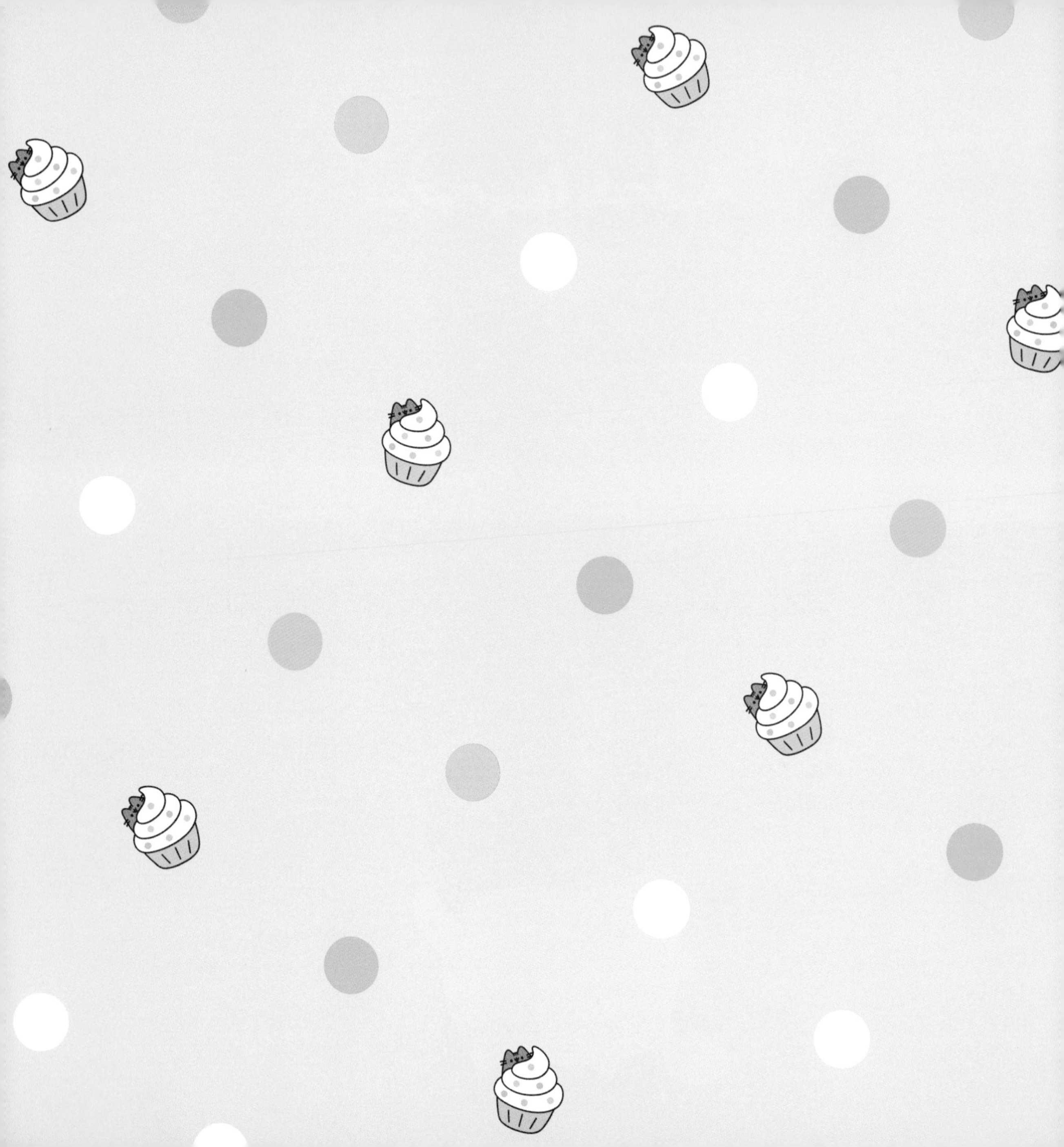

Baking Glossary

BATTER: Batter comes from the French word *battre*, which means to beat, and usually refers to the beaten mixture of ingredients, e.g., eggs, flour, sugar, and other components used in baking.

BEAT: In baking, to beat means to rapidly stir a batter to thoroughly incorporate the ingredients, along with air.

BEET POWDER: Beet powder is a natural pink food colorant derived from ground dehydrated beets. It can be homemade or purchased online and from health or baking supplies stores.

CANDY MELTS: Candy Melts are a trademarked type of compound coating often used to coat cake pops because they are easy to use—just melt and dip—and do not need to be tempered. They are not real chocolate but made from sugar, milk solids, and vegetable oil, and have a sweet, milky flavor. For coloring the Candy Melts, oil-based food coloring should be used instead of water-based food coloring.

CHANTILLY CREAM: Chantilly cream refers to whipped cream that is sweetened or flavored.

CHIFFON CAKE: In this book "chiffon cake" refers to a light and airy sponge cake that uses vegetable oil in place of butter. Its fluffy texture comes primarily from egg whites that are whipped and then folded into the cake batter before baking, similar to angel food cakes.

COCOA POWDER (NATURAL, DUTCH, AND BLACK): Natural cocoa powder is the powder that occurs when cocoa beans are roasted and the fat (or cocoa butter) is removed. Light brown in color, it is acidic and bitter, and when used in baking requires baking soda, an alkaline, to react with it, which helps with leavening.

Dutch cocoa powder, or dark cocoa powder, is cocoa powder that has been treated with an alkaline solution to neutralize its acidity, and therefore it does not require baking soda when used in baking. Alkalizing cocoa makes it darker in color and less bitter, and helps it dissolve more easily into liquids. The recipes in this book that call for dark cocoa powder are referring to this alkalized, or "dutched," cocoa powder.

Black cocoa powder refers to heavily alkalized, or dutched, cocoa powder. It is extremely black and has a milder, unbitter taste. Black cocoa powder can be used as a substitute for black liquid food coloring.

COMPOUND CHOCOLATE: Compound chocolate contains cocoa powder and vegetable oil instead of cocoa butter, and is commonly used to coat cake pops or candy. It is cheaper than regular chocolate and easier to use for coatings, as it does not need to be tempered but still has a sweet, chocolaty flavor. For coloring the chocolate, oil-based food coloring should be used instead of water-based food coloring.

COUVERTURE CHOCOLATE: Couverture chocolate is high-quality chocolate that contains cocoa butter (at least 31 percent) and has velvety, strong chocolate flavor. Good-quality couverture chocolate is used to make rich-tasting chocolate ganache and mousse.

CREAM: In baking, creaming refers to beating fats and sugar together until the mixture is light, pale in color, and greatly increased in volume. It is important for incorporating air, which is needed for leavening, and helps to produce light and fluffy baked products.

CREAM OF TARTAR: Cream of tartar, or potassium hydrogen tartrate, is an acidic by-product of the wine-making process. Cream of tartar is added to beaten egg whites, which increases stability and volume.

DANGO: Dango is a Japanese sweet dumpling that is often served on a skewer. It is similar to mochi except that dango is made from rice flour while mochi is made from pounded intact grains of rice.

FOLD: In baking, folding refers to the technique of gently combining a delicate lighter mixture—e.g., whipped egg whites—into a heavier mixture without deflating the air bubbles in the lighter mixture. The lighter mixture is placed on top of the heavier mixture, then the two are combined by passing a flexible spatula down through both mixtures to the bottom of the bowl, from one side to the other, and gently folding them over until the mixtures are combined.

FONDANT: There are two kinds of fondant: rolled and poured. The fondant in this book refers primarily to rolled fondant, which is a doughlike sugar paste that can be rolled out, colored, and used to cover cakes of all shapes with a smooth finish. It can also be used to make decorations.

GELATIN LEAVES: Gelatin comes in both sheet form (leaves) and as a powder, and both need to be bloomed. Gelatin leaves are preferred over powder because they are easier to measure, odorless, and set clearer and finer. Blooming refers to soaking the sheets in cold water to hydrate and soften them. Once pliable, squeeze out any excess water, add to the liquid you wish to gel, and heat to about 122°F/50°C until completely dissolved.

HEAVY CREAM: Heavy cream, also known as heavy whipping cream, is the thick part of the milk that rises to the top due to its high fat content. For whipping, try to get cream with greater than 35 percent fat content for a silky, airy end product.

INSTANT YEAST: The recipes in this book use instant dry yeast (or rapid rise yeast), which is finer in texture and activates faster than active dry yeast. It can be mixed right into dry ingredients, unlike active dry yeast, which needs to be dissolved in warm water before using. Be sure you are using instant yeast, as proofing times for active dry yeast may be much longer.

KNEAD: Kneading means to work the dough, usually by hand or using the mixer with a dough hook, for the purpose of developing the glutens in the flour, which helps give baked goods their texture. The dough is put on a floured surface, pressed and stretched with the heel of the hand, folded over, and rotated through 90 degrees repeatedly, until the dough is elastic and smooth.

LOTUS PASTE: Lotus paste is a sweet and smooth filling made from dried lotus seeds, popular as a filling for mooncakes. It can be purchased online or at Asian grocery stores. Other pastes, such as red bean paste, can be substituted. Lotus paste can also be made by pureeing boiled lotus seeds and then frying them with oil until a sticky dough is formed.

MATCHA POWDER: Matcha powder is made from dried and finely ground green tea leaves, and can be used as a natural green food colorant with tea flavor. Pure matcha powder may start to turn dull after a day of light exposure, so careful storage in a dark-colored container is recommended to prolong its shelf life.

MERINGUE: Meringue refers to silky-smooth, shape-holding foam made from whipped egg whites and sugar, and occasionally an acid such as cream of tartar or lemon juice. The key to a good meringue is the formation of firm or stiff peaks by denaturing the protein in egg whites through whipping, and stabilizing the foam structure gradually with sugar.

MOUSSE: Mousse is a chilled dessert made of cream that has been whipped until it's light and airy, which is then combined with other ingredients.

PURPLE SWEET POTATO POWDER: Purple sweet potato powder is a natural purple food colorant derived from cooked purple sweet potato that is then dried and ground into a powder. It can be homemade or purchased online and from health or baking supplies stores.

RIBBON STAGE OR RIBBONS: Ribbon stage in baking means that when you lift the whisk over the mixture you have been whisking, the batter should fall slowly, forming a ribbon that will hold its shape for a few seconds. This is usually used to test the texture of an egg-and-sugar mixture that has been beaten until pale and extremely thick.

RICE FLOUR, GLUTINOUS RICE FLOUR, AND COOKED GLUTINOUS RICE FLOUR: Rice flour is ground from the long-grain white rice that is commonly eaten. The rice grains are typically opaque. Glutinous rice flour is ground from sweet white rice that is solid white, and is also called sweet rice flour. Both rice flour and glutinous rice flour are available from Bob's Red Mill and various Asian brands, and are available online and at Asian grocery stores. Cooked glutinous rice flour is made by frying glutinous rice flour over low heat or steaming it for 45 minutes until pale yellow.

SIFT: Sifting refers to passing dry ingredients such as flour through a fine-mesh sieve to remove lumps or large particles. It also helps to aerate the ingredient.

STIFF PEAKS AND FIRM PEAKS: "Stiff" and "firm" peaks describe the consistency of whipped cream or egg whites. Stiff peaks stand straight up when the whisk or beaters are lifted out of the bowl and held upright. Firm peaks are just stiff enough to stand up firmly, but with a slight curl at the tip.

TEMPER: For heat-sensitive foods like eggs, tempering refers to combining a hot liquid into the eggs so that it doesn't scramble them. This is done by slowly raising the eggs' temperature by adding the hot liquid bit by bit while whisking continuously.

With chocolate, however, tempering has a different meaning. It refers to a process of heating and cooling melted chocolate, which aligns the chocolate's crystals to make it smooth, silky, and glossy, and gives it that familiar "snap" when you bite into it. The recipes in this book don't use tempered chocolate because coating or compound chocolate makes it unnecessary.

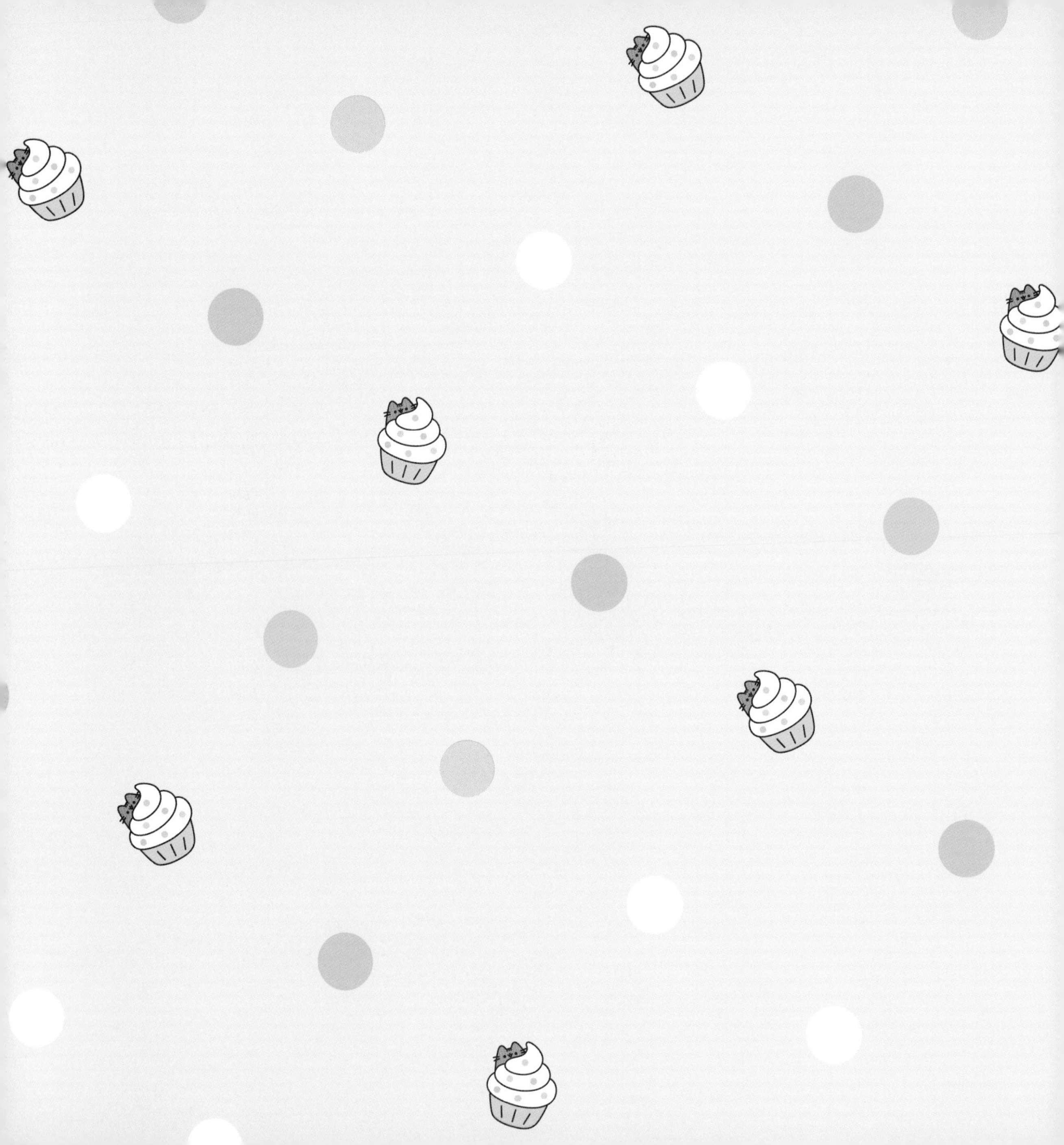

About the Authors

PUSHEEN is a tubby tabby cat who brings smiles and laughter to people all around the world. She became famous through her animated comics and GIFs posted on Pusheen.com, as well as through her widely used animated stickers on Facebook, Instagram, iMessage, and other platforms.

CLAIRE BELTON is an artist and entrepreneur based in Chicago. She spends her time petting cats, drawing cats, and pursuing cat-related endeavors.

DR. SUSANNE NG is a scientist-turned-chef based in Singapore. She loves experimenting in the kitchen and making delicious, cute treats. She is the founder of Deco Chiffon Cakes, and her creations have been featured on media outlets all over the world. You can find her on Instagram @susanne .decochiffon.

Templates

1

2

3

4

Top shell

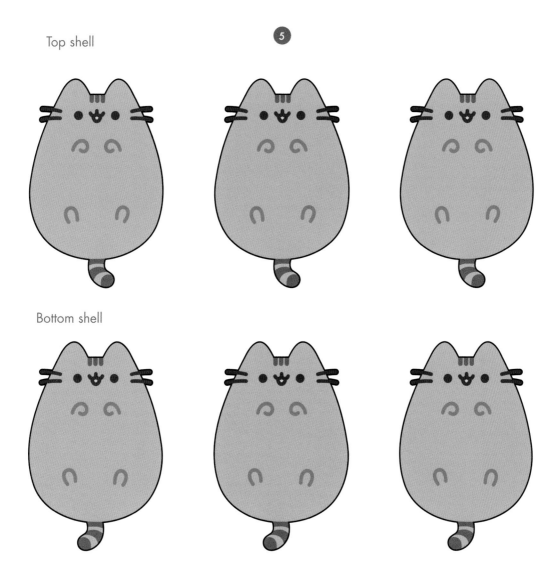

Bottom shell

6

Top shell

Bottom shell

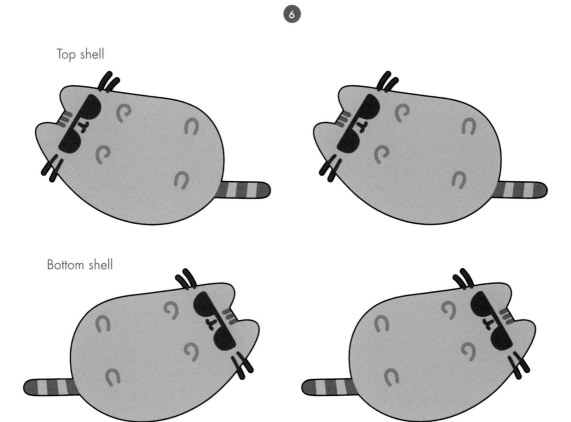

201

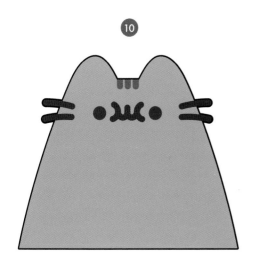

14

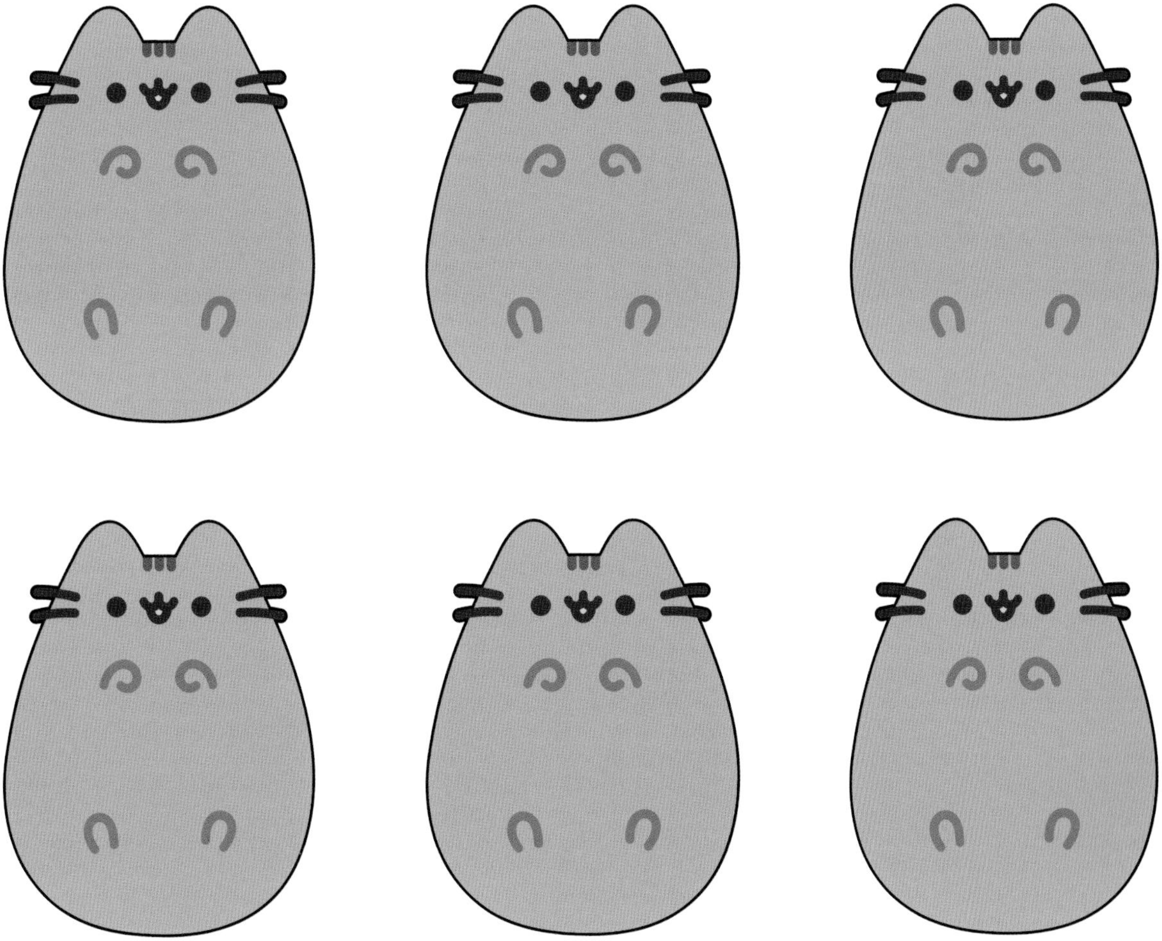

15

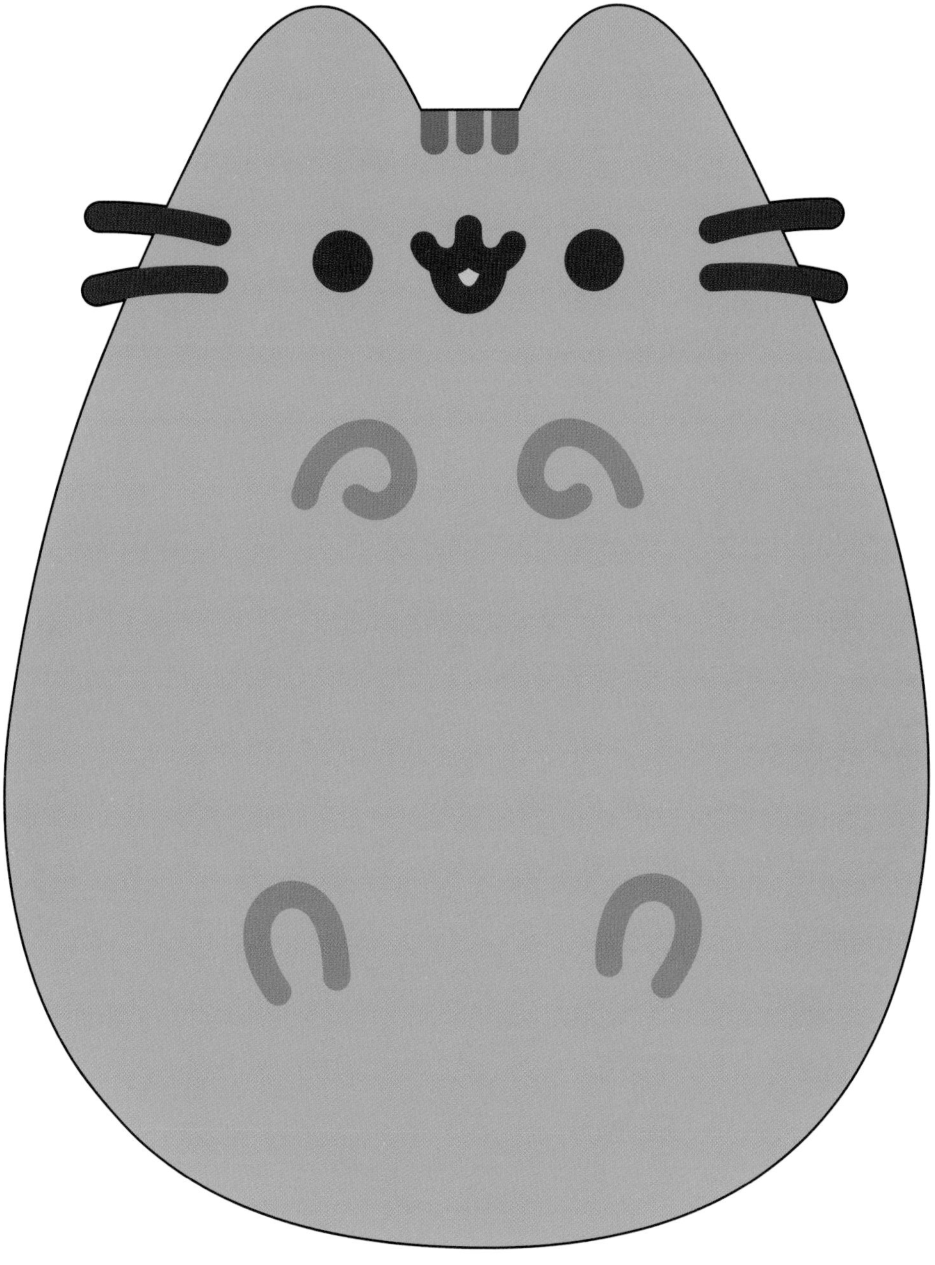

More from Pusheen

Pusheen™
COLORING BOOK

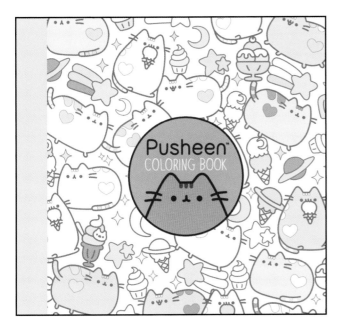

"Funny, weird, and lovably adorable." —Matthew Inman, founder of The Oatmeal
I Am
Pusheen the Cat
Claire Belton

Mini
Pusheen™
COLORING BOOK
46 tear-out pages inside!

Available wherever books are sold or at SimonandSchuster.com